Zarqawi

Zarqawi

THE NEW FACE OF AL-QAEDA

JEAN-CHARLES BRISARD

WITH DAMIEN MARTINEZ

OTHER PRESS • NEW YORK

All excerpts from English language sources have been translated from the author's French versions.

LIBRARY OF CONGRESS CATALOGING-IN-PUBLICATION DATA

Brisard, Jean-Charles.
  [Zarkaoui, le nouveau visage d'Al-Qaida. English]
  Zarqawi : the new face of al-qaeda / Jean-Charles Brisard with Damien Martinez.
    p. cm.
  Includes bibliographical references and index.
  ISBN 1-59051-214-6 (pbk. : alk. paper) 1. Zarqawi, Abu Musab, 1966–
2. Terrorists–Biography. 3. Qaida (Organization) 4. Terrorism–Middle East.
5. Terrorism–Europe. 6. Terrorism–United States. I. Martinez, Damien. II. Title.
  HV6430.Z37B75 2005
  956.7044'3'092–dc22

                                                        2005006964

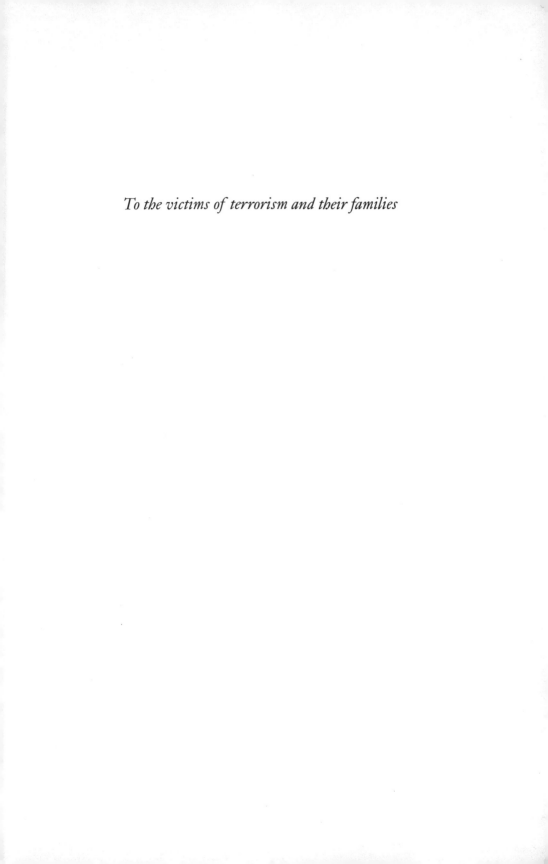

To the victims of terrorism and their families

The author wishes to thank all those without whom this book would not have seen the light of day and expresses his gratitude to the many witnesses who, for personal or professional reasons, prefer to remain anonymous.

Contents

Preface

If circumstances are what create notoriety for terrorists, Iraq is for Abu Musab Al-Zarqawi what Afghanistan was for Osama Bin Laden: violence and more.

Afghanistan and Iraq are two jihadist countries with worldwide stakes. In the former, Bin Laden got himself accepted on the basis of his strategic intelligence; in the latter, Zarqawi predominates by main force. Bin Laden worked out a pragmatic position; Zarqawi advocates chaos as a form of politics. Bin Laden thinks of himself as bringing people together; Zarqawi is exclusionary.

When it comes to violence, Zarqawi brings terrorism back to its original meaning: terror. Always one war behind, he never succeeded in his undertaking until he found in the Iraqi conflict an outlet for his frustrations and complexes and a way to undo his failures. Draped in his personal religious convictions, he has declared war against the world and everyone in it. "I am global," he states, so as not to have to admit that all he can do is depict worst-case scenarios in order to justify his existence, this man who was never more than the shadow of his religious or military masters, starting with Osama Bin Laden, and who was always constrained, be it in the jails of his country or in acts of local terrorism.

The insignificance of his battles explains why, in his lifetime, the most hunted man in the world was just one more name on the endless list of candidates for jihad, and why no one, from Jordan to the United States, noticed the genesis of a criminal. He was let out of prison in the belief that confinement would drive him mad, but what actually happened was that a murderer, already fascinated by death, was uncaged. This blindness went on for a long time: as of the beginning of November 2004 he was still not the subject of a "red notice," that is, a worldwide arrest warrant issued by Interpol.

Behind the mask of the bloody executioner who terrifies the planet vicariously on the Internet, Zarqawi is a terrorist with an atypical, chaotic career, profiting from the rout of Al-Qaeda to create a personal role for himself and build "his" organization, supplanting the Bin Laden networks in many countries.

Zarqawi became a professional terrorist, a cold-blooded killer, by learning a lot from others. First there was Al-Qaeda, which gave him scope for his ambitions and made him one of its leaders before letting him go off on his own. He took advantage of the weakness of several governments, or their ambiguous position toward terrorism and Islamic radicalism, to establish himself, protect himself, and, today, to extend his influence.

He is neither the tool of Saddam Hussein, as the Americans have claimed, nor the henchman of Osama Bin Laden, but an extremist exceptionally favored by circumstances. Zarqawi does not intend to make a career; what he is trying to do is take revenge on life. He follows no logic other than that of a violence that almost makes the Taliban seem like a band of jokesters in turbans. Zarqawi gives lessons to hell, to use André Malraux's expression, and others take him as a model. Iraq could be his tomb, but he himself sees it as a stepping stone. It is time to become aware of him.

This is how and why I set myself the task of understanding the personality and acts of Abu Musab Al-Zarqawi.

·   ·   ·

It all began in October 2002. Four months earlier lawyers for the families of victims of the attacks of September 11—ten thousand such relatives—had put me in charge of an international investigation aimed at bringing to light and justice the people physically or morally supporting Al-Qaeda. My team had been relentlessly tracking the financial and logistical underpinnings of the terrorist group. From the mountains of Afghanistan to the desert of Yemen, by way of Chechnya and Bosnia-Herzegovina, more than fifteen investigators had been providing daily reports on Islamic terrorism, sometimes to the great displeasure of the official intelligence services.

One morning an investigator of ours in Afghanistan, a man who, several weeks earlier, had asked for automatic pistols, machine guns, and a dozen bodyguards for his protection, handed over to me a box stamped SECRET-AFG and containing a batch of unpublished documents he recovered from the administrative quarters of a training camp that had been deserted after the American offensive. What I found there, all jumbled together, were individual military tags, a handbook for the manufacture of chemical and bacteriological substances, an anti-Western pamphlet, and a practical guide to Al-Qaeda in Afghanistan for new recruits.

This last document, thirty pages in length, was a real treasure trove. It listed useful telephone numbers, detailed the methods of communication and code names to be used, and named people to be contacted, whether religious and military leaders or those responsible for lodgings. In addition to the already identified members of the organization, I noticed a name that had never attracted our attention: Abu Musab Al-Zarqawi. He might have been an insignificant figure had he not had a place on this list, between the military chief of Al-Qaeda and the person in charge of Bin Laden's terrorist training camps.

After several days of research, it turned out that the man called Zarqawi, whose real name was Ahmad Fadil Nazzal Al-Khalayleh, was being sought in Jordan and appeared on a list of Al-Qaeda members who had fled to Iran.

In January 2003, one of my colleagues, whose task is to look into the new leaders of Al-Qaeda, was assigned the AMAZ file and began to seek information about Zarqawi, his intermediaries, and his men. Since that time, over ten thousand pages of documents have been gathered, emanating from the judicial, police, and intelligence services of more than ten countries ascertaining the doings of the "Zarqawi network." Over one hundred witnesses have been questioned, including not only magistrates and members of the police and intelligence services, but also relatives and close associates of Zarqawi, in order to define the nature of this man's career and the reality of his network. Over ten trips to the Middle East, especially to Jordan, were required to gather the elements of the investigation presented in this book. Most are unpublished, and some have had to be expurgated so as not to harm ongoing governmental investigations into the man who has become the world's most wanted fugitive.

PART I

Genesis of a Terrorist

Ambition for which one has no talent is a crime.
—RENÉ DE CHATEAUBRIAND

CHAPTER 1

Zarqa and the Zarqawi Tribe

THE IMAGE WENT AROUND THE WORLD. ON SEPTEMBER 6, 1970, two airplanes, one from Swissair and the other from TWA, were hijacked and forced to land at the so-called "Revolutionary" airport, a disused military facility at Zarqa, in Jordan. Three days later, a British plane was diverted to this same airport. Once the passengers were let go, two Palestinian terrorists, Wadi Haddad and Layla Khalid, blew up the cabins. This first dramatic gesture on the part of the PFLP[1] triggered the onset of Black September, the fierce repression undertaken by King Hussein against the Palestinian fedayeen who had taken refuge in Jordan.

Unprecedented and spectacular, this act of piracy came as a shock to international opinion. The filmed images of the dynamited planes, the first of their kind, lent this view of terror unexpected impact. From now on, the most skillful terrorists would make use of the media to disseminate their message of death. The messages evolved over time, ending, thirty years later, in images of barbarous cruelty broadcast over the new digital channels.

In Zarqa, in 1970, the airplanes were empty. In Baghdad, in 2004, a man born in Zarqa slit the throats of other men, and the sequence shots were as unbearable as they were interminable.

Despite its efforts in the struggle against terrorism, the Kingdom of Jordan was unable to anticipate the growing Islamist danger in the 1990s. A nation at the crossroads, at the heart of a region in crisis, Jordan was confronted head-on by the repeated attacks of various extremist movements. On the periphery of the capital, Amman, cities like Maan or Zarqa became refuges for the harshest of Islamist causes. Terrorist groups formed and disbanded there, and alliances were sealed. Activists were arrested, tried, sentenced, and often released, alongside the spread of Salafist ideology, which advocated the return to the roots of Islam and took as its ultimate goal the establishment of an Islamic state in Jordan.

At Maan and Zarqa, the two largest cities in the kingdom after Amman, poverty makes the people receptive to the siren song of extremism. Palestinian refugees have been crowding into Zarqa since the 1950s and leading a precarious existence there. Although it is the major city in an area economically important by Jordanian standards, its rate of unemployment, too, is one of the highest in the kingdom,[2] and the rate of criminality there breaks all records, to the point where Zarqa is often described as the Jordanian Chicago. Public facilities are left in a state of neglect, in contrast to Amman, where brand-new buildings come up every month.

The dusty hills of Zarqa extend as far as the eye can see around Amman. The city shelters Jordan's largest community of Palestinians: in Camp Schneller (also called Camp Hattin) and Camp Mushairifeh refugees have lived in exile since 1948, the year of the creation of Israel. These camps are in fact incorporated as population centers. In the eastern part of Jordan, resentment has been piling up for almost fifty years against both Jordan and Israel. Palestinian identity is a strong social bond, but it is also a force favorable to the politicization of Islam. Since 1948 the Hashemite Kingdom has been trying to sustain a fragile equilibrium between Bedouin tribes and Palestinian refugees. But despite the integration programs put in place by the state, the Palestinians of Jordan stand apart from regional and national political structures, even if, on paper, they possess all the rights of Jordanian citizenship, including the Hashemite passport.

The discontentment of the population of Zarqa had been growing since the early 1990s. In tandem with political developments in certain neighboring countries like Syria and Saudi Arabia, and with the worsening of the Israeli–Palestinian conflict, the large Palestinian population centers in Jordan became radicalized. Fanaticism gradually spread through Jordanian society. Honor crimes punishing women began to multiply, sermons by extremist imams filled the mosques, and terrorist movements recruited an ever-growing number of candidates to carry out suicide attacks in Israel. The Afghan mujahidin called for the coming of an Islamic state, a caliphate; the Muslim Brotherhood took over the universities and the centers of national power; politico-religious leaders organized protest marches against the policies of Israel. Hamas infiltrated the Palestinian enclaves in Jordan.

Several facts bear witness to this increase in fanaticism, especially in Zarqa. Shortly before the attacks of September 11, 2001, a 22-year-old Jordanian Palestinian called Saeed Hotari, described by those close to him as a calm, poised young man, left for Israel to earn a living. On June 1, 2001, he blew himself up in front of the Dolphinarium Discotheque in Tel Aviv, killing twenty-one young Israelis. Saeed Hotari had grown up in Zarqa, like so many other members of Hamas, the organization claiming responsibility for this bloody attack.[3]

The other Palestinian terrorist groups did not want to be outdone, beginning with Al-Qaeda. Thus a young Jordanian Palestinian hailing from Zarqa, Mohammed Salameh, is serving a life sentence in the United States for his part in the first attack on the World Trade Center in 1993. Having entered the U.S. on a tourist visa on February 17, 1988, on the very day of the attack he tried to get reimbursed for the deposit on the van used in the crime. The American courts had established that he belonged to the inner circle of the organization led by Omar Abdel Rahman, which had planned the attack.[4] Salameh's family in Zarqa had saved up so that he could obtain his visa.

The destinies of these hundreds of Palestinian activists are often similar, whether they join the ranks of Hamas or the Brigades of the Al-Aqsa Martyrs. And the city of Zarqa had already paid a high price to Islamist terrorism before the appearance on the international media scene of Abu Musab Al-Zarqawi, literally, Abu Musab from Zarqa. But Zarqawi's own militarism has nothing in common with the political activism of the young Palestinians. Zarqawi is a professional killer who does violence with his own hands. Atypical and elusive, the man escapes all the scenarios of the antiterrorist services, including those of Jordan.

And yet at the beginning of the 1990s the formidable General Intelligence Department (GID) of Jordan had undertaken systematic, methodical surveillance of radical movements operating in that country, with particular attention to the one led by Zarqawi. At that time Jordan was going through one of the most serious political crises of its modern history. Shaken by a deep Islamist current inspired by the Muslim Brotherhood, the Kingdom of Jordan had reacted firmly, taking measures against the various terrorist groups inciting the suburbs of Amman. But this repressive logic did not subdue Abu Musab Al-Zarqawi, who, after being arrested, was freed thanks to a general amnesty applying to political prisoners. Thus one of the most emblematic terrorists since Osama Bin Laden left a Jordanian prison on March 29, 1999, never to return.

In contrast to other Arab countries such as Algeria and Tunisia, Jordan had legalized several Islamist political parties from 1989 on. The most important of these, the Islamic Action Front (IAF), is a direct offshoot of the Muslim Brotherhood. The IAF has political responsibilities at the highest level, including several ministerial portfolios.[5] On a number of occasions this party has attempted to bend the political direction of the kingdom in the direction of fundamentalism. Intervening in the reform of school texts and controlling several municipalities, the IAF established itself in the course of the 1990s as a partner necessary to the Jordanian monarchy. Yet it is merely the legal front for the Muslim Brotherhood.

Weakened in the elections of November 1993, the IAF came back in force after the peace treaty signed in October 1994 between Jordan and Israel and denounced as a betrayal by the Islamists. It then increased its influence in the large Palestinian cities of Jordan, especially in its stronghold, Zarqa. The mayor of the city, Yasser Omari, is a high official in the IAF.[6]

The IAF was sharply critical of the peace treaty and the decisive role played by the United States in getting it signed. IAF militants delivered a fundamentalist message in the suburbs of Amman. At the same time other activist groups, such as the Hizb Al-Tahrir Al-Islami (Islamic Freedom Party) and the Jaysh Mohammed (Mohammed's Army), encouraged their militants to commit acts of violence against Jews and Westerners. Several of Zarqawi's companions in arms in his first terrorist group, Bayt Al-Imam, had belonged at one time or another to these organizations, though they were illegal in Jordan. Most of them were veterans of Afghanistan. Terrorists of this new kind in Jordan liked to be called *imam* without, however, being able to justify this title. On the whole they had received only vague religious instruction.

Thus the Jordanian political context in the 1990s was like a nutrient broth in which Islamist organizations and radical currents proliferated, especially those of the Salafist persuasion. For, soon after the war in Afghanistan against the Soviets, Salafism became fashionable in Zarqa. In this city alone, the three candidates from the IAF won 85 percent of the votes in the elections of 1993, following a clearly anti-Israeli campaign. The Jordanian Islamist current made common cause with the Palestinians in the occupied territories,[7] while, throughout the decade, the city of Zarqa sank deeper and deeper into a social and economic crisis.[8]

Abu Musab Al-Zarqawi (alias Ahmad Fadil Al-Khalailah, Ahmad Fadil Nazal Al-Khalayleh. Abu Ahmad, Abu Muhammad, Abu Muhannad, Al-Muhajer, Muhannad, Sakr Abu Suwayd, and Garib) was born in Zarqa, under his real name of Ahmad Fadil Nazzal Al-Khalayleh, on October 20, 1966.

He belongs to the clan of the Khalayleh, whose name he bears. This family of Bedouin origin settled in Jordan over two centuries ago and occupies one of the highest positions in the political arena of Zarqa. And so let us note from the outset that Zarqawi does not come from a Jordanian Palestinian family, as was claimed by U.S. Secretary of State Colin Powell in a speech at the United Nations on February 5, 2003. All the available documentation and testimony on Zarqawi are quite clear on this point.[9] Moreover, in 2004 Jordan decided to revoke his nationality, as Saudi Arabia had done with Osama Bin Laden in 1994.

Comprising several thousand people, the Khalayleh clan inhabits a very large part of the city of Zarqa and also forms various population centers on the outskirts of Amman. As if to distance themselves from the actions of their *enfant terrible*, the representatives of the clan sent a message to King Abdallah II on May 29, 2004, in which they condemned these acts of his and renewed their vow of allegiance to the king and the kingdom.[10]

The Khalayleh clan belongs to the Bedouin tribe of the Bani Hassan, with over 200,000 members one of the most numerous Jordanian tribes.[11] Sharing power with the Bani Hamida and the Hedwan, it also extends over other countries of the Near and Middle East, including Iraq.

Though it is established in a number of areas distributed over several countries, the Bani Hassan clan has a unity and political capability of its own, to the point where, on July 16, 2002, the representative of the tribe firmly condemned the "diabolical policy of the United States" against Iraq. Other representatives of the Bani Hassan have proclaimed themselves "strongly determined to protect

Iraq and Arab rights everywhere" and "to continue the sacrifice until…American–Zionist plans [fail] in the region."[12] The community is constituted along self-sufficient lines so as to defend its own interests. Thus there is a charitable organization in Zarqa called Bani Hassan Islamic Society, devoted to aiding the most needy members of the clan. The Bani Hassan are a crucial link in the sociopolitical system of Jordan.

CHAPTER 2

"The Green Man"

Abu Musab Al-Zarqawi grew up in the Ma'soum district with his seven sisters and one of his brothers, Mohammed,[13] in modest surroundings steeped in conservative Islam. Ma'soum is a dormitory suburb in which traditional Bedouin culture exists alongside modernity. The skyscrapers of the capital are a few minutes away by car. The district is the cradle of the Bani Hassan tribe. At the very center of Zarqa, extending across the hills above the city, it is poor but not destitute. The arid landscape is overwhelmed by the sun's burning heat.

Ahmad Fadil was born in Ma'soum on October 20, 1966. The family's large, middle-class house with two stories overlooks the dilapidated town cemetery, with its long-neglected graves. Like many members of the Khalayleh clan, Zarqawi's father, Fadil Nazzal Mohammed Al-Khalayleh, born in 1926 and a veteran of the 1948 war, for which he had volunteered, was employed by the municipality of Zarqa as a *mokhtar*, that is, a conciliator to whom people turned in order to resolve their quarrels.[14] The patriarch died two years after his retirement in 1994,[15] and the family profited from the goodwill of the municipality, which decided to award the clan a pension. Nevertheless, the large Ma'soum villa was sold in favor of a more modest house in the Al-Ramzi district of Zarqa.

Thus the man who was still called Ahmad Fadil Nazzal Al-Khalayleh grew up opposite the municipal graveyard. His young manhood was spent in constant sight of this moonscape strewn with graves, a likely influence on his personality and, if we are to believe several people who knew him in his youth, one that aroused in him a real fascination with death.[16] With its dusty alleys and barely paved roads, Ma'soum stood in sharp contrast to nearby Amman and its business centers. On Friday, the day of prayer, almost all the women were veiled, and most of them wore robes down to their ankles.

Young Ahmad Fadil was an average student. His teacher describes him as a pupil with "a few" intellectual inclinations.[17] Between the ages of 6 and 11 he rarely achieved a grade as high as B at the King Talal Ben Abdallah Elementary School.[18] He was then admitted to Al-Zarqa High School.

Equivalent to our junior high school, this was the largest scholastic establishment for boys in the Zarqa region, Ahmad Fadil sat in the fourth row on the left, next to the window. According to his teacher at the time, he was a dreamy boy who took no interest in his courses. The school backed onto the city's main Palestinian quarter along the highway leading to Amman and was maintained by the United Nations Relief and Works Agency (UNRWA), which established the primary public services for the city's Palestinian refugees.

Zarqawi pursued his studies up to ninth grade. In his final school year, 1982, his scholastic average was a mediocre 51.6 out of 100 in general studies. He distinguished himself only in sports and art.[19] The school then decided to expel him and orient him toward vocational education, but Zarqawi refused, preferring to end his studies without giving any explanation to those around him. At loose ends, he spent most of his time in the Ma'soum cemetery.[20]

His mother, Um Sayel, who was born in Zarqa in 1940 and whose real name was Dallah Ibrahim Mohammed Al-Khalayleh, was deeply religious. Up to the time of her death from leukemia on February 29, 2004, she regretted that her son hadn't gotten a diploma. As if to exonerate him, Um Sayel also declared that the youngest of her three boys, presented by the Western media as a fine strategist, hadn't attained a high level of instruction, yet she recalled that he had genuine intellectual abilities. Shortly before her death, she was still uncertain about why he had left school: "We tried to persuade him to continue his studies, but he refused. Even if he didn't have to pay anything, he said he wouldn't continue and wouldn't go to college."[21]

Zarqawi preferred the school of the streets. His pals remember him as just one of the boys playing soccer in the back streets of Ma'soum.[22] Busy painting the town red with the other youngsters in the neighborhood, Ahmad Fadil did not attend religious services. Witnesses agree in describing him as a rowdy and violent teenager, rebellious, undisciplined, and quick to pick a fight. As his cousin, Muhammad Al-Zawahra, puts it, he wasn't so much physically strong as he was ill-tempered.[23]

Soon after dropping out of school, Zarqawi began his working life as an employee in a paper factory, in charge of the chemicals involved in making paper, but he was let go two months later for leaving his machines unmonitored. He then got a job in the maintenance service of the municipality of Zarqa. Like his father before him, he was favored with a flimsy position granted by city hall because he was one of the Khalayleh clan,[24] many of whose members are in the army as well as the police and other local institutions. In this way the kingdom maintains social equilibrium among the various tribes.[25]

National and local Jordanian institutions, however, were to be among Zarqawi's first targets when he headed the terrorist organization Bayt Al-Imam.

Like so many young Jordanians of his generation at the end of the 1980s, as a civil servant Zarqawi was overcome by idleness and fear of the future. The grand economic reforms and the beginnings of privatization plunged young people into financial and social uncertainty.[26] According to the testimony of his friends at the time, the position Zarqawi occupied did not correspond to his deep aspirations. He is described as an idealistic young man, irascible and hard to control. He received two warnings for inciting quarrels and, in 1983, was finally fired after six months on the job.[27]

One of his neighbors, Ibrahim Izzat, sees him as "a man of a modest social class, isolated and hardly socialized."[28] Zarqawi was looking for a way to break free of the dead-end situation in which he felt he was stuck, a way to give meaning to his life and shape his destiny. In 1984 came the time of his obligatory military conscription, and the 18-year-old served for two years. Back in Zarqa in 1986, he was again at loose ends and led a dissolute life. The undisciplined civil servant had become the neighborhood lout, feared by the other young people. Those who knew him in those years say that he drank like a fish and covered his body with tattoos, two practices condemned by Islam. They called him "the green man" on account of his many tattoos, especially on his forearms and shoulders. He even sported an anchor on his left hand, a symbol of his attachment to the sea, and three blue dots at the base of one of his thumbs.[29] He clearly had the need to distinguish himself from the narrow world of Zarqa in which he had grown up unwillingly. In 1998 he would try to erase these marks with acid.[30]

In the space of a few months Zarqawi won the reputation of a cantankerous hoodlum. On several occasions he opposed the local police, to the great displeasure of his father, a leading figure in the city, although he was the latter's favorite son. His father and one of his uncles had to pick him up at the police station repeatedly. In 1987 he wounded a young man of the district with a knife. In police custody for four days before being sentenced to two months in prison, he was eventually let go upon payment of a heavy fine.[31] He was arrested several times for shoplifting and drug dealing, and was even questioned in connection with an attempted rape. In this period of his life, Zarqawi was not at all religious. On the contrary, everything in his attitude contradicted the basic tenets of the Koran. In full crisis, this adolescent was seeking his path in the alleyways of Zarqa.

CHAPTER 3

The Great Departure

A FEW HUNDRED YARDS AWAY FROM THE SCHOOL ZARQAWI LEFT prematurely is the Al-Falah Mosque, located within the precinct of Zarqa's main camp for Palestinian refugees. Enjoying full autonomy in the camp, the mosque brought together the most radical of the Palestinian youth. Zarqawi made new friends, people who promoted a highly politicized Islam. He adopted their principles with the same fervor that he had until just recently brought to fighting and drinking. Now, however, he spent months frequenting this Palestinian enclave in Zarqa. Although he was a Jordanian born and bred, he rapidly gained the trust of the young Palestinian refugees, establishing himself as a respected leader.

To bring her son back to the right path, his mother enrolled him in religious instruction at the Al-Husayn Ben Ali Mosque in the center of Amman. This is where he spent most of his time at the end of the 1980s. In those years this place of worship, with its Salafist leanings, was considered a necessary stage in preparation for the "holy war" in Afghanistan against the Soviets. The Salafist sheikh Jarrah Al-Qaddah, who was the preacher there, recalls having met Zarqawi before he became a practicing Muslim. He recalls how Zarqawi, eager to have a turn at the adventure in Afghanistan, quickly submitted to the most basic religious requirements, forgoing alcohol and regularly attending the inflammatory sermons of the imams.[32] The prospect of fighting in Afghanistan offered Zarqawi the best way out, the possibility of finally choosing his destiny.

In 1989, after some months of preparation, Abu Musab Al-Zarqawi greatly displeased his relatives by joining other young men leaving Jordan for Afghanistan by way of Peshawar in Pakistan. At this time Zarqawi was not yet a convert to extremism; he contented himself with conscientiously assimilating the precepts of Salafist ideology. This decision to leave brought about a violent conflict with his father, who was convinced that his best interests lay in undertaking a "real career" in Jordan. Zarqawi would bear the scars of this conflict for a long time.[33]

Zarqawi and his comrades soon settled in Hayatabad, a town on the outskirts of Peshawar that had become the rear base of the Afghan and Arab mujahidin. Hayatabad lies at the foot of the Khyber Pass, an eminently strategic site leading to Jalalabad and the Afghan battlefields. Throughout the 1990s the town was the hideout of Al-Qaeda, and when Zarqawi arrived in Hayatabad Osama Bin Laden was already there, in District 4, setting up the first networks of his organization, which had been constituted a few months earlier, in September 1988.

A garrison town, Hayatabad brought together the legions of Arab jihadists who had come to strengthen the Afghan ranks. The most visible Islamist combatants, like Abdallah Azzam, Gulbuddin Hekmatyar, and Abu Mohammed Al-Maqdisi, were lodged in the town's "guest houses." These were actually safe houses, sheltering preachers and fighters under the same roof.

The intellectual leaders of the jihad were in charge of organizing the fighters and taking in hand the young people who flocked in from all over the world. The first stage was the Service Bureau

(*Makhtab Al-Khedamat*) and the team of Abdallah Azzam. They were then directed to camps located in the zones controlled by the various Afghan warlords, namely Gulbuddin Hekmatyar, Abdul Rasul Sayyaf, and Burhanudin Rabbani. In the face of this rigorous supervision, some of the trainees occasionally remained in Peshawar, giving up the idea of fighting against their Arab brothers on the other side of the border.[34]

In the spring of 1989, after several days in transit, along with other young fighters Zarqawi was sent to Khost, in eastern Afghanistan. When he arrived the war against the Soviets had just come to an end. He just managed to be present at the fall of Khost so as to be able to enter as a liberator. The city, however, would remain in play as a major strategic site; two years later, in 1991, rival factions to the pro-Communist regime of Najibullah were still clashing in violent battles, and Zarqawi would take part in capturing the city a second time.[35]

Ever since 1988, the Soviet Army had been withdrawing all of its troops from Afghanistan, and in February 1989 it had in fact abandoned the Afghan mountains. But Zarqawi arrived too late to fire against the Russians. After several years of petty delinquency in Zarqa, the young Jordanian missed his initial rendezvous with destiny, the first war in Afghanistan. Yet he would participate in the battles of Islamist factions against the pro-Communists until 1993, at which time Afghanistan was plunged into full-scale tribal war for the capture of Kabul.

A few weeks after setting foot on Afghan soil, Zarqawi decided to prolong the adventure. He increased the number of trips he made back and forth among the Afghan war zones and Hayatabad. On each side of the Khyber mountain, the "Arabs" were then reveling in the status of victor, occupying a position of strength in both countries. It was in this context that Zarqawi made several decisive acquaintanceships, especially the one with Mohammed Taher Al-Barqawi, alias Abu Mohammed Al-Maqdisi, whom he met at the time of his arrival in Peshawar in 1989.[36] From 1992 on, Maqdisi was to become a spiritual father for Zarqawi. In a letter to Zarqawi dated 2004 and written in the Jordanian prison of Kafkafa where he was incarcerated, Maqdisi speaks at length of their friendship and their meeting in Peshawar at the home of Abu Walid Al-Ansari, another theoretician of the jihad.[37]

Maqdisi was 38 when he left Kuwait for Pakistan.[38] Unlike Zarqawi, he already had solid Islamist references. Born in 1959 in the town of Borqa, near Nablus on the West Bank of the Jordan, Issam Mohammed Taher Al-Barqawi emigrated to Kuwait at the age of three with his family and lived there until the mid-1980s. He then went to Iraq to pursue Islamic studies. Considered a Salafist hostile to the Baathist and secular regime of Saddam Hussein, he was arrested and deported to Saudi Arabia. Maqdisi then settled in Mecca, where from 1984 on he accomplished various missions on behalf of the World Islamic League, which operates in Afghanistan. In 1988 Maqdisi formed close ties with another radical organization located in Kuwait, the Jam'iyat ihya' al turath, also known as the Society of the Revival of the Islamic Heritage (SRIH).[39] On a number of occasions beginning in the early 1990s, this Kuwaiti "charitable" organization has been associated with Islamic terrorism. Today it is banned in Russia, and Great Britain suspects it of supporting terrorism.[40] Moreover, the SRIH was denounced as a terrorist organization by the United States Treasury Department on September 1, 2002,[41] and its assets have been frozen by the Egyptian government.

Maqdisi is one of the most influential ideologues of Salafist thought in the Middle East, a source of inspiration for many candidates for martyrdom. Thus some eighteen articles and publications by Maqdisi were found in Hamburg among the personal effects of Mohammed Atta, the operational coordinator of the attacks of September 11.

Maqdisi was to remain in Peshawar for three years. On the basis of his solid religious knowledge, he was invited to Pakistan by the group Badafit Al-Mujahdin (or Badafat Al-Mujahidin) as a professor

of religion. Two months later he left this group to join the fundamentalist center Jami Al-Rahman, also in Peshawar. During this time
Zarqawi followed the religions teachings of Maqdisi, and the two
men quickly became fast friends,[42] Zarqawi being extremely eager to
study with this first-rank ideologue.

Throughout the 1990s Maqdisi proved to be both a theoretician
and a formidable practitioner of radical Islamism. Indeed, he was the
founder of various Sunni terrorist organizations, and he was implicated in a number of attacks or attempted attacks. His name appeared, for example, in the confessions of one of the four Saudis
arrested in 1996 following the Al-Khobar attack, mounted against
American interests in Saudi Arabia in November 1995, in which five
Americans were killed. In 1996, before his execution, the Saudi terrorist Abd Al-Aziz Fahd Nasir Al-Mi'thim declared;

> In Riyadh I met young men whose names I already gave during the
> inquest. They had taken part in the Afghan jihad. In Afghanistan
> they met people of different nationalities and were influenced....
> Together with these young men, we were accustomed to receiving
> propaganda documents from Mas'ari, Osama Bin Laden, and also
> Abu Mohammed Isam Al-Maqdisi. We also read and exchanged
> books declaring that the Arab leaders were "unbelievers," such as
> the book entitled *Clear Evidence of the Infidel Nature of the Saudi State*
> and the book *The Faith of Ibrahim*, written by Abu Mohammed Al-
> Maqdisi. Once I read the book *The Faith of Ibrahim* I was eager to
> visit Abu Mohammed Al-Maqdisi, and I in fact met him several
> times in Jordan and was convinced by his ideas.[43]

At the end of the 1980s several currents of radical Islamist doctrine were flourishing. One of the most famous jihadist theoreticians
of this time was Abdallah Yussuf Azzam (alias Abdallah Azzam).
Born in 1941 in the province of Jenin, in Palestine, Azzam was a
highly gifted student. After pursuing Koranic studies in Syria, he was

awarded the prestigious diploma of *sharia* at Al-Azhar University in 1971. (*Sharia* is the law code based on the Koran.) After teaching Islamic jurisprudence at King Abdel Aziz University in Jeddah, Saudi Arabia, in 1979, he joined the Afghan jihad at the beginning of the 1980s. He established his base in Peshawar, where he met Osama Bin Laden and soon became his mentor.

But Abdallah Azzam was not the only ideologue of Islamist terrorism at the end of the 1980s. Other radical theologians took part in forming Al-Qaeda, Maqdisi among them. The Saudi inquest into the Al-Khobar attacks revealed the active role played by Maqdisi in preparing the operation.

In May 1997 a professor at the University of Yarmuk, Dr. Osama Yassin Abu Shamah, was arrested by the Jordanian secret service in the Suwaylih district of suburban Amman. Abu Shamah had close ties with Maqdisi, and the authorities proved that he helped to finance the Al-Khobar operation. He was thus working for the Bayt Al-Imam group.

According to the Jordanian police, in 1997 some of Maqdisi's terrorist activities were personally financed from Afghanistan by Osama Bin Laden.[44] The two men, said to be close, often met in Afghanistan at that time and especially in Pakistan, the rear base of the Arab forces. One of Osama Bin Laden's top associates in Afghanistan, the Algerian mujahid Abdallah Anas, now in exile in London, recalls sharing a meal in Islamabad with Bin Laden, Abdallah Azzam, and Maqdisi.[45]

In short, Maqdisi was at the heart of Al-Qaeda. That he was so right from the beginning is confirmed by Jamal Al-Fadl, a repentant terrorist who had a leading position with Osama Bin Laden and whose testimony had provided top-level information on Maqdisi's role in Al-Qaeda.

Al-Fadl, a regular witness for the U.S. Department of Justice in Al-Qaeda cases, said in connection with the Ennaam Arnaout case that he met Maqdisi in the context of Al-Qaeda activities. Maqdisi had just published *Irrefutable Proofs for Undertaking Jihad*. Close to certain Arab fighters in Pakistan and Afghanistan, he maintained a solid friendship with another terrorist called Azmiri.[46] Azmiri would later be accused of participating in the so-called Bojinka plot to crash several airplanes simultaneously over the United States. Foiled in 1994, this plot anticipated the attacks of September 11. In addition, Azmiri would later meet in Manila with the originator of the September 11 attacks, Khaled Sheikh Mohammed. He is also said to have taken part in an aborted attempt to assassinate President Bill Clinton during a trip to Africa in 1998.

Maqdisi's second close friend in Pakistan, Mohammed Shobana (or Shabana) put out the Islamist magazine *Al-Bunyan Al-Marsus* (*The Impenetrable Edifice*), in which Abid Sheikh Mohammed, brother of the September 11 mastermind, also took part. This publication, run by the friends of Sheikh Abdallah Azzam, was said to be close to the mujahidin and the central organization of Al-Qaeda. Thus as early as its July 1989 issue the magazine published an editorial announcing the real aims of Al-Qaeda; the obligation of every Muslim, it said, is to fulfill the goals of jihad until America is reached and liberated. This was one of the first declarations calling for jihad against the United States. And it was the man at the head of *Al-Bunyan Al-Marsus*, Mohammed Shobana, who, on Maqdisi's recommendation, recruited the young Zarqawi several weeks after the latter's arrival in Pakistan—Zarqawi who wrote Arabic so badly.

Zarqawi's other decisive meeting in Pakistan was with Saleh Al-Hami, a fighter in the Arab legions who would later become his brother-in-law. Sporting a long black beard and an artificial leg, Al-Hami had been a combatant from the outset. Likewise a Jordanian, he had studied journalism at the University of Irbid in that country. Until 1992, when he left Pakistan to return to Jordan, he worked as a correspondent for the magazine *Al-Jihad*, founded by Abdallah Azzam, the mentor of Osama Bin Laden.

While convalescing in a hospital in Peshawar after stepping on a landmine in the mountains of Khost, in Afghanistan, Saleh Al-Hami met Zarqawi. Present where the accident took place, Zarqawi had taken part in evacuating Al-Hami across the Khyber Pass to Peshawar. Admiring the courage of the wounded man, he visited him regularly in the hospital. Al-Hami recalls that Zarqawi, who had seen him covered with blood when he was hit, came to see him when he recovered, introducing himself by saying that he worked as a correspondent for *Al-Bunyan Al-Marsus* and wanted instruction in the techniques of reporting and publishing. Al-Hami was happy to comply, and this was the beginning of their relationship.[47]

Zarqawi was then 23 years old. The journal that employed him was based in Peshawar itself, and he made regular round trips between Pakistan and Afghanistan.

At this time Zarqawi was a thin young man with a dark gaze, five feet nine inches tall, who traveled all over Afghanistan to gather direct testimony from the Arab combatants, victors in a war he missed by several months. The journal for which he was writing was the ideological spearhead of Al-Qaeda. A makeshift reporter with no journalistic experience or cultural credentials, he tried to construct an identity for himself alongside the fighters he admired so much. People who knew him at this time speak of a young man searching for orientation points of identity and terribly eager to learn. In the evenings, at the fireside, he would take refuge in the Koran and then spend his nights in prayer.

As the months went by, Zarqawi became increasingly close to Saleh Al-Hami. As a token of friendship, he offered his new companion the hand in marriage of one of his sisters back in Jordan. Al-Hami agreed, and in 1991 the young woman came to Peshawar for the wedding. (It is a tradition among the Khalayleh to give their daughters in marriage to fighters for Islam, and two of Zarqawi's other sisters became the wives of diehard jihadists. As we have seen, Alia, born in 1968, married Khaled Al-Aruri, one of Zarqawi's closest lieutenants in Afghanistan and later in Iraq, and Mariam married

Haytham Mustafa Obeidat, alias Abu Hassan, a veteran of the Afghan jihad.) This marriage sealed the friendship between the two men.[48] Upon his return to Jordan, Al-Hami and his wife settled close to the house of the Zarqawi family in the Al-Ramzi district of Zarqa.

Zarqawi and Al-Hami liked one another and shared the same vision of a triumphant Islam. Al-Hami still considers Osama Bin Laden a model today: "He is a great man, an example for all of us. He is the new caliph. It is as though the Prophet Mohammed had returned to earth from the seventh century to arrive among us."[49]

Al-Hami recalls that Zarqawi told him about a dream while they were spending a night in a cave: he had had the vision of a sword splitting the sky, the word "jihad" engraved on its blade.[50]

The two men spent several months together in Afghanistan before Al-Hami returned to Jordan; according to him, his wife thanked God because she was married to an impaired man, for "God honors the handicapped and the mujahidin." Later, when her brother was declared an international terrorist, she would be stopped for six hours on the border between Jordan and Saudi Arabia on a pilgrimage to Mecca, on the grounds that she was the sister of Abu Musab Al-Zarqawi. The zeal of the Saudi police on that occasion angered Al-Hami, who still recalls the fine moments spent with his brother-in-law in Afghanistan: "It was a marvelous thing, a terrific life, the best thing I've ever experienced in my life....I felt I was being reborn when I went there. That was really living."[51]

This first trip to Afghanistan was truly an initiation for Zarqawi. He found a country in ruins and came face to face with others, especially the many Arab or Afghan warlords, to whom he owed respect and deference. The big shot of Zarqa was learning about life. But the Afghanistan of the late 1980s, coveted by rival factions, Arab legions, and Afghan fighters, was a country where a lot was at stake. The young Zarqawi did not possess the cultural wherewithal to make a name for himself in this complex environment, and he was also financially strapped. So he set about forming ties with those veterans who were likely to support him during his stay in Afghanistan, following the example of Maqdisi, who opened the doors of the Islamist organizations to him.

The war against the Soviet regime was now completely over. With outside help, the jihad had won. But another struggle, an internal one among rival factions, was soon raging. Each clan defended its own plan for government according to its tribal, ethnic, regional, ideological, and religious specificities. The confrontations came to a head during the fight over control of Kabul. In May 1992 Ahmad Shah Massud, a moderate Tajik Islamist, entered the capital with several thousand men and became minister of defense. Tensions remained very lively, and one year later there was still open conflict. Despite a peace treaty among the rival factions, fighting continued south of Kabul. On May 7, 1993, Ahmad Shah Massud resigned, and a new government formed around the radical leader Gulbuddin Hekmatyar, mentor of the Taliban—and protector of Al-Qaeda.

Although Zarqawi had just missed the war against the Soviets, he took part in the second wave of fighting in this civil war. He quickly chose to join the camp of the Pashtun Gulbuddin Hekmatyar, who represented the majority ethnic group. Thus, shortly after beginning his first journalistic experience with the extremist *Al-Bunyan Al-Marsus*, he put down his pen and took up arms alongside Jalludin Haqqani, the Afghan warlord who, since 1995, had won renown for training Taliban cadres in the madrasa (Koranic school) Dar Al-Uloom Islamiya in the town of Sharsadda. In a speech delivered on the Al-Jazira network Osama Bin Laden would later lament the fact that the U.S. strike forces in Afghanistan had killed Haqqani, the "hero... who rejected the American occupation in Afghanistan."[52]

Zarqawi attended a number of military training camps in Afghanistan, in particular Sada (Echo), where he learned how to handle weapons like the Kalashnikov or RPG (rocket-propelled grenade launcher).[53] Sada was led by an Iraqi jihadist called Abu Burhan Al-Iraqi, a close collaborator of Abdul Rasul Sayyaf, the head of

Hizbul-Ittihad El-Islami (Islamic Union Party), which controlled the combat zone around Kabul in 1993.[54] Sayyaf's troops were known to be among the harshest of the Afghan factions, practicing rapes and beheadings. He was largely responsible for establishing Al-Qaeda facilities, opening several military training camps in the service of the "Arabs."

Zarqawi made the trip to the Sada camp in the company of one of his Zarqa comrades, Mohammed Wasfi Omar Abu Khalil.[55] Abu Khalil would later be arrested, tried, and sentenced in connection with the dismantling of the first terrorist group led by Zarqawi, Bayt Al-Imam. Zarqawi and Abu Khalil were to be prison mates in Suwaqah, in Jordan.

Besides Zarqawi, other top-ranking terrorists visited Sada at this time, in particular Khalid Sheikh Mohammed,[56] who, as time went by, had become a close associate of Abdul Rasul Sayyaf before winning the full confidence of Osama Bin Laden and masterminding the operation of September 11.

For many years Sada, located on the border between Pakistan and Afghanistan, was an obligatory stage in the training of terrorists coming from all over the world to swell the ranks of Al-Qaeda. Another emblematic figure who spent many weeks in this camp was Ramzi Yussef, who devised the first attack on the World Trade Center on February 26, 1993.[57] Extradited from Pakistan to the United States, Ramzi Yussef was sentenced to life imprisonment in 1998.

At this time, then, Zarqawi was coming as close as possible to the nerve center of Al-Qaeda. He was not in the inmost circle, however, for, although Sada was a cornerstone of the Al-Qaeda military apparatus with regard to the training of the "Arabs" in Afghanistan, it merely provided the ordinary share of fighters. There was a second, so-called long-term, camp under the control of a military council, where the most promising mujahidin were trained, and Zarqawi was not a part of it. It was at this time that he formed friendships with a number of other Jordanian combatants, including a certain Salem

Saad Salem Ben Suweid, whom he recruited some ten years later in the murder of the American diplomat Laurence Foley in Amman.[58]

Up to the time he left Afghanistan in the course of the year 1993, Zarqawi read and heard on tape the inflammatory sermons of the jihad theorist Abdallah Azzam, who had been killed by a car bomb in September 1989. According to his brother-in-law Saleh Al-Hami, as reported in *Al-Jazira*, he found himself in perfect agreement with the thoughts of this Palestinian, the spiritual father of contemporary Salafism and the mentor of Osama Bin Laden. Impressed by Azzam's implacable rhetoric, he spent hours on end steeped in the Salafist message, to which he later referred when he claimed credit for the attacks in Iraq: rejection of modernity, return to the roots of Islam, proclamation of the caliphate.

He had come a long way from the streets of Zarqa. In Afghanistan, he filled himself with the spirit of jihad, no matter what the cause: for the liberation of Afghanistan, for Islam, for the liberation of Iraq, or on any other grounds. Zarqawi discovered in himself the personality of a fighter.

In the early 1990s the border between Afghanistan and Pakistan was already porous, and the Arab legions were setting up their quarters in Karachi and Peshawar. Zarqawi made several stops between Hayatabad and Peshawar, where he visited the Zayd Ben-Harithah Mosque. The imam recalls a young man saturated with religion who spent many hours praying with his Arab brothers, especially during the month of Ramadan. Before setting out on a pilgrimage to Mecca in 1992, Zarqawi even asked the imam to pray that God would "forget him a little."[59]

It is on the basis of his experience in Afghanistan that he decided to return to Jordan.

CHAPTER 4

The Return to Jordan

UPON HIS RETURN, EARLY IN 1993, ZARQAWI FOUND THAT JORDAN
had changed a great deal. The kingdom had become freer both po-
litically and economically. It had embarked on a peace treaty with Israel and was stabilizing its position in the region. In September 1991
the first Jordanian veterans of Afghanistan began to come back to
their country and felt it to be their duty to work for the renewal of
the Islamic cause.

In the space of a few months the enemy had changed identity.
The men who had left full of enthusiasm for fighting the Soviet occupation returned with a fierce hatred of the United States and the
Israeli government. It was a very different time. The most highly mo-
tivated mujahidin were already orienting themselves toward new
lands of jihad, including Bosnia-Herzegovina.[60] Many Jordanians
were inclined to wage holy war between Sarajevo and Tuzla. Zarqawi did not go along with them but returned home to Zarqa. After
missing the war against the Russians, he missed a second opportunity
to take part in jihad, this time with the Arab forces of Bosnia.

A goodly number of these young veterans were under surveillance by the forces of order in their own countries. In Egypt, Morocco, Tunisia, and Jordan, the security agencies often had precise knowledge of the identity of the mujahidin. Even before leaving for Afghanistan most of the fighters had been the objects of special attention on the part of the intelligence services. Ordinary criminals or fanatic Islamists, it was not by chance that they were setting out for Afghanistan. And so the states in the region grew anxious at the return of the "Afghans," especially Egypt and Algeria, where Islamist groups of veterans were rapidly forming again. The anxiety reached its peak when the ISF (Islamic Salvation Front) threatened to win the elections in Algeria in 1991 after a democratic vote.

But if the early 1990s mark the advent of religious fanaticism on the Algerian political scene, they were also marked by increased activism on the part of radical and violent groups struggling against the government and the Coptic Christians in Egypt. Egyptian Islamists returning from the jihad in Afghanistan soon had to seek refuge in the Islamic state of Sudan or in Saudi Arabia. The Islamist wave shook up all the Arab countries in the great Mediterranean arc.

Starting in 1991 the kingdom of Jordan paid ongoing attention to "its" mujahidin, whose commitments ran counter to the political direction taken by the government both on the domestic level, since the Islamist parties were severely restricted by the king's cabinet, and on the international level, given the diplomatic rapprochement between Jordan and Israel.

The heads of the Jordanian intelligence service began to be worried by the activism of the "Afghans" at the beginning of 1991.[61] Information was pouring in to indicate that hundreds of returned veterans had started recruiting young Islamists and training them in the desert. On the political scene, the "Afghans" spoke up, denouncing Jordan's involvement in the American talks that were likely to lead to a peace treaty in the Middle East. They advocated the destruction of Israel in concert with the Jordanian branch of the Muslim Brotherhood (Al Ikhwaan Al-Muslimoon), a political party that had been banned in all other Arabic countries. From 1991 on, the most highly organized "Afghans" came together in the Army of Mohammed (Jaysh Mohammed), a Sunni terrorist group that soon held sway in the Hashemite Kingdom. Other veterans joined the ranks of Islamic Jihad and Hamas in the territories occupied by Israel.

The judicial authorities in Jordan set out to understand these new threats so as to be better able to combat them. Large-scale attacks were foiled by the government, and five organizations were dissolved. The twenty-two terrorists comprising the cell of Khadir Abu Hawshar were arrested; they had been planning to strike tourist sites at the moment of transition to the year 2000. Militants of the Army of Mohammed, whose aim was to destroy the Jordanian government, were arrested at the end of 1991 in the vicinity of Amman.

The organization called Al-Hashayibakah (the Jordanian Afghans) planned terrorist attacks in Jordan between 1991 and 1993. On December 21, 1994, its members received harsh sentences from the State Security Court of the Hashemite Kingdom of Jordan. Among them was the Saudi businessman Muhammad Jamal Khalifa, the brother-in-law of Osama Bin Laden. From 1986 to 1994 he had headed the charity IIRO (International Islamic Relief Organization) in the Philippines. Suspected of having ties to Islamist terrorism, which he denies,[62] he was sentenced to death in absentia. He fled to Jeddah, in Saudi Arabia, where he has since opened a seafood restaurant.

Another armed group, Harakat Al-Islah Wal-Tahaddi (Movement for Reform and Change), created in Jordan in 1997, saw its activists convicted of terrorism by a military tribunal on July 22, 2001. On the list of those convicted was the religious leader Abu Qatada (whose real name is Omar Mahmud Uthman Abu Umar),[63] an associate of Osama Bin Laden and Maqdisi. Sentenced in absentia to life imprisonment by the Jordanian courts, and sought by the Egyptian and Algerian police, Abu Qatada was leading a life of quiet retirement in London when he was arrested by the British police and placed under temporary detention in October 2002. From 1995 to

2001 he had taken part in the establishment of the Al-Qaeda network in Europe as well as in several operations by terrorist cells there, including the one by Al-Qaeda in Spain.

Finally, another group of jihadists, Al-Buq'ah, was dissolved in 1998 by the Jordanian police.[64] The aim of these different movements was to overthrow Arab governments, in particular that of Jordan, replacing them with a fundamentalist caliphate. This resolutely simplistic project united the most radical of the Islamists.

On November 10, 1992, two independent, dissident Islamist leaders, Layth Shubaylat and Yaqub Qarrash, were sentenced by a military tribunal to twenty years in prison for illegal possession of firearms and an attempt to overthrow the government. On November 23, 1992, King Hussein announced that he would do everything in his power to protect the state. Many Jordanian statesmen at that time were worried about the radicalism of these young veterans back from the Afghan jihad. Ahmed Oweidi Abbadi, a Bedouin member of the Jordanian Parliament and a former officer, issued a solemn warning to the kingdom in November 1992 on the occasion of a speech before the Parliament. These people, he said, claim that their weapons are to be used in the fight against Israel, but their intention is ultimately to overthrow the monarchy.[65]

Illegal armed groups proliferated, increasing the number of violent actions against the kingdom. Several sectors were aimed at, including tourism, so as to dry up the leading source of foreign currency. A French national, a diplomat by profession named Gilbert Heines, was stricken by this wave of violence.[66] When Heines and his wife visited the tourist area of Mujeb, about sixty miles from Amman, in February 1995, they were hit by bullets fired from the mountain. Gilbert Heines was wounded. The gunmen, Salem Khakhit Abdallah, 31, and Ahmad Khaled Kassen, 23, were immediately arrested and sentenced to life in prison and ten years in prison, respectively. According to their statements, they were trying to contest the peace treaty signed in October 1994 between Jordan and Israel.

. . .

ABU MUSAB AL-ZARQAWI RETURNED HOME TO ZARQA AND, LIKE the other "Afghans," was put under surveillance. In his case, however, he had been well known to the local police as an ordinary delinquent before his departure.

He went back to his house, number 13 on Street 6 of the Al-Ramzi quarter, a large two-story house surrounded by a high wall, where he was rejoined by his wife Intisar, whom he had married in 1988 and who is called Um Mohammed (Mohammed's mother), as well as his oldest son and his daughter Aminah, born in 1991. His mother, some of his sisters, and his brother Mohammed were also living in the family home.

Zarqawi returned deeply marked by Afghanistan. The young neighborhood tough had been replaced by a hardened man. An authoritarian, he quickly imposed a drastic religious rigor on those around him. The women of the family had to conform to the religious practices that he himself had adopted during his years in Afghanistan. From that time on, the members of the Zarqawi family could be recognized in the street, since they alone wore traditional Afghan clothing, and this remains the case today.[67] Men who are not part of the family were forbidden to enter the house. Similarly, Um Mohammed reports that, from the time of his return from Afghanistan, Zarqawi made his brothers stay away from television because the programs "corrupt the younger generation."[68]

Beside the Zarqawis other veterans lived in the Al-Ramzi quarter, such as Abu Qudama, whose home was close by, and several future members of the terrorist group Bayt Al-Imam. Like them, the Khalaylehs are very pious, and the only decorations adorning the inside of their house are verses of the Koran and a plaque on which is inscribed "Allah." The Zarqawi family house is certainly smaller and less comfortable than the one in the Ma'soum quarter, but it is in perfect keeping with middle-class standards.

To earn a living, Zarqawi opened a video rental business that seems to have been unsuccessful. But this veteran had other ambitions. For shortly after his arrival, he found his old companions again and spent a lot of time spreading his ideas among the young Jordanians and Palestinians of Zarqa. Once again he visited the mosques of Al-Falah and Hussein Ben Ali, talking about his Afghan experience and attracting an increasing number of unemployed young men to his views.

One of the Salafist leaders in Amman, Sheikh Jarrah Al-Qaddah, remembers him as an impassioned young man who shouted in Zarqa's crowded streets in order to spread the good word. This behavior must have seemed unusual, to say the least, to the inhabitants of a town in which public sermons were forbidden.

In any event, these excesses soon made it possible for him to gather around himself defenders of the most violent causes. Saleh Al-Hami, who returned from Afghanistan in 1992, recalls that this was the time when tensions began to arise between Zarqawi and the Jordanian regime. Waging jihad, he says, had become like oxygen for these men, and it was difficult to forgo it.[69] After the Afghan war and jihad, Zarqawi was clearly resolved to carry on the struggle in his own country. The Jordanian services knew this and stepped up their vigilance.

The man known to everyone in Zarqa as Ahmad Fadil Nazzal Al-Khalayleh was now called Abu Musab (Musab's father), although his last son, who would bear this name, wasn't yet born. The turbulent adolescent had made quite a change and was now a feared man with overweening ambitions. It is rare that an inhabitant of Zarqa bears the name of his town, but the new name Abu Musab Al-Zarqawi (that is, of Zarqa) reflected the intentions of the man who would do anything to represent his clan and his city. He borrowed his name from one of the prophet Mohammed's warriors, Musab Ben Umayr, considered the patron saint of suicide bombers, who lost both hands at the Battle of Yathrib, an episode Zarqawi has mentioned a number of times.

Only a few months after his return to Zarqa, he tried to find Maqdisi, the Palestinian preacher whose sermons inflamed the "Arabs" of Peshawar. In 2004 Maqdisi wrote a letter in which he speaks of the reunion with Zarqawi: "As soon as he got back from Afghanistan, Zarqawi paid me a visit....Abu Walid was the one who gave him my address in Jordan....We then worked together, and I gave religion courses in several Jordanian cities. We thought up tracts."[70] From that time on, Issam Mohammed Taher Al-Barqawi, alias Abu Mohammed Al-Maqdisi, became an ideological crutch and, at the same time, a spiritual father and intellectual reference point for Zarqawi. All other things being equal, he played the same role for Zarqawi as Abdallah Azzam did for Osama Bin Laden.

Maqdisi had finally come to roost in Jordan, in Yajouz on the outskirts of Amman, near the Sohaib Mosque. After Kuwait, Iraq, Saudi Arabia, Pakistan, and then Kuwait once again, he settled for good in Jordan in 1992. His move coincided with the return of the Jordanians who had fought in Afghanistan and with Zarqawi's return at the beginning of 1993. The two men were glad to meet again and cultivated their friendship amid shared memories of Pakistan.

In this way the simple man from the Amman suburbs became the associate of one of the most conspicuous theoreticians of jihad in the early 1990s, for Maqdisi was already a celebrity in the small world of radical theologians. He had just published *Democracy Is a Religion*. According to this scathing diatribe against the West and its form of government, democracy is a social innovation condemned by the Koran, one that conveys a heretical message. The citizens of democratic states are "infidels" soon to incur destruction. "Democracy is a religion that is not the religion of Allah....It is a religion of pagans,...a religion that includes other gods in its belief....In the democratic religion people are represented by their delegates to Parliament.... They and their associates legislate in accordance with the religion of democracy and the laws of the constitution on which the government is based."[71]

Together with the older radical Saudi preachers Hamud Bin
Uqla Al-Shuaibi and Ali Al-Khudeir, Maqdisi advocated a return to
the origins of Islam and a firm repudiation of everything that was
not Muslim. But this extremist rhetoric was not limited to a few
feverish publications. Starting in 1991 Maqdisi was personally involved in the recruitment and training of young Jordanian veterans
with terrorism in mind. His participation in various terrorist organizations, including the Army of Mohammed and Al-Islah Wal-
Tahaddi, was explicitly confirmed by the Jordanian legal system and
would lead to repeated judicial convictions.

Imprisoned for his participation in Bayt Al-Imam, Maqdisi was
freed in 1999, only to be arrested and jailed again in December 2002
for masterminding the rebellions that broke out in Maan. In addition, in July 1991 the Jordanians had established his ties to the Army
of Mohammed, whose members were being trained in Afghan
camps. The six leaders of the group were quickly sentenced to death
for their role in attacks on Jordan. Their sentences were commuted,
however, following a royal amnesty.

Although Jordan was vigilant, in 1991 it was still unable to grasp
the full extent of the threat. The veterans were not really taken seriously by the judicial authorities, who pronounced sentences they
then failed to carry out. Yet the intelligence services were still keeping track of the reentry of the veterans into civilian life.

At the time they got together again, both Maqdisi and Zarqawi
cherished strong personal ambitions and a common aim, the pursuit
of jihad against "infidel regimes." In the course of the year 1993, new
enemies and new targets became clear: Israel and the kingdom of
Jordan. Like hundreds of veterans, the two men felt deep hatred for
the Jordanian government because of what they saw as its guilt in
colluding with the enemy.

That same year history speeded up for Maqdisi, Zarqawi, and
some three hundred other Jordanian veterans of Afghanistan. Their
militant faith had remained strong. Frustrated because they could

not wage "their" war, they constituted a terrorist cell. Toughened by battle and lacking real social bonds in their country of origin, they declared themselves "ready for a confrontation with the [Jordanian] government on the basis of their beliefs."[72] They violently disapproved of the peace treaty with Israel that was about to be signed. All of them had received military training, sometimes in camps, like Salah Eddin in Jalalabad, affiliated with the Muslim Brotherhood. Some, like Zarqawi at Sada, were trained in the very first camps established by Al-Qaeda. In 1992–1993 the camps of the Saudi Osama Bin Laden, with their abundant facilities and equipment, were considered the most sophisticated and elite in Afghanistan. Costly air-to-ground Stinger missiles, for example, were often available for use during training. What was taught was the relentless imposition of Islamic law, if necessary by force.

This was the context in which Zarqawi introduced Maqdisi to some of his friends in Zarqa, all veterans of Afghanistan. Among them were Sherif (also known as Abu Ashraf), Suleiman Taleb Damra, Khaled Al-Aruri, Nasser Fayez and his brother Nafez, Mohammed Rawashdeh, Amer Sarraj, and Nasri Tahayinah,[73] who formed Zarqawi's inner circle and would soon constitute Bayt Al-Imam (Allegiance to the Imams), his terrorist group. It has been claimed that the Jordanian authorities learned only in 1997, during the interrogation of the activist Osama Yassin Abu Shamah, professor at Yarmuk University and financier of the organization, that Osama Bin Laden provided funding for the formation of this terrorist cell.[74]

In the course of his initial confessions before the Jordanian judiciary on August 31, 1994, Zarqawi described in detail how he and Maqdisi had organized Bayt Al-Imam. Maqdisi provided religious instruction, teaching political views hostile to the Jordanian regime. The message of this Palestinian ideologue, leader of the Salafist sphere of influence in the Middle East, is based on the idea that each individual must lead his life in accordance with the Koran, and that the Arab governments, particularly that of Jordan, do not honor this precept. This is why the Jordan regime must disappear.

Together with Zarqawi, Maqdisi gave an increasing number of speeches in the homes of group members and in places of worship won over to the cause of jihad, for example the Hamuri Mosque in Awajan, a suburb of Amman, not far from the Zarqawi family home. Here he tested out all his arguments: the decline of Jordanian sovereignty in the face of Israel, American interference in the region, the need for jihad, the struggle against the infidels. As Zarqawi stated before the prosecutor Mahmud Obeidat, his group opposed the United States because that country rejects Islam.

Maqdisi's talent and eloquence and Zarqawi's charisma and the fear he inspired attracted new disciples. The group kept expanding as it recruited in the Jordanian provinces. On one occasion Zarqawi, accompanied by his friend Al-Aruri, traveled to the Karak region on the banks of the Dead Sea near the village of Al-Qasr. There they enrolled Abdul Majid Al-Majali. Mustafa Hassan Musa, Maqdisi's brother-in-law and a veteran of the Army of Mohammed that had been dissolved in 1991, soon brought them his skills in explosives.

Zarqawi has reported that one day, while his group was meeting at Mustafa Hassan Musa's home, the latter touched a spark to a sediment of acetone peroxide, an explosive in the form of a white powder, thereby producing a slight explosion. This was just one way of illustrating his project, which was to send a booby-trapped "Christmas card" to Walid Abu Daher, the editor of the Arabic magazine *Al-Watan Al-Arabi*, whose offices were in Paris. He never managed to bring this off,[75] though he was convicted of the attempted attack. Walid Abu Daher died in 2004.

As the meetings and theological discussions continued, the members of the group began to grow impatient to proceed to true terrorist action. At the instigation of Zarqawi and Maqdisi, a plan was drawn up for a suicide mission against Israeli targets. But in order to succeed they needed equipment.

Shortly before settling in Jordan in 1992, Maqdisi, as we know, had lived in Kuwait. As it happened, at the time of their retreat Saddam Hussein's troops had left behind quantities of munitions, and Maqdisi had bought a large supply of these on the black market. When he moved to Jordan he slipped five antipersonnel mines, seven hand grenades, and several antitank rockets among his household possessions. He would later confess to Jordanian investigators that his aim was to use this equipment in an attack on Israel.

To carry out operations the right way, Zarqawi suggested that Maqdisi hide the weapons in the large house in the Ma'soum district in which part of his family lived at the time. Maqdisi refused. After trying in vain for two weeks to conceal the equipment around the cemetery, Zarqawi returned most of it to Maqdisi, keeping just a few explosive charges for which he constructed a hiding place, a double wall, in the family home.[76] He wanted to keep these weapons, he said, "to use them in a suicide mission in the territories occupied by the Zionists."[77] He had, in fact, persuaded his two faithful colleagues, Suleiman Taleb Damra and Abdel Hadi Daghlas, to carry out a suicide mission on the border between Israel and Jordan. But the latter was arrested by the Jordanian authorities before this first terrorist action planned by Zarqawi could be put into effect.

Some of his accomplices in Bayt Al-Imam describe Zarqawi as ambitious but certainly not a visionary. Thus the Jordanian activist Yussef Rababa recalls a man who, unlike Osama Bin Laden, had no long-term projects. His lawyer at the time, Mohammed Dweik, goes as far as to state that his client never struck him as especially intelligent.[78] It was Maqdisi who served as the group's mentor, while Zarqawi took charge of military operations.

The arrest of Abdel Hadi Daghlas threw everything back into doubt. For, at this time, Bayt Al-Imam was composed of only a few men, basically Maqdisi, Zarqawi, Khaled Mustafa Khalifa Al-Aruri, Suleiman Taleb Damra, the brothers Nasser and Nafez Fayez, Mohammed Rawashdeh, Amer Sarraj, Nasri Izzedin Mohammed

Al-Tahayneh, Mohammed Wasfi Omar Abu Khalil, Nabil Abu
Harthiyeh, Sharif Abdul Fatah, and Ahmad Yussef. In addition, the
hard core of the group were the men around Maqdisi, Zarqawi,
Aruri, and Abu Khalil, and differences were beginning to arise
among them.

The dissent came primarily from Khaled Al-Aruri, the third in
command. Originally from Ramallah in Palestine, he was 27 years old
at the time of these events. An employee of the Saudi organization
IIRO in 1991, he returned to Zarqa in 1992. He supported Zarqawi but
did not subscribe to all his projects, such as the plan to assassinate Ali
Berjak, a member of the powerful antiterrorist intelligence service
GID, and Yakub Zayadin, honorary president of the Jordanian Communist Party. Nor did Al-Aruri approve of the idea of setting fire to
the GID headquarters.[79]

Following several secret meetings of the members of Bayt Al-
Imam, Zarqawi undertook to carry out the operations. He provided
Aruri and Damra particulars on Berjak and Zayadin, collecting information on these two targets and locating Berjak's personal residence.[80] Eight years later, on February 28, 2002, two people were
killed in the explosion near Berjak's residence of a booby-trapped
car belonging to his wife.

IN ANY EVENT KHALED AL-ARURI HAS RETAINED ZARQAWI'S TRUST
throughout his career as a terrorist. His name came up in the context
of the inquiry into the Casablanca attacks of May 16, 2003: it was he
who sent Aziz Hummani, a Moroccan Salafist, the $70,000 needed to
carry out the attacks.

The members of Bayt Al-Imam did not fear prison so much as
the tough methods of the GID, whose aim, two years after the return
of the first veterans, was to destroy these rebel groups. Tracked by
the Jordanian government and weakened by the arrest of Abdel
Hadi Daghlas, Bayt Al-Imam was driven into a corner. Zarqawi and

Maqdisi then planned to flee Jordan with false papers. To this end Zarqawi contacted Mahmoud Hassan Hadjawi, who lived near the Huseyn Mosque in Zarqa, to obtain a false passport. It cost him 100 dinars and a photo, and a week later he received the document in the name of Ali Ahmad Abdullah Majali.

As operational leader of the group, Zarqawi was able to use his contacts to the advantage of Maqdisi and Aruri. Maqdisi soon got a false Jordanian passport in the name of Fayez Al-Hafi.[81] He and Zarqawi then hastened their preparations for flight, since, as Zarqawi would later confirm to the prosecutor who interrogated him, they knew they had been under observation by the Jordanian Secret Service for several days.[82]

Zarqawi was aware that, ever since his return, he had been a priority target of the service on account of his fiendish personality and his relationship with Maqdisi. He received a summons from the headquarters of the service to appear at his Al-Ramzi residence but had already decided not to obey it. His reaction, as he himself described it during his interrogation, reveals a great deal about the kind of man he was: "I would have done anything not to go there and to resist if they decided to bring me in. When I knew I was summoned, I bought a submachine gun and paid 800 dinars for it. I did this with the aim of resisting if the police came to my house....I had three rounds for this weapon and thirty-five cartridges."[83]

Despite his firm intention not to be caught, Zarqawi was arrested on March 29, 1994. Five days later Maqdisi, too, was arrested by the police at home in Yajuz. During the search conducted under the direction of Captain Mustafa Awad, Maqdisi asked that his parents be allowed to leave the house so as not to learn that their son had hidden explosives in the family home.[84] The explosives in question were found in a false ceiling especially constructed for the purpose, as well as in the curtain rods. Maqdisi himself climbed up onto a barrel to point out the cache to the policemen.

The lawyer Fouad Badawi, who was officially appointed to defend

Zarqawi and Maqdisi, refused to do so and was soon replaced by Mohammed Dweik. During their interrogations the terrorists came up against the GID's severity, to the point where Maqdisi had to ask several times not to be hit.[85]

In preparing the case, the military prosecutor Mahmoud Obeidat raised several charges against them, including participation in an illegal organization, unauthorized possession of explosives and weapons, falsification of passports, and impugning the honor of the king. Another military prosecutor, Muhannad Hijazi, who had been on the scene at the Ma'soum house, retained a precise memory of the way Zarqawi addressed him. Zarqawi was shackled at the time and under the surveillance of the security forces when the prosecutor came over to him. Although Hijazi wasn't wearing his badge or official insignia, Zarqawi called him by his name. Surprised, Hijazi asked how he knew his name, and Zarqawi replied that he had seen him at work in a number of court cases and had noted the pertinence of his closing speeches.

Hijazi recalls a hardened boy with a piercing gaze, his body covered with tattoos. In his opinion Zarqawi was more of an ordinary delinquent at this time than an international terrorist; his reputation was that of a hoodlum with vague religious learning. When he was apprehended Zarqawi had tried several times to pass messages to his family members, who were watching from the balcony of the house. He had tried especially hard to let his brother know where the explosives were hidden; he had told the police that the weapons were in a dry stream bed below the family home near the Zarqa cemetery, whereas they were within the precincts of the house itself. Before this Zarqawi had pretended for several hours that he no longer remembered the hiding place.[86]

His brother Omar, too, was eventually arrested in connection with the investigation of the Bayt Al-Imam network and spent prison time in Suwaqah.

Hardened as he was, Zarqawi signed detailed confessions before the military prosecutor Mahmoud Obeidat on August 31, 1994, declaring himself guilty of having possessed bombs and mines without official permission, and of having forged and used a false passport.[87] Maqdisi, in turn, signed similar confessions and went as far as to condemn terrorism: "The bombs, mines, and weapons I had at my disposal were not destined for terrorist actions in Jordan but for resistance against the Israeli enemy, and I am against all persons committing terrorist acts against the police, agents of the intelligence services, movie theaters, and stores selling alcohol."[88] We do not know under what circumstances Maqdisi made this statement. In any event, the actions undertaken by Bayt Al-Imam come under the heading of terrorism as that term is ordinarily understood and were primarily aimed at the Hashemite kingdom.

After this initial arrest Maqdisi continued to support the Salafist cause and Islamist attacks perpetrated around the world, taking special pleasure in the terrorist actions of September 11 in Washington and New York. Although he is once again incarcerated in Jordan, he continues to spread his extremist views on his Web site.

THUS, IN THE COURSE OF THE YEAR 1994, THE BAYT AL-IMAM group was dissolved by the Jordanian police, and its leaders, Maqdisi and Zarqawi, were convicted and imprisoned. This group had been one of the gravest extremist threats hanging over Jordan, and the authorities breathed a sigh of relief. But scarcely three years later, in 1997, new investigations pointed to a reactivation of Bayt Al-Imam centering around four young Jordanians, Mujahid Abd Al-Rahim, Isa Al-Khalayleh, Ali Al-Khalayleh, and Saud Al-Khalayleh. The last three belong to the Zarqawi clan, Saud being Abu Musab's own cousin.[89]

CHAPTER 5

At Suwaqah, the Desert Prison

THE OPERATION AGAINST ZARQAWI AND HIS GROUP WAS A GREAT success for the Jordanian security forces. The thirteen terrorists came before the Court of Military Security, presided over by Colonel Yussef Fawri, in November 1996.

During the trial Maqdisi seemed to revoke his confession, shouting, "*Allahu akhbar* [God is great], history will record the secret of our jihad, the voice of jihad will not weaken." When Colonel Fawri pronounced the sentence of fifteen years in prison for the leaders of the group, Maqdisi recited verses from the Koran. Before leaving the room, he cried, "Your penalties only strengthen our faith in our religion. Victory until jihad!"[90]

Abu Musab Al-Zarqawi received his first oppressive prison sentence in his own country only three years after returning to it. From that day on he cherished a virulent hatred against that power, which he considered to be corrupt and in the pay of the Americans. In 1995, however, these same Americans would express concern about the poor conditions under which the Jordanian prisoners at Suwaqah were detained.[91]

At the trial Zarqawi seemed mesmerized by the Salafist views in which he had immersed himself since his return from Afghanistan. He challenged Jordanian power along with all forms of public authority. He did not want a lawyer at his side and refused to listen to the judge, whose verdicts, he said, were contrary to the teachings of God. He tried, quite awkwardly, to be his own defense attorney, asking his judges to repent and get back in touch with the spirit of jihad. He had obviously lost awareness of reality: his was a confused, disturbed personality, saturated with an ideology adroitly distilled by his intellectual mentor, Abu Mohammed Al-Maqdisi. The court-appointed lawyer for Zarqawi and Maqdisi, Mohammed Dweik, cast a jaundiced eye on the two men: "At the time Ahmed [Zarqawi] had the same ideas as Maqdisi...; he [Zarqawi] could have admitted to being Maqdisi's clone. But Maqdisi is a thousand times more dangerous than Zarqawi. He had charm and charisma and could have convinced anyone."[92]

After the madrasas in Pakistan, the landmines in Afghanistan, and the suburbs of Amman, Zarqawi found a new battleground: the Jordanian prisons. And it was in prison that his magnetism and strength appeared in a new light. Sentenced on November 27, 1996, to fifteen years of confinement, he was immediately transferred to the high-security prison of Suwaqah, one of the most heavily guarded in Jordan, located in the middle of the desert between Amman and Aqaba.

He had already spent over two years there since his arrest in 1994. On the third tier of the third cellblock, he occupied cell number six opposite the office of the prison director.[93] This large collective cell, scattered with steel beds, held various "Islamists" including certain members of Bayt Al-Imam. One of Zarqawi's cellmates recalls seeing him set up his bed as a tent by hanging the blankets down from each side of the mattress; seated on the ground, Zarqawi would try to memorize the verses of the Koran.[94] Maqdisi reports that, "on the level of the religious sciences [he] wasn't a model student, but he learned the Book of God by heart."[95]

Maqdisi was incarcerated in the same prison at the same time. But now Zarqawi was the one with the influence. In 2004 Maqdisi gave a very mild version of this transfer of authority: "The brothers chose me as emir [chief]. I remained in that role unwillingly for a year before dedicating myself to the religious sciences. I decided to give my position to Zarqawi. Contrary to what certain people have written, [this] was not the result of a quarrel between us but the result of an agreement, so that we could speak with one voice to the heads of the prison."

Zarqawi became a curiosity for his jailers and cellmates alike. Who was this man, his body covered with greenish tattoos, who spent his time reading the Koran? And why did he say so little? Intriguing and fascinating, he quickly made sure he had a network of relationships both inside and outside the prison. The outside relationships were easy. Maqdisi was able to compose and circulate his writings while in prison, be it at Suwaqah, Al-Salt, Jafar, or Kafkafa. In 2004 he explained that "in each prison it was possible for us to have letters sent out and books brought in…. The government imprisons us, and God gives us everything we need."

Though the ways of God are impenetrable, corruption is often widespread in prisons. As for the regular transfers from one prison to another, according to Maqdisi they enabled the inmates "to get close to [our] brothers" and "strengthen ourselves in our convictions." He adds, moreover, that the Jordanian government "does not suspect that prison makes our fight stronger."

Sheikh Jarrah Al-Qaddah, who visited Zarqawi in prison, recalls seeing him shortly after he was found guilty. Zarqawi, he says, had the reputation of loving his brothers in arms more than the members of his own family, and he shouted a great deal inside the prison, just as he used to do in the streets of Zarqa when he got back from Afghanistan.

In just a few months' time he became a respected ringleader in Suwaqah on the basis of his past in Afghanistan, his religious positions, his physical strength, his defiance of the prison authorities, and his often summary treatment of his fellow inmates. Layth Shubaylat, a more moderate Islamist opponent of the Jordanian regime, was incarcerated at the same time for having been a member of the Army of Mohammed. The two men often crossed paths in the corridors. Although they were both Islamist militants, Zarqawi looked down on this former member of Parliament accustomed to political methods and involved in the democratic system. A faithful pupil of Maqdisi, Zarqawi believed that democracy was in no way compatible with the Koran.

Layth Shubaylat, for his part, recalls a man steeped in religion. On several occasions Zarqawi's sense of commitment led to rather sharp conflicts with the prison staff. For example, the supervisors required all the inmates, with the exception of some political prisoners, to wear uniforms. Zarqawi and his sidekicks refused, the uniform being in their view a symbol of submission to the authority of the regime. According to Shubaylat, the army sent troops into the prison one day in order to make sure the rule was respected. The situation turned into a clash, and Zarqawi's side finally had to give in. Mad with rage, he turned to the soldiers, hurling abuse at them and calling them infidels. According to the same source, right from the beginning of his incarceration Zarqawi established himself as one of the most influential ringleaders.[96]

Layth Shubaylat was freed a few months later by decree of King Hussein and redoubled his attempts to have his Islamist companions released. He later reported his conversation with the king on the occasion of an audience the latter granted him shortly after he was freed:

—Your Highness, let me give them good news.

—About whom are you speaking?

—About the prisoners, the political prisoners, or let me say the Islamists, or let me say the Afghans.... Sir, let me tell you that you and I are responsible for these people.

—How?

—For fifty years you have taught them to stand up to Zionism. Would you expect them to change overnight? For me, as a moderate Islamist, you have failed. You haven't allowed me, or those who think the way I do, to develop one or the other part of our program. And so, Your Highness, you now have to expect that people worse than I am will call you an infidel.

As recounted by Layth Shubaylat, the anecdote says nothing about the king's reaction.

While Shubaylat was pleading the Islamist cause before the king, the "democratic" Islamist forces, including the Jordanian branch of the Muslim Brotherhood, were launching into an intensive campaign of lobbying various political forces in the kingdom, and Zarqawi was entrenching his position inside the prison. As one day followed the next, his hatred of the regime and his rage against the "infidels" increased. Yet Zarqawi did not forget his family (especially his mother, Um Sayel, and his wife, Um Mohammed), to whom he regularly sent letters and drawings. Written in the first years of his detention, this correspondence shows how hardened he was becoming in prison. The deprivation of liberty strengthened him in his notion that he was on the right path in his struggle and had to remain steadfast in his beliefs. Nearly two years after his arrest by the Jordanian police Zarqawi showed no regret for his ideological choices or remorse for his first attempted attack.

His fellow prisoners drew closer to him, and Zarqawi noted which of them were the most faithful. The ties that formed during these years became indestructible, all the more so because they were based on a remorseless ideology. A Jordanian journalist, Abdallah Abu Rumman, the future editor in chief of the weekly *Al-Mira'ah*, shared Zarqawi's everyday life during their stay in Suwaqah. He recalls that in September 1996 Zarqawi was still the leader of the group of Islamist prisoners, especially those who came from Bayt Al-Imam.

At that time Zarqawi and his partisans were being held in a cell next to that of the journalist. They had their own social system following strict rules set up by Zarqawi, who attended to all aspects of the group's organization. In this same wing of the prison there were of course other factions, inspired by convictions different from Zarqawi's. According to Abu Rumman, internal wars would often break out between the clans, each accusing the other of apostasy. Prison opened a new battlefield for these warriors of God.

Thus in the early 1990s Suwaqah was a formidable breeding ground in which the most divergent Islamist causes were thrown together. The various movements represented there resembled gangs offering their members protection and survival insurance. Each group occupied its own space, recruiting new members, distributing its own proselytizing tracts, and meeting in specific places at the hour of prayer on Friday.

Several groups, all illegal, shared the central wing of the prison. Among them was the Islamic Liberation Party, whose leader, Ata Abu Al-Rashtah, was also the founder of the Al-Jun and Al-Mujib groups. Offshoots of the Jordanian Islamic Brotherhood, they coexisted with several Islamist mavericks like Layth Shubaylat. And then there were the "Afghans." These men were a group apart, determined to impose the caliphate in Jordan and throughout the Middle East, starting with Suwaqah Prison. Unpredictable and bold, the members of this movement had networks running from one wing to another of the prison and hence were feared by the other inmates. Zarqawi headed the group's hierarchy together with Abu Mohammed Al-Maqdisi.

Looking on at this fundamentalist organization reconstituted inside the prison, Abdallah Abu Rumman stressed the influence Zarqawi gradually achieved among the "Afghan" prisoners to the detriment of the ideologue Maqdisi.[97] Even though he had inspired Zarqawi's Islamist vocation, Maqdisi now saw his control and influence diminishing. Unlike the theoretician Maqdisi, Zarqawi was glad to play the strongman and provoke the guards and administration of the prison. He even tried several times to organize uprisings, maintaining the aggressivity of the group of inmates sharing his conditions of detention. Summoned to the office of the head of security at Suwaqah, he looked him straight in the eye on each occasion.[98]

Zarqawi's outbursts earned him not only close surveillance inside the prison but also the special attention of his jailers. The wing in which the members of Bayt Al-Imam were held soon enjoyed privileges such as exemption from the morning roundups in the prison yard and, eventually, from the need to wear a uniform. According to Abdallah Abu Rumman, the "Afghans" were also freer to move around within the prison, visiting other inmates without fearing reprimands.[99]

FLAUNTING HIS DEFIANCE OF THE GUARDS, ZARQAWI ATTRACTED the admiration, or at least the respect, of his comrades. Unlike the other inmates, he behaved like a rebel. But, by the same token, he found it hard to take criticism.

One of the inmates, Yussef Rababa, incarcerated at the same time for his ties to the illegal organization Ajlun Minds, often wrote for the prison magazine. When he published articles critical of Zarqawi, the latter replied with his fists. According to Rababa, this is all Zarqawi was capable of, being unable to view a situation objectively and use words in support of his actions.[100] In contrast, some reports describe an impassioned man carried away by a vision, the vision of the advent of the caliphate. But the majority of eyewitnesses recall a violent Zarqawi who could not tolerate contradiction and religious differences. According to his comrades, on several occasions he even struck some of his fellow prisoners for having read books other than the Koran.

One of these men, Abu Doma, convicted of throwing a bomb at civilians, has an unpleasant memory of Zarqawi. One day the latter came upon Abu Doma, who was reading *Crime and Punishment*. "Why are you reading this book by a heathen?" he asked. Some time later

Abu Doma received a threatening letter from Zarqawi, reproaching him for having immersed himself in Dostoyevsky's masterpiece. Next, according to Abu Doma, Zarqawi sent him a letter in very bad Arabic, as though it had been written by a young child, ordering him to stop reading "Doseefsky."

Zarqawi came and went freely in the prison, wearing his traditional Afghan garments. He took credit for the great Afghan battles against the Russians, although he had not actually experienced them. In the course of the secret meetings and long afternoon discussions in cell number six, he maintained the myth of the "Arabs" of Afghanistan, forging a legend for himself. Unable to hold his own in the political debates established among the Islamists, he created a different impression by lifting makeshift weights he cobbled together out of pieces of his bed and olive oil cans filled with pebbles. His cellmates clearly recall his muscle-building exercises. To keep himself fit, he ran in the prison yard every day. His physical strength became a way for him to ensure his power; he liked "to have his authority in his hands," Yussef Rababa confirms.[101] Zarqawi later demonstrated this in Iraq, during the darkest hours of the execution of hostages.

As the months went by Zarqawi developed the body of a fighter. He became an essential figure in the small world of Suwaqah, taking on a social role by distributing meals to his fellow inmates, participating regularly in housekeeping chores, and on occasion bathing his sick cellmates.[102] In this way he won the forty prisoners around him over to his cause. He then extended his sphere of power by recruiting among the ordinary delinquents and the drug addicts, whom he considered "victims of society."[103]

In the course of 1997 Zarqawi and the political prisoners at Suwaqah were transferred to the prison of Al-Salt and, in early 1998, they were finally incarcerated at the high-security prison at Jafar, one of Jordan's harshest penal institutions, which was reopened for the occasion.[104] There Zarqawi asked to consult the prison doctor. One of his relatives was diabetic, and he wanted to know his own blood sugar

level. The physician on duty, Dr. Basil Abu Sabha, still remembers
how great an influence Zarqawi exerted; during that visit the doctor
observed that Zarqawi was able to give orders to his fellow inmates
solely by blinking his eyes, and that the others did not go to the in-
firmary unless they had gotten his permission in advance.[105] Abu
Sabha also noted that Zarqawi had tried to remove his tattoos, in-
delible as they were, with hydrochloric acid.

In that same year, 1998, when Al-Qaeda struck the American embassies in Tanzania and Kenya, Zarqawi mentioned to his cellmates
his firm intention to join in the attack on American targets.

ZARQAWI GAINED HIS INDEPENDENCE IN SUWAQAH PRISON. WHILE
he was shaping his body and radicalizing his ideas, his wife, Um Mohammed, his oldest daughter, Aminah, and his mother, already seriously ill, were impatiently awaiting his return to the family home in
Al-Ramzi. The people close to him were worried about his situation,
but Zarqawi himself was not anxious in prison. Quite the contrary,
he felt comfortable there. In the intermittent letters he sent to his
family, he explained that he had become reconciled with himself—
and with God.

Over the course of the year 1998, Zarqawi dedicated more and
more time to praying among his comrades. After each Friday prayer
he prolonged the sermon by speaking up against the unbelievers and
the injustices committed by the Arab and American regimes. Yussef
Rababa, observing developments from the outside, noticed a profound change in the relationship between Zarqawi and Maqdisi at
this time; it became increasingly strained as Zarqawi grew envious of
the recognition accorded the theologian by those around him. At the
end of the year Maqdisi remained alone in Suwaqah after Zarqawi's
transfer to Jafar.

Since the time of his arrest in 1994, Zarqawi had most definitely
not calmed down. Unlike Osama Bin Laden, who advocated the fight

against the Jews and the Crusaders, Zarqawi swore the destruction of all unbelievers, which assured him quite a large range of potential targets to aim at once he was released.

For Zarqawi, the term "unbeliever" covers a rather heterogeneous set of people, including not only Christians and Jews but also Shiites, Hindus, and, more generally, all those who do not strictly adhere to the tenets of Salafism. By the end of his incarceration in Jordanian prisons he had been won over to the Manichean idea that there are two worlds: the world of Sunni Muslim believers of the Salafist persuasion and the world of the others, the *kafirs* or unbelievers, among whom he counts Muslims themselves when they collaborate with the "implacable" enemies: Israel and the United States. No individual belonging to the second category deserves to live. Shortly before his release from prison Zarqawi confided to Rababa that it was his duty to attack unbelievers wherever they might be and without distinction, whether Europeans or Shiite Muslims.

While Zarqawi was swearing the fulfillment of his dark plans, the Jordanian intelligence services were deeply concerned about this man who was unclassifiable, determined, and hardened by five years of imprisonment. For Zarqawi was unpredictable. He did not fit into any preestablished schema or partisan logic but seemed to obey an instinct of destruction. On this last point the militant Zarqawi is very far from the sophisticated objectives of Al-Qaeda and the ideological directions taken by Osama Bin Laden. The various terrorist operations undertaken by Al-Qaeda at this time conformed to a longstanding political and military strategy worked out and executed by Bin Laden himself. At this stage Zarqawi, like Maqdisi, lacked the means to put his ambitious terrorist program into action.

At first, therefore, Zarqawi would have to content himself with a terrorism of expediency.

PART II

Full-Time Terrorist

He was a sort of hoodlum in the city of Zarqa. He did not have the reputation of being an intelligent or brilliant man. All of a sudden, when he was just a criminal and a drunk, he found himself in the nets of Al-Qaeda.

—KING ABDALLAH OF JORDAN,
SEPTEMBER 27, 2004

CHAPTER 6

A New Departure

AMMAN, JANUARY 1999. KING HUSSEIN WAS DEAD; LONG LIVE King Abdallah, who ascended to the throne of the Hashemite Kingdom of Jordan. Abdallah had spent his childhood between Jordan and England, primarily in Surrey, with his English mother, Antoinette Avril, who converted to Islam and took the name Mouna. Schooled at St. Edmond's and then at the military academy Sandhurst, he returned to Jordan only in 1984. Until he was named to the position of brigadier general in the Jordanian army in 1994, Abdallah pursued his studies in the most prestigious Anglo-Saxon universities, including Georgetown in Washington, D. C. It goes without saying that the most Westernized of Arab leaders in the Middle East was quickly denounced by Islamists of every stripe as the pawn of the Americans. As for Abdallah, he wanted to open his country to the outside world and liberalize the Jordanian economy.

In spite of the dissent, the coming to power of the young king worked in favor of regional stability at first. For Abdallah was quick to distance himself from the rigid directions his father had taken when it came to foreign policy. He aligned himself closely with

Washington in the hope of a lasting diplomatic rapprochement with the United States. Though Abdallah refused to let his country become the rear base of the Americans in their project of destabilizing the regime in Iraq, the alliance with the United States took on a special dimension after September 11, 2001, when Jordan headed the list of the Arab nations taking an active part in the antiterrorist struggle waged by Washington. On the regional level Abdallah undertook to pursue Jordan's efforts in the context of the peace treaty of 1994, maintaining peace with Israel. Yet the peace accords remained the subject of strong criticism among the people of Jordan, and even more so in the Islamic world in general.

From the beginning of his reign Abdallah had to work things out with the Islamists, and in particular with the Muslim Brotherhood. A full-fledged institution in Jordan, the Muslim Brotherhood is one of the top-level political forces in the kingdom. Established in Amman in 1946 as a political party, it defends a fundamentalist vision of Islam. Persecuted in Saudi Arabia, Syria, Egypt, and Algeria, the Brotherhood positioned itself under Jordanian protection in the 1970s. This same group, however, had stood by without lifting a finger when the Palestinians of Jordan were crushed in 1970. They followed a policy of docile submission with regard to the king. Given their apparently harmless nature, King Hussein had opened the doors of democratic representation to them in the 1989 election. After an unexpected landslide, the Muslim Brotherhood now dominates the Jordanian Parliament and occupies several ministerial positions.

From 1989 on, then, the Jordanian ruler had to come to terms with the Brotherhood. Its role in Jordanian society had become too important to be ignored or neglected. By 1995 the fraternity employed over one thousand people and controlled entire sectors of society: some thirty schools, eighteen health clinics, and two hospitals.[1] Moreover, the Muslim Brotherhood controls some of the Palestinian refugee camps, including the one in Zarqa, one of the largest in the kingdom. It is said to play a role in the writing of textbooks and the development of educational programs. In book after book it spreads an anti-Semitic and anti-Christian message, in contrast to the king's efforts in the direction of openness.

Like his father, Abdallah undertook a politics of compromise with the Islamists, receiving the heads of Hamas, for example, on March 18, 1999, in the presence of Abdul Majid Zuneibat, the leader of the Jordanian branch of the Muslim Brotherhood (Hamas is the Brotherhood's Palestinian branch). On this occasion Hamas had to repeat the oath of allegiance to Jordan it had made in 1992. As a token of goodwill, the new king granted early release to twelve imprisoned militants of the movement. On August 31, 1999, however, he was forced to close the Jordanian branch of Hamas under American and Israeli pressure.

In the first weeks of his reign Abdallah received a great many requests from Parliament, the Muslim Brotherhood, and various Islamist committees to free political prisoners, that is, fundamentalist Muslims being held in Jordanian penal institutions. This pressure was all the stronger for being supported by public opinion. Faced with this groundswell and the intensive lobbying deployed by Islamist movements, Abdallah was cornered, especially since, traditionally, a royal amnesty is extended forty days after the death of the sovereign. That time was drawing near.

On March 23, 1999, the television news opened with the announcement of a general amnesty for Jordanian prisoners. The king had given in, and, to Washington's great displeasure, the amnesty included the Islamist prisoners. The royal decree was approved by a vote of Parliament on March 18, 1999.[2] The pardon excluded only individuals imprisoned for drug dealing, slavery, treason, rape, murder, or terrorism. Not a word about the Islamists.

Ultimately three thousand prisoners were freed, Zarqawi among them. The heads of the various Jordanian security services were bitter about this general amnesty. One of them stated confidentially that "many of the freed men are recidivist hoodlums and delinquents who will remain a burden on Jordanians after their release."³ This statement was very close to the truth.

The Islamists in power hastened to get their activists out of prison. The amnesty decree went into effect on March 18, 1999, and two days later fifteen members of the Islamist Action Party were freed. Abdul Majid Zuneibat took credit for the king's decision. On the basis of this success, several Islamist groups in Parliament, for example the Committee on Public Freedoms and Human Rights under Muhammad Al-Azayidah, demanded the immediate release of their people. Al-Azayidah asked for the immediate discharge of the "Afghans" being held in Jordanian prisons, and, on March 29, 1999, Zarqawi and his comrade Khaled Al-Aruri were free men.

Sentenced to fifteen years in prison, Zarqawi did not expect this early release, and it was almost with regret that he left his cell in Jafar. Given his determination to take action against the "unbelievers," his former associates were waiting to have him rejoin them. A few weeks later Maqdisi left Suwaqah Prison, was kept under surveillance by the GID, and, in 2002, was sent back to prison, where he remains.

Not a single day had gone by in Suwaqah without Zarqawi's promising the destruction of the infidels. Later on he often told those around him, especially his brother-in-law Saleh Al-Hami, that he hadn't really been glad to regain his freedom. In accordance with the profile of the psychopath who gradually gets used to incarceration to the point where he needs it for his sense of stability, as time went on in prison Zarqawi had gained an increasingly comfortable position based on his reputation. Outside of the world of prison, he had to start all over again. He confided to his brother-in-law that his detention caused him less distress than living as an ordinary Jordanian, which seemed highly monotonous to him. Hardly out of prison, Zarqawi struck Al-Hami as a man overcome by his lassitude and unemployment, once again eager to leave his own country. "I sensed the spirit of jihad deep within him," Al-Hami later reported.[4]

Set free at seven o'clock in the evening, Zarqawi did not return home to kiss his mother until eight the next morning. He intentionally spent an extra night in prison to share a few more hours with his cellmates.[5] Later—too late—King Abdallah would admit that his release "was perhaps a mistake," adding, however, that "no one could have suspected at the time what would become of him." On the contrary: there was every reason to believe that Zarqawi was on the point of lapsing into religious violence.

Zarqawi spent only one month with his relatives,[6] the time he needed to prepare for his departure. He made a show of trying to find a job, but after his two previous career failures he was under no illusions. For a time he toyed with the idea of buying a truck and selling fruits and vegetables, but this plan went nowhere. He attended the mosques of Zarqa once again, trying to mobilize a new set of young men, but his mind was elsewhere. Already planning his revenge, he joined the preparations for the attacks scheduled for the millennium. (As we shall see, these were foiled in October 1999.)

Convinced that Jordan was becoming too dangerous a country for him and his sidekicks,[7] and that sooner or later he would fall into the hands of the GID, he organized his departure for Pakistan, where he planned to stay on a six-month visa.

Before leaving he withdrew his children from the school system and ordered them to learn the Koran thoroughly. His mother would later say that his decision to leave early was mainly due to the fact that the GID kept on investigating him after he left prison.[8]

In setting out for Pakistan in the summer of 1999 Zarqawi put behind him his family life, his past as a delinquent, and his country. He also distanced himself for awhile from Abu Mohammed Al-Maqdisi. With the exception of a few isolated terrorist projects aimed at his country of origin, he never went back to Jordan. Abu Musab Al-Zarqawi was entering a life of secrecy and engaging in "global jihad."

Several years later, in a message broadcast in Iraq, he described his departure in these terms: "Although I yearn for the cradle of my childhood and feel a burning desire for my parents, my brothers, and my childhood friends, I am global and have no land that I can call my country. My fatherland is wherever God's word takes me." He added that he "left the land of [his] memory, emigrating to the land of hope where the religion of God was established on earth, and then to the land of Afghanistan in obedience to Allah."[9]

Zarqawi told his lawyer at the time, Mohammed Dweik, that Afghanistan was his only chance. Indeed, in the opinion of Yussef Rababa, his former cellmate in Suwaqah, "Because of his ideological orientations there was no longer a place for him in Jordan."[10] And shortly before he left, Zarqawi said this to Saleh Al-Hami: "Do you remember my dream? Do you remember the sword that fell from the sky, with the inscription 'jihad' engraved on the blade?"

AND SO ZARQAWI LEFT JORDAN A SECOND TIME, HEADING FOR Hayatabad,[11] where he had stayed during his first trip to Pakistan between 1989 and 1993. Nostalgic for the grand time of the mujahidin, he was happy to find himself once again in this frontier city, a stopping place familiar to many Arab fighters who had received medical attention there.

Hayatabad is on the outskirts of Peshawar, near the border with Afghanistan. One of Zarqawi's sisters lived there, married to a teacher of religion. His mother says that she accompanied her son to Hayatabad in 1999 and stayed there for a month.[12]

Even more than Peshawar, Hayatabad is a fallback position for Al-Qaeda. The Wafa Organization, one of the Islamic humanitarian groups implicated in Al-Qaeda's functioning, was established in this city. Originally in Jordan, this radical nongovernmental organization (NGO) was characterized as "terrorist" by the United Nations committee on sanctions against Al-Qaeda and the Taliban. Moreover, during the German proceedings against Zarqawi's terrorist networks, known as Al-Tawhid, one of Osama Bin Laden's lieutenants, Shadi Abdalla, confirmed that Zarqawi had received major assistance from the Wafa Organization in Pakistan: "In addition to providing false papers and planning clandestine trips, the members of Al-Tawhid take care of providing money for the fighters. For that, the Pakistani Wafa Organization plays an important role with its office in Kabul."[13]

According to the repentant terrorist Jamal Ahmed Al-Fadl, a former top-ranking leader in Al-Qaeda who became an informer for the United States government, Hayatabad is definitely one of the primary nerve centers for Al-Qaeda in Pakistan. At the end of the investigation into the attacks directed against the American embassies in Africa, a criminal trial against Osama Bin Laden and those in charge of the attacks was held in the United States in February 2001. In the course of this trial Al-Fadl gave one of the most precise accounts of Al-Qaeda.

Thus, when asked about what kind of support the terrorist group had in Pakistan, Al-Fadl replied that Al-Qaeda had had guest houses at its disposal in Hayatabad since 1991.[14] And it was in Hayatabad that the Tanzanian Ahmed Khalfan Ghailani, the Al-Qaeda member in charge of the attacks on the American embassies in Kenya and Tanzania, was arrested on August 19, 2004. Other important members were also captured in this fiefdom of Osama Bin Laden.

ONCE IN HAYATABAD, ZARQAWI TRIED TO PUT HIS PERSONAL LIFE back together and reconstitute his networks in the shortest possible time. His jihad could wait no longer; the fanatic Islamist was impatient to make up for the time lost in Jordanian prisons. He made more and more contacts, renewing his ties with his former friends from the time of the mujahidin and returning to his former quarters in Hayatabad's most extremist places of worship, the very ones he had stayed at in the early 1990s.

But the situation had changed since then. Peshawar in 1999 had become the rear base of the Taliban. The Afghan mullahs were recruiting on a large scale in the mosques and places of worship. And the Taliban leaders would take refuge there in 2001 after the coalition began bombing Afghanistan.

CHAPTER 7

Entering Al-Qaeda

AT FIRST UM MOHAMMED AND HER CHILDREN MOVED INTO A modest three-room house in the Al-Kasarat district north of Zarqa, but she soon joined Zarqawi in Pakistan.

Hayatabad is also the city that welcomed Osama Bin Laden at the start of the war against the Soviets. According to several reports, in the mid-1980s the Saudi had settled in the Fourth District with his wives and children. From 1987 on, Hayatabad was his rear base.

Zarqawi's return to Pakistan coincided with Al-Qaeda's rise in power. The network had emerged with new strength after the attacks on the American embassies in Kenya and Tanzania in August 1998, attacks that left two hundred and twenty-four victims. Osama Bin Laden was now focusing his group's activities on the border between Pakistan and Afghanistan, specifically between Peshawar and Jalalabad.

It was not by chance that Zarqawi had come there. He knew that if he wanted to plan large-scale operations he had to get closer to Al-Qaeda's decision center and especially to Osama Bin Laden himself. Since his visa permitted him to stay in Pakistan for only six months, his time was running out. And so each evening he would go to the central mosque in Peshawar to pray and to try, in his own way, to force destiny. But the Pakistani authorities were watchful.

In 1999 the international community was greatly concerned with the aid Pakistan was providing for the Islamists. Pakistan and its central intelligence organization, ISI (Inter-Services Intelligence) were accused of playing into the hands of the terrorists, or at least of the Taliban government next door. Moreover, the parts of Pakistan adjacent to Afghanistan were inevitably succumbing to what has been called a kind of Talibanization. This was causing anxiety around the world, exacerbated by the fact that Pakistan was now a nuclear power. The Taliban ideology moved easily across the porous borders of the Afghan mountains as Afghanistan was torn apart by an endless civil war following the peace agreements with the USSR.

The fundamentalist Pashtun regime governing Afghanistan at that time was close to Islamabad. Kabul was under the yoke of fundamentalist leaders whose faces remained unknown, photographs and photocopies being forbidden by the Taliban. The prerogatives of the state were strictly limited to Islamic law, and, with its neighbor's blessings, Afghanistan had become the first caliphate in modern history.

The Taliban regime was supported by a major segment of Pakistani religious leaders like the mullahs of Peshawar, who advocated an updated interpretation of Deobandism, a school of fundamentalist thought that had originated in Deoband, India, as a branch of Sunni Islam promoting the struggle against the British colonizers there. The Pakistani mullahs preached hatred and violence against the infidel Western governments trying to reproduce the colonial pattern in Central Asia.

Saudi money, which had continued to flow in since the end of the war against the Soviets, made it easier to operationalize these precepts. Between 1994 and 1999 almost 100,000 Pakistanis passed through Afghan training camps,[15] and an alliance was soon formed between the Taliban and the opposition party of Pakistani Islamists, Jamiat-Ul-Ulema-e-Islam (JUI). In July 1999 between six and eight thousand Pakistani militants joined the ranks of the Taliban. Stonings occurred every week in the streets of Kabul, and all women wore the veil. Thus the Taliban regime was supported by Pakistan and Saudi Arabia, two of Washington's traditional allies.

But Pakistan went too far in providing support. From 1993 to 1999 the government of Benazir Bhutto became increasingly discontent with the political danger posed by its troublesome neighbor. Shortly before she was overthrown by the coup d'état led by General Pervez Musharraf in October 1999, Bhutto undertook a series of purges aimed at Arab militants still present on Pakistani soil. These operations were a response to requests and pressures coming not only from the United States but also from Arabs who hoped to reclaim their "lost soldiers." Going against its traditional policy, Pakistan carried out several raids in Peshawar and above all in Hayatabad, where Zarqawi had recently settled.

In the wrong place at the wrong time, Zarqawi was once more arrested by the police, in this case the Pakistanis. Between May and July 1999 several dozen Arab activists like him were held in the central prison in Peshawar awaiting expulsion to Egypt, Tunisia, and Algeria, which were for the most part their countries of origin.[16] A number of these extremists would nevertheless manage to escape with the help of ISI, which secretly continued to support the government of the Taliban.

When Zarqawi settled in Pakistan in the spring of 1999, the situation of Jordanian nationals had already become complicated. For several months the Jordanian government, with the help of the American FBI, had been stepping up its pressure on Benazir Bhutto to arrest the American-Palestinian national Khalil Al-Deek.[17] Said to be close to Osama Bin Laden's lieutenant Abu Zubaydah, Al-Deek was the operational head of the terrorist cell that planned the so-called millennium attacks in Jordan, a project aimed at the Radisson Hotel SAS in the heart of Amman.

The attention of the Pakistani security forces was therefore focused on Jordan, and as a result Zarqawi was first monitored and then arrested. He spent about a week in prison in Peshawar. During this time, if we are to believe her, his mother in Amman was sure he was selling honey in the city markets.[18] He was eventually released and, though he was listed as a terrorist by the security forces of his own country, given an exit permit by the Pakistani authorities. In any event, he left Peshawar for Karachi.

Once in Karachi, Zarqawi had to make a choice: Should he go back to Jordan or rejoin the Taliban in Afghanistan? As far as he was concerned, Jordan was now just a target of destruction, and his heart was inclined toward the Islamic emirate of Afghanistan. All he had dreamed of these past years was finally being realized in this state, ruled by the discipline of the mullahs, where women were entirely covered—in short, where sharia (Islamic law) was applied, and nothing but sharia.

And so, at the end of the summer of 1999, Zarqawi returned to Afghanistan. He first moved into a house near Wazir Allbar Khan Square.[19] Um Mohammed remained in Pakistan with the children for the time being, but she would soon join her husband in Kabul. Shortly before coming to Afghanistan for the second time, however, Zarqawi had met Asra, a young Palestinian who was the daughter of Yasin Abdallah Mohammed Jarad, an instructor at the Herat training camp in eastern Afghanistan, who would later be killed in Iraq.[20] Zarqawi fell in love with Asra, who was then 13, took her with him to Kabul, and married her when he was heading the camp at Herat. According to a document from the German security services, Zarqawi also got married a third time, to a girl of 16 whom he met in Iraq, her native country, in 2003.[21]

A memorandum from the United States National Security Council, dated April 29, 1999, claims that at this time Al-Qaeda was using the city of Herat to stockpile nuclear material,[22] a detail indicating the crucial role of this city on the Iranian border for the terrorist group.

In the fall of 1999 some young Arab activists who had not fought against the Soviets planned a meeting in Kabul. The word was spread through the circuit of extremist places of worship in Europe and over the Internet: Al-Qaeda was recruiting. A new holy war was in the offing, this time in Afghanistan, against Western interests in the world. Facilities for receiving new recruits, directed by the Jordanian Abu Zubaydah in Pakistan, were moved to Afghanistan in June 1999. At the end of that year Abu Zubaydah, who was now in charge of Al-Qaeda's military operations in Kabul, met with the group of Jordanians under Zarqawi.

On the basis of the charisma he had displayed at Suwaqah and his knowledge of the small world of Jordanian Islamists, Zarqawi had established himself as the leader of the group of Jordanians who came with him to Afghanistan. These included not only his first comrades from the time of Bayt Al-Imam, Khaled Al-Aruri and Abdel Hadi Daghlas, both of whom had left prison in 1999, but also all sorts of future fighters. In the space of a few weeks he had shown surprising skill in reconstituting an operational group and bringing his partisans into Al-Qaeda.

Zarqawi then moved into a "guest house" large enough for his group of about forty Jordanians in the village of Logo, several kilometers west of Kabul, an area traditionally under the control of the extremist leader Gulbuddin Hekmatyar.[23] He leaned on Al-Qaeda, of course, at first to take advantage of its equipment and logistical support so that he could plan large-scale operations. The man who opened the door of Bin Laden's structure to this group of Jordanians was a Jordanian himself, Abu Zubaydah, Al-Qaeda's head of operations.

By the end of 1999 and the beginning of 2000 Zarqawi had proved himself an important part of the Al-Qaeda apparatus in Afghanistan, and in 2001 he took the oath of allegiance to Bin Laden.[24] To avoid any conflict between dissident factions (in particular the Algerian groups), starting in May 2001 the Taliban required all heads of training camps who wanted to pursue their activities to swear allegiance to their regime.

Having taken this step, Zarqawi had to conform to the ideological line set by Osama Bin Laden. The oath of allegiance was a way for Bin Laden to rein in rebellious spirits, but it was primarily a way to bring the different "Islamo-nationalist" groups together under a single banner. The oath, written by Bin Laden himself, is as follows: "I recall the commitment to God, in order to listen to and obey my superiors, who are accomplishing this task with energy, difficulty, and giving of self, and in order that God may protect us so God's words are the highest and his religion victorious."[25]

Since its creation in 1988 the Al-Qaeda organization has functioned according to a complex system of interpersonal relationships. Each group present in Afghanistan—Jordanians, Egyptians, Algerians, Tunisians, and Kurds—obviously had its own concept of jihad, often linked to plans for action aimed at the destruction of the political regime in its country of origin. By making these different groups swear an oath of allegiance, Bin Laden unified them under a single banner and avoided conflicts of interest. Like the other leaders of foreign groups, Abu Doha for the Algerians or Abu Iyad for the Tunisians, Zarqawi had to line up under the flag of Al-Qaeda. There was no choice.

There were three levels in Al-Qaeda at the time. At the top, of course, were Osama Bin Laden and his right-hand man, the Egyptian Ayman Al-Zawahiri. Around them, in a second circle, a managerial staff took shape, each man assigned to a specific mission (security, intelligence, ideology, planning). The third level of the hierarchy consisted of several hundred operational members, many of whom had come up through the Afghan training camps. They ran autonomous terrorist cells in Arab or Western countries that were nevertheless ideologically aligned with the positions of Al-Qaeda.

According to a confidential document of the Spanish antiterrorist unit UCIE (Unidad Central de Informacion Exterior), at the end of the summer of 1999 Zarqawi joined the second circle, the circle of Bin Laden's lieutenants. By this time he was no longer an unknown or marginal figure. He was assigned the planning of the group's operations,[26] and as such was in charge of several dozen militants.

Shadi Abdalla, Bin Laden's former bodyguard, later told the German intelligence services that Zarqawi's rise within the Al-Qaeda hierarchy owed a great deal to Abu Zubaydah, who was himself very close to Osama Bin Laden. Both men were Jordanians; both were inspired by a visceral hatred of the Hashemite regime. Zarqawi is said to have assisted Zubaydah in the preparation of the so-called millennium attacks against Western interests in Jordan. During this first terrorist operation on the international level he would win the trust of the Al-Qaeda staff and of Bin Laden in particular.

Several witnesses agree that Zarqawi was in Kabul at the beginning of 2000, but the report of Saïd Arif is especially significant. This 37-year-old Algerian, imprisoned in Syria since July 2003 for his alleged membership in Al-Qaeda, took part in several Al-Qaeda staff meetings held in Kabul at the beginning of 2000. In the context of a judicial commission of inquiry with Syria concerning the file on the so-called Chechen Ring, French antiterrorist judges happened to have the opportunity to consult the confessions of Arif, who recalled having lunch with Ayman Al-Zawahiri and Abu Doha in Kabul in 2000.

Abu Doha, whose real name is Rashid Bukhalfa, was born in Constantine, Algeria, on November 24, 1969. He was an old friend of the Salafist leader Abu Qatada, based in London and today in prison. Both were in charge of Algeria House in Jalalabad, the main function of which was to facilitate the entry and reception of Algerian fighters who had come to join Al-Qaeda. At this luncheon, Arif says, he talked with the members of the Zarqawi group while Zarqawi himself was in the company of Abu Doha. Since Zarqawi's house in Kabul was right next to Zawahiri's, it is plausible that such a meeting took place.[27]

Maqdisi's shadow was still hovering over Zarqawi's career path. Though the two men had gone through a period of tension and conflict when they were incarcerated together in Suwaqah, their fates seem to be irreparably linked. Zarqawi's progress within Al-Qaeda was determined by several factors: not only his strength of character and his charisma, but also his perfect knowledge of the Jordanian networks and his connection to Maqdisi. After the bombing in Afghanistan at the end of 2001, a number of documents were recovered from the "guest houses" belonging to Al-Qaeda. Since its founding in 1988, that group has kept meticulous and up-to-date records on the progress of its activities. The name of Abu Musab Al-Zarqawi appears in these documents. He is always presented as "the friend of Al-Maqdisi," and the young recruits arriving in Afghanistan are directed to him.[28]

A few months after arriving in Afghanistan Zarqawi was a member of the managerial staff of Al-Qaeda. This brought him close to the networks of the Algerian AIG (Armed Islamic Groups) and the Tunisian TIF (Tunisian Islamic Front). Beginning in 2000 the Tunisian activists belonging to Al-Qaeda were led by Seif Allah Ben Hasin, also known as Abu Iyad. Arrested by the German police in 1993, Abu Iyad was found to be in possession of a forged Dutch passport. He told the German authorities that he belonged to the Saudi charitable organization Al-Haramain, most of whose offices abroad had been designated as terrorist fronts by the United States government and the United Nations. In 1999 Abu Iyad, who would later become one of the leaders of the Darunta training camp, which is said to manufacture and experiment with chemical weapons, undertook a major rapprochement with Abu Qatada, who is considered to be the leader of Al-Qaeda in Europe.

Zarqawi's name appears in one of the letters, seized in 2002, that Abu Iyad sent to Abu Qatada. In this correspondence, Abu Iyad kept Abu Qatada informed of the progress of Al-Qaeda activities in Afghanistan. Although he is openly critical of the decisions of a certain

Abu Walid regarding the running of the camps, he praises the results obtained by Zarqawi, whom he calls "an honest, generous person who would be happy to sacrifice his soul and property for you." He goes on to say that Zarqawi and his group "have decided to protect you against any attack if you decide to come."[29]

After spending several months convincing Bin Laden of his trustworthiness, Zarqawi developed his own network with the financial and material support of Al-Qaeda. He eventually left Kabul and settled in Herat, the third largest city in Afghanistan and an important business center bordering Iran and Turkmenistan, directly opposite Kabul on the map.

In moving to Herat Zarqawi distanced himself geographically from the Al-Qaeda staff. This raised doubts at the highest level of the organization; for several months certain dignitaries had suspected him of being "turned" by the Jordanian services during his five years of incarceration.[30]

Zarqawi was a maverick, as we know, and his autonomy was making the hierarchy anxious.

CHAPTER 8

Origins of the Zarqawi Network

AT THE BEGINNING OF THE YEAR 2000, THEN, ZARQAWI MOVED to Herat with his second wife, the young Palestinian. Far from Al-Qaeda headquarters in Kandahar, the Herat training camp was slowly growing larger and receiving an increasing number of Arab recruits from eighteen different countries, including Jordanians and Palestinians. The camp was situated on the Iranian border near the customs house and the offices of the governor of the city, Abdel Manan Khawajazai, with whom Zarqawi had a good relationship.[31] At the time it was disguised as a religious school[32] and contained ten barracks. At the entry to the camp was a banner reading *Tawhid wal Jihad* (Unity and Jihad), which would become the name of Zarqawi's organization in Iraq.

In directing the camp he surrounded himself with people close to him. The faithful lieutenants at the heart of his network were Abdel Hadi Daghlas, Khaled Al-Aruri, Isam Yusif Al-Tamouni (alias Abu Hareth, who died in Afghanistan in 2001), Abu Hamza, and Azmi Abdel Fatah Yussef Al-Jayusi (alias Abu Ata).[33]

Zarqawi made frequent round trips between Herat and Kabul on behalf of Al-Qaeda. Herat was a strategic site for the terrorist group, opening the way to Iraqi Kurdistan via Iran. Thanks to a diplomatic rapprochement between the Iran of the mullahs and the Afghanistan of the Taliban, the border between the two countries, called "Islam Qila," had been reopened in November 1999.[34] The agreement on free circulation across the border was signed in Herat and ended a period of sharp political tensions between the two governments, triggered by the assassination of nine Iranian diplomats the year before at Mazar-E-Sharif in Afghanistan.

Nevertheless, though the border was open for business dealings and the influx of Afghan refugees, the detente between Kabul and Tehran was only on the surface. The two regimes were full of mutual resentments, and the fearsome Iranian secret service, Savak, was keeping a close eye on the jihadists based on the other side, in Herat. The Iranian consulate in Herat kept a record of the movements of groups linked to Al-Qaeda, Zarqawi's in particular. In addition, the Iranian government was financing an anti-Taliban Shiite militia in the northeastern part of Afghanistan.[35] Zarqawi's missions on behalf of Al-Qaeda were thus known to the Iranian authorities.

As a strategic crossroads of trade and commerce, Herat offered Zarqawi a good opportunity to extend his activities. Control of this Afghan city right in the heart of Central Asia makes it possible to oversee several routes for jihad, including the one leading to the Caucasus via Turkmenistan. As early as 1996 the Russian authorities had emphasized that certain Chechen rebels were being trained in the camp at Ziaraj, located in the province of Herat.[36] A transit city for the Sunni mujahidin, Herat was also marked by a strong Shiite tradition.

Several months after Zarqawi's arrival it was clear that the camp, situated outside the city, was being run successfully, with recruits being taught the handling of arms, explosives, and chemical weapons. The news quickly reached Bin Laden. Summoned by his chief of staff, Zarqawi went to Kandahar in 2000. He needed money to carry out his activities, especially one close to his heart: he wanted to mount an attack on Israeli soil at any price. His first attempt, in 1993, as we recall, had ended in bitter failure and led to his incarceration. This time he intended to succeed.

He got $35,000 from Al-Qaeda to organize the attack and, soon after his trip to Kandahar, sent two of his closest associates on this suicide mission. The Jordanians Firaz Sulaiman Ali Hijir and Ahmed Muhammed Mustafa were arrested at Van, in Turkey, under melodramatic circumstances in February 2002. The two men, accompanied by a Palestinian called Ahmet Mahmoud, refused to comply with a routine check. They took flight and were caught by the Turkish police. Interrogated at the police headquarters in Van, all three confessed their plan, formulated in Kandahar in 1999, to mount an attack in Israel, where they were heading by way of Iran and Turkey. They revealed to the police that they had been convicted by the Jordanian courts in connection with the Bayt Al-Imam affair in 1994.[37] The two suicide bombers sent by Zarqawi, who happened to be childhood friends of his from the Ma'soum district of Zarqa, turned out to be failures. Once again a terrorist operation planned by Zarqawi ended up as a fiasco.[38]

But Zarqawi persisted in his supervisory task. He recruited a goodly number of Jordanians, including some of his former friends from Bayt Al-Imam. In 2000 Zarqawi's Jordanians were a distinctive group on the regional chessboard. Based in Herat, they were mobile and well trained, able to travel to Iraqi Kurdistan by way of Iran. In contrast to the Algerians, who were destroying each other in power struggles in Jalalabad, and the Tunisians of the Darunta camp, the Jordanians were both the scouts and the missionaries of Al-Qaeda on the new front of Iraqi Kurdistan. For all these reasons Zarqawi saw his way clear to gaining his ideological—and also operational—independence very quickly.

In the past he had been careful to keep his distance from Maqdisi. Now he was trying to get free of the political line imposed by Osama Bin Laden himself and especially by Ayman Al-Zawahiri. This wish for independence was reinforced by the geographical distance of the Herat camp and the recurrent criticism of Bin Laden on the part of many jihadists. The Saudi had the reputation of constructing his own myth to the detriment of the common cause aimed at restoring the caliphate, and two "foreign factions" in Afghanistan, one of which was Zarqawi's, were said to be hostile to him.[39] But in 2000 Bin Laden's financial and political support was still indispensable to Zarqawi, and he would have to be patient for another few months before breaking free. For it was only when he fled Afghanistan for Iran and then Syria that his expenses would be paid by his networks in Europe and the Middle East.

In Europe Zarqawi was already relying on two important support cells that were forming in Germany and Italy. In the Middle East he was receiving support from people in Syria and Jordan, one of whom was Bilal Mansur Al-Hiyari, a Jordanian national who would be accused by his country's security court of having participated in financing Zarqawi's group in Iraq.[40]

For the moment the Herat camp was a training camp quite like the others. But Zarqawi was beginning to surround himself with the faithful. Some of the Jordanians who joined him came from the Palestinian refugee camps of Lebanon and belonged to the terrorist organization Asbat Al-Ansar (League of Partisans).[41] Formed in the Ein Al-Hilweh refugee camp, Asbat Al-Ansar was headed in the early 1990s by Ahmad Abdul Karim as-Saadi (alias Abu Muhjin). Several attacks on Western interests in Lebanon in the course of that decade bore the mark of this group, whose Salafist ideology was close to the precepts imposed by Al-Qaeda on its members. It was also Zarqawi's ideology.

Beside these Jordanians most of the people close to Zarqawi were Iraqis and Palestinians. These men were much too young to have known the years of jihad against the Soviets.

Like Bin Laden, Zarqawi required the new recruits to take an oath of allegiance. His strong personality ensured a unified, homogeneous, and trustworthy group. Thus it was not long after the establishment of the Herat camp that a number of Zarqawi's associates were implicated in attacks or attempted attacks in Jordan, Iraq, and Israel.

Five Jordanians, in particular, were among those who joined Zarqawi in 1999. Some of them came from Chechen combat zones, others directly from Jordan to strengthen the ranks of Al-Qaeda in Afghanistan. The father of one of them, Nidal Arabiyat, has testified to the conditions under which his son joined Zarqawi.

Nidal Arabiyat had completed his primary education before enlisting in the Jordanian Army for two years. After an auto accident he sought refuge in religion and began to read widely on the subject of jihad. He soon built a wall of silence around himself, remaining alone for days on end, until he announced to his father that he was going on a pilgrimage to Mecca. His father thought at the time that he would never return. After fighting alongside Zarqawi and Bin Laden in Afghanistan, Nidal Arabiyat returned to Iraq by way of Iran and Iraqi Kurdistan. This lieutenant of Zarqawi's, a specialist in laying car bombs, was eventually killed in the course of an American operation in the northern part of Baghdad in February 2004.[42]

One of the most determined Jordanians, Muammar Al-Jaghbir (also known as Moammar Ahmed Yussef Al-Jaghbir) came from Al-Salt, a city west of Amman controlled by the Muslim Brotherhood. One of Zarqawi's companions at arms, he would eventually be arrested in Iraq and sent back to the Jordanian authorities in May 2004. He was accused of taking part in the assassination of the American diplomat Laurence Foley in Amman in October 2002. Like Zarqawi, Al-Jaghbir was sentenced to death by the Jordan courts; like Zarqawi before him, he benefited from an amnesty in 2000 under pressure from the Islamist deputies of Balqa.

Another of Zarqawi's partners was arrested in Baghdad at the same time. Ali Mustafa Yussef Siam, one of the terrorists who took part in the Foley assassination, also joined Zarqawi in planning the assassination of Ali Berjak, head of counterterrorist operations in the

GID, the state intelligence department.[43] He too had been freed in the royal amnesty.

Then there was Azmi Al-Jayusi, who on April 26, 2004 would try to set off a chemical explosion in central Amman that, according to the authorities, would have killed 80,000 people. In his confessions, broadcast in their entirety on Jordanian television, Al-Jayusi explained how it all began: "At Herat I started training for Abu Musab. The training included handling high-level explosives and learning about poisons. I then took an oath of allegiance to Abu Musab Al-Zarqawi and agreed to work for him without asking questions."[44]

Another Jordanian from Al-Salt, the city that would provide Zarqawi with twenty of his fifty associates, was Ra'id Khuraysat (alias Abu Abdel Rahman Al-Shami), who quickly became one of Zarqawi's right-hand men. On Zarqawi's order Al-Shami and three other young recruits from Al-Salt, Mahmoud Muhammad Al-Nusur, Mutasim Musa Abdallah Muhammad Al-Darikah, and Ibrahim Khuraysat, soon left the camp at Herat to extend the group's range of action to Iraqi Kurdistan.[45] This mission, coordinated by Zarqawi and, from above, by Osama Bin Laden himself, was intended to reorganize the "Islamist resistance" in Iraqi Kurdistan.

The purpose of this small community of jihadists established in Iraqi Kurdistan was to repeat the experience of the Taliban in this area and prepare a possible fallback position for the Al-Qaeda terrorists. On September 1, 2001, Al-Shami and his three associates took part in the creation of the Islamist group Jund Al-Islam; several weeks later they fought against Jalal Talabani's Patriotic Union of Kurdistan. Jund Al-Islam, soon to be renamed Ansar Al-Islam,[46] would ensure the retreat of Zarqawi and his partisans after the American bombing in Afghanistan.

Zarqawi's interest in Iraqi Kurdistan is not surprising, for he was acting on behalf of Al-Qaeda, which was planning a progressive redeployment of its members to Kurdistan in anticipation of the turmoil to follow September 11. As early as 2000, Bin Laden knew that the attacks of September 11 would be devastating, and that the American reaction would be proportionately severe. A prudent man, Bin Laden therefore instructed Zarqawi and his partisans to infiltrate the region of Iraqi Kurdistan.

Parastin, the primary Kurdish intelligence agency under the Democratic Party of Kurdistan (DPK) of Massud Barzani, had long taken an interest in Ansar Al-Islam. One of the officials of the agency, Dana Ahmad Majid, stresses the fact that the terrorist organization was inseparable from Al-Qaeda: "Before September 11, Al-Qaeda planned to secure a new base for itself to which it could retreat after the attacks…, because they [Al-Qaeda] knew very well that they would be attacked in Afghanistan after the September 11 attacks and would have to find another territory…. They thought the Kurdish government was weak enough that they [Al-Qaeda] would be able to take control."[47]

In 2000 Zarqawi increased the number of his trips between Kabul and Herat, gradually imposing his authority over the Islamic resistance in Iraqi Kurdistan. He controlled the road that passes through Mashhad, in Iran, and leads to the Kurdish mountains. He also took charge of the Sargat training camp in Iraqi Kurdistan, identified several times as a place where chemical weapons and biological toxins were manufactured. Tests performed by the United States Army after the bombing of Iraqi Kurdistan would reveal the presence of very powerful neurotoxic agents like botulin and ricin in the Sargat camp.[48]

To ensure his control of the Islamist factions in Iraqi Kurdistan, Zarqawi called on his companions from early days, the men who had been part of Bayt Al-Imam and were released along with him in 1999, especially his former neighbors from Zarqa, Khaled Al-Aruri (alias Abu Ashraf) and Abdel Hadi Ahmad Mahmoud Daghlas (alias Abu Ubaydah). These two men were living in Iran at the time, on the border with Iraqi Kurdistan. They would soon become the coordinators of Ansar Al-Islam's operations, taking orders from Zarqawi, their chief. The group of about fifteen men, mostly Jordanians, under their direction had been set up in Iran by Zarqawi himself. Their task now was to help Ansar Al-Islam mount attacks in Jordan and fight against the Democratic Party of Kurdistan. At the same time Ansar Al-Islam profited from the ability of the organization's founder, Mullah Krekar, to mobilize funding.

FOR THE JORDANIAN SERVICES IN CHARGE OF COUNTERTERROR-ism this was a bitter picture. It was clear in retrospect that the royal amnesty of 1999 had had grave consequences. Only one year after releasing Zarqawi, Maqdisi, Aruri, Daghlas, Al-Jaghbir, Firaz Sulaiman Ali Hijir, Ahmed Muhammed Mustafa, and the others, the GID saw a revival of the threat of Islamist terrorism, a threat that was all the more direct because the group was planning to kill officers of the GID itself,[49] most importantly Ali Berjak, the head of the counterterrorism unit.

Between the amnesty freeing the members of Bayt Al-Imam in March 1999 and the reconstitution of Zarqawi's organization, only one year had gone by. In the meantime Zarqawi was strengthening his support in Iran, Afghanistan, and Iraq. From now on the Jordanian services would have to confront an extremely serious threat, countering a campaign of attacks directly aimed at Jordan. In short, the Jordanians of the Muslim Brotherhood, who had lobbied intensively at the beginning of 1999 for the freeing of the Islamists, had truly achieved their ends. The terrorists, more hardened now, were free—and in a position of strength.

In accord with Al-Qaeda, the Ansar Al-Islam organization would eventually be placed under the control of a triumvirate: Zarqawi in Afghanistan; Al-Shami in Iraqi Kurdistan; and Mullah Krekar, who had taken refuge in Norway in 2002. The operational members of the organization were based in the mountains of Iraqi Kurdistan, but the network was in Iran and consisted almost entirely of Zarqawi's associates.[50]

Even while he set up his network in Iraqi Kurdistan in coordination with Al-Qaeda, Zarqawi continued to direct the Herat training
camp on an autonomous basis. This wish for independence would
become stronger in the course of 2001, as the proximity to Iran and
his enduring relationship with Ansar Al-Islam inspired him to extend his own networks in Europe, especially in Germany and Great
Britain. These terrorist cells, which the European judicial authorities
would later call Tawhid (Unity), were in fact only an extension of
the Ansar Al-Islam networks. The Tawhid organization was to have
a twofold function under Zarqawi: mounting attacks on European
soil and ensuring support at the time of his flight from Afghanistan
after "Operation Enduring Freedom."

CHAPTER 9

A Regional Terrorist

From now on Zarqawi would represent a serious threat, as became evident in several attacks and attempted attacks organized in the Middle East between 1999 and 2004. After arriving in Pakistan in 1999, he organized a series of terrorist operations whose primary target was the kingdom of Jordan, still a source of bitterness for him. Thus, before occupying center stage as an international terrorist, Zarqawi made himself a reputation on the regional level.

One of the first attacks he organized after leaving prison was aimed at tourist sites in Jordan. Although the name of Ahmad Fadil Nazzal Al-Khalayleh does not appear on the list of guilty parties sent by the government of Jordan to the Committee on Counterterrorism of the United Nations on January 29, 2002, Zarqawi's participation was later confirmed by the Jordanian courts. Moreover, on February 11, 2002, Zarqawi was sentenced in absentia to fifteen years in prison for his role in this planned attack, which was known as the millennium plot.

The millennium plot had been planned in its entirety by Jordanians working for Al-Qaeda in Afghanistan. Fresh out of Jordanian prisons, Zarqawi did not have enough power at the time to coordinate an operation; this task fell to the head of military operations in Al-Qaeda, the Jordanian Zayn Al-Abidin, also known as Abu Zubaydah. In 1999 Abu Zubaydah received a visit from two Jordanians determined to conduct jihad in their own country: Ahmad Al-Riyati and Ra'id Hijazi. Abu Zubaydah agreed to help, taking the two men and training them in the Al-Qaeda camps to handle explosives. In November 1999, when Zarqawi left Pakistan prematurely for Afghanistan, he met the two young Jordanians in Kabul on the advice of Abu Zubaydah. Zarqawi had the full confidence of Abu Zubaydah, who was himself one of the chief lieutenants of Osama Bin Laden.[51]

From that time on, Zarqawi, together with his faithful comrade in arms Khaled Al-Aruri, took part in the plans for attacks at the time of the millennium. Among the targets were the Radisson Hotel SAS in the heart of Amman, the place where Jesus was baptized on the banks of the Jordan River, and the King Hussein Bridge connecting Jordan to Israel.[52]

These were ambitious aims, perhaps too large in scope for the abilities of this group of Jordanians inexperienced in matters of terrorism. Despite the financial support of Al-Qaeda and Zarqawi's technical assistance, the Jordanian police would soon discover the plot and sentence the guilty parties, including Zarqawi. Abu Zubaydah was eventually captured by the American special forces on April 12, 2002, and sentenced to death by the Jordanian court. In the course of his interrogation he confirmed Zarqawi's involvement in the attempted millennium plot.

During his trial, the Jordanian court established the identities of various terrorists implicated in the operation. The military prosecutor in charge of the case, Colonel Fawas Al-Buqor, indicted the military leader of the Kurdish terrorist network Ansar Al-Islam, Najmuddin Faraj Ahmad, better known as Mullah Krekar. Mullah Krekar had provided aid to several members of the cell accused of implementing the attacks, chief among whom was the Jordanian

Ahmad Mahmud Saleh Al-Riyati. Since there is no extradition agreement between Jordan and Norway, where Mullah Krekar was living in exile, the leader of Ansar Al-Islam is still a free man.

Some of the twenty-seven terrorists found guilty of the plot were arrested in Syria and Jordan. When he pronounced the verdict, Judge Tayel Raqad announced that Hijazi, one of the leading terrorists of the group, had been sentenced to death. Hijazi, who was present in the courtroom, exclaimed, "God is great" then turned and addressed the judge as follows: "Where is God's will? Why are you sentencing me to death? You are running the country against the citizens of Jordan. [Ariel] Sharon does not sentence his people to death. You are fighting your own fellow citizens for a few dinars."[53]

Zarqawi, for his part, was sentenced for the second time to fifteen years in prison, this time in absentia. The millennium plot reveals the state of mind of the militant extremists of Al-Qaeda, resolved to fight a regime they considered corrupt and collaborationist.

Despite this setback Zarqawi pursued his bloody plans, more determined than ever to strike at the Israeli government. He once again decided to attempt a suicide mission. As we have seen, ever since he arrived in Afghanistan and joined Al-Qaeda, he had been planning an operation similar to the one that had failed in 1994, and with the same partners, his neighbors from the Ma'soum district of Zarqa, Firaz Sulaiman, Ali Hijir, and Ahmed Muhammed Mustafa. The same causes produce the same effects: the two men were arrested in Turkey.

These two aborted attempts did not discourage Zarqawi, who, from Syria, coordinated an action targeting Jordan in 2002. The plan was to strike at American interests in that country, and, more specifically, to assassinate the American diplomat Laurence Foley in Amman. The operation called for support and a complex organization of which Zarqawi became the manager.

To implement this operation, he gathered around him several of his own associates and members of the Al-Qaeda network: Salem Saad Salem Ben Suweid (alias Abu Abdallah); Yasser Fatih Ibrahim

Freihat (alias Abu Firas and Abu Maaz), a Jordanian living in Rasifa; Mohammed Amin Ahmad Said Abu Said, a Libyan national also living in Rasifa; Neaman Saleh Hussein El-Harach, a Kuwaiti national living in Amman; Shaker Yussuf El Abassi (alias Abu Yussuf), a Palestinian living in Syria; Mohammad Ahmad Tyura (alias Abu Ouns), born in Syria and living in that country; Mohammed Issa Mohammed Daamas (alias Abu Oman), living in Rasifa; Muammar Ahmad Yussef Al-Jaghbir (alias Abu Mohammed), a Jordanian who would later be killed in Iraq; Ahmad Hussein Assoun (alias Abu Hassan); and Mahmoud Abdelrahman Zaher (alias Abu Abdelrahman), who, like Abu Hassan, was a Syrian national in flight from the law.

This planned attack against the diplomat was partly based on the special relationship between Suweid and Zarqawi. A veteran of Afghanistan, Suweid had met Zarqawi in the Sada training camp in 1989. He also met Osama Bin Laden, Ayman Al-Zawahiri, and Abdallah Azzam, likewise in Afghanistan. Zarqawi's jihadist companion in the early 1990s, Suweid volunteered to join him in carrying out a terrorist operation on Jordanian soil. Zarqawi had support from Al-Qaeda as well as weapons and financial resources.

In radical Islamist circles Suweid already had the reputation of being a professional. The subject of an arrest warrant in Libya for his participation in a group of Islamist activists, he had fled with his wife to Syria, then to Jordan, in 1992. He would remain in Jordan for five years, during which he regularly met with Zarqawi in the Bilal Mosque in Ujan. The two men were solid friends until Zarqawi's incarceration in Suwaqah. In August 1997 Suweid left Jordan and returned to Syria, settling in Damascus, though he made regular trips to and from Jordan with the aid of false Tunisian passports.

Suweid was gradually consolidating his own group of activists, bringing in Yasser Fatih Ibrahim Freihat, his future accomplice in the Foley assassination. Suweid and Freihat had met in Jordan at the end of 1997. But Suweid was especially close to the Syrian Mohammed Ahmad Tyura, who helped him obtain a forged passport in the name of Ali Lafi so that he could leave Syria. In April 2002 Suweid had asked Freihat to learn how to handle explosives and manufacture chemical weapons. Freihat then contacted Tyura in order to get this training. The next day, Tyura took Freihat to one of the "military barracks"[54] of Damascus, a camp where Freihat spent a week. Under the supervision of three soldiers, he was trained in the use of submachine guns and pistols and in the manufacture of bombs with ammonium nitrate.

Other members of Zarqawi's group, including Daamas and Harach, also trained in Syrian military barracks in 2002. Along with Freihat, they learned how to use M16 assault guns, offensive grenades, and Kalashnikov rifles.

After his training, Freihat returned to Suweid in Jordan. On Zarqawi's advice the two men rented an unassuming house in Rasifa, on the outskirts of Amman. In June 2002 they were joined there by the Syrian Tyura. Their house also served as a hiding place for the five Kalashnikovs and other weapons needed for the operation. From neighboring Syria Zarqawi provided funds for the dormant cell in Rasifa, sending sums of $1,000 and later $5,000.

Zarqawi wanted to oversee the operation personally and soon ordered his two faithful lieutenants, Daamas and Al-Jaghbir, to bring Suweid back to Syria. When they met in June 2002, Zarqawi gave Suweid a seven-millimeter pistol, a silencer, and seven rounds. This was the pistol used to kill Foley.

Later, at the trial, the defendants stated that in the summer of 2002 "Zarqawi was living in Syria," although U.S. Secretary of State Colin Powell placed him in the Olympic Hospital in Baghdad, where Zarqawi claimed to be receiving medical treatment between May and July of that year.[55]

To verify that all was in order, Zarqawi entered Jordan secretly from Syria in September 2002 and spent several days in Tarfa with Suweid and Daamas. The operation was taking shape. Zarqawi gave Suweid $13,000, asking him to enlist additional recruits in order to ensure the success of the assassination. He promised to send Suweid arms and explosives from Iraq[56] and to deliver missiles with a view toward a second operation.

One month later, in October 2002, Zarqawi did indeed send Suweid important sums from Iraq: $10,000 and then $30,000. The money was intended to finance a series of terrorist operations on Jordanian soil, including the Foley assassination, and came to the terrorists through the Rafidain Bank. Ultimately over half of the funding for the operation would be sent by this bank, which was held by the Iraqi government at the time.[57]

At Zarqawi's request the group simultaneously prepared an attack against the United States. To this end Zarqawi kept watch on the military airport at Marqa, from which American planes would take off to bomb Afghanistan. He even made provision for transporting missiles that could shoot a plane down during takeoff. The operation proved too complex and was eventually abandoned.

On October 28, 2002, Laurence Foley, a 60-year-old American diplomat attached to the United States Agency for International Development (USAID) was killed in his garage by eight bullets fired point blank by Suweid. This action was the first of its kind directed against a foreign diplomat working in Jordan.

From the very beginning of the inquest, the Jordanian Minister of Information, Mohammed Adwan, noted the lead to the terrorists: "Whatever its motives, this is an attack on the country and its national security." The GID was quick to find not only the gunman, Suweid, but also Freihat, who was waiting for him in his car, and to identify the commander, Abu Musab Al-Zarqawi.

During his initial interrogation at the GID, Suweid stated that he had killed Foley "because he was an easy target for us."[58] On orders from Zarqawi, Suweid and Freihat had first carefully followed their intended victim, studying all his movements in Amman. In short, the terrorists had carried out a painstaking analysis of the terrain on the model of the "Homo" operations conducted by classical intelligence services. Once the target had been "neutralized," Suweid called Al-Jaghbir, Zarqawi's lieutenant in Iraq, to confirm the success of the operation.

The means employed by Zarqawi and his team to implement the assassination seemed almost disproportionate, and the Jordanian antiterrorism investigators were struck by their professionalism. Until then Zarqawi had taken part only in attempted attacks, but after the Foley killing the threat he represented was taken very seriously. On April 6, 2004, after his trial in absentia as the ninth defendant, "Ahmad Fadil Nazzal Al-Khalayleh," as he was referred to, was sentenced to death by hanging.[59]

The Foley incident marked a turning point in Zarqawi's career. He had proved capable of coordinating an operation from abroad and profoundly destabilizing his country of origin, Jordan. But his campaign of terror was only beginning.

The operation had revealed Syria's role, previously unrecognized, in supporting Zarqawi's networks. According to the Jordanian indictments, Zarqawi had been in Syria between May and September of 2002, availing himself of access to the "military barracks" in order to train his recruits; he possessed a Syrian passport and had been able to travel more or less freely from Syria to Jordan and Iraq. In addition, the Jordanian inquest revealed that the Foley operation had been planned almost entirely from Damascus by Zarqawi and his closest collaborators.

Although these accusations are much more serious than those leveled at any time against the regime of Saddam Hussein, up to now they have not been mentioned. Zarqawi's presence in Syria is also attested to by at least one Western intelligence service, which has established on the basis of telephone taps that he was in the Damascus area during this time.

But this is not all. When Zarqawi returned to Iraq in September 2002, he let Suweid know that he could be reached in Baghdad should the need arise. Foley's murderer stated that he was to come to the Al-Ghouta restaurant, a short walk from the Hotel Palestine in Baghdad, and mention the name "Al-Khalayleh" so that the owners of the restaurant could put him in contact with Zarqawi.[60] This upscale establishment in the Iraqi capital is owned by Syrians.

As chance would have it, the actor Sean Penn, writing in his travel journal after his return from Baghdad,[61] used these Syrian owners of the Al-Ghouta restaurant and the presence of Iranian tourists to illustrate "the irony of the Iraqi situation" at a time when the neighboring states were placing all their hopes on the fall of the regime.[62] This is one more piece of reality that seems to have escaped the Americans, unless they knowingly evaded it.

AT DINNERTIME ON APRIL 26, 2004, WHEN THE WAR IN IRAQ WAS raging, the Jordanian national television channel began the evening news with a "special program." To their horror, the Jordanians learned that they had had a close brush with death.

The threat had a name: Azmi Al-Jayusi. The terrorist who was speaking in front of the camera was a man with a round face, an ordinary-looking but articulate Jordanian. On the occasion of this televised forced confession, he described in detail how he had planned a chemical attack in Amman that, if successful, could have killed 80,000 people and wounded 160,000. The scenario was similar to that of the attack on Foley two years earlier, in that Al-Jayusi said he had received his orders, false passports, and money from Zarqawi. This time, however, the means and ends were different, the targets being none other than the building in which the prime minister had his offices, the headquarters of the GID, and the American embassy in Amman.

To carry out these attacks the terrorist group had manufactured twenty tons of chemical explosives, packing them in containers that were carefully placed on trucks. The overall operation was directed from Iraq by Zarqawi, who had provided the necessary funding and personnel.

On April 20, 2004, shortly before the group carried out the operation, which would have been the largest terrorist undertaking ever brought to completion, the Jordanian police brought Al-Jayusi in for questioning. The other members, Muwaffaq Adwan, Hassan Simsmiyyeh, Salah Marjehm, and Ibrahim Abu Al-Kheir, refused to surrender and were killed during the assault launched by the Jordanian police.

Like others before him, Al-Jayusi had met Zarqawi in Al-Qaeda training camps in Afghanistan. And, like the others, he had been trained in explosives at Herat. He too had sworn an oath of allegiance to Zarqawi, promising "to obey without asking questions and always be at his side."[63] After the fall of the Taliban, Al-Jayusi had joined Zarqawi in Iraq, where, with the help of one of his associates in Syria, Khaled Darwish (alias Abu Al-Ghadiyyeh), Zarqawi gave him the wherewithal to constitute his own cell in Jordan.

Soon after this meeting in Iraq, Al-Jayusi had slipped into Jordan together with Adwan, another man close to Zarqawi. Using funds collected by the logistical support group in Syria, he gradually bought all the material needed to manufacture chemical weapons. Through a complex system of messengers, Zarqawi had the sum of $170,000 sent to the group in charge of the operation. New recruits joined the project, including Ahmad Samir, who was directly involved in making explosives near Ramtha Bridge. Finally, Al-Jayusi bought several vehicles, one of which was a yellow truck sturdy enough to break through the gates of the GID and explode inside the compound. All in all, the operation cost more than $250,000; according to the German intelligence services, this money was brought in from Syria.[64]

The group members contacted one another using prepaid phone cards, and they took draconian security measures during their communications. An even more trustworthy method involved the use of messengers recruited in Syria, where the logistical base of the Zarqawi network was located.

As the months went by, some of Al-Jayusi's neighbors in the Al-Barha district near Irbid had noticed a change in his behavior. He seemed to be withdrawing from society and isolating himself. The group soon moved closer to its targets, with Al-Jayusi arranging the final details of the operation, such as the RPG rocket launchers which would be used to shatter the gates when the time came. All the men around him were determined to carry through to the end, if need be destroying themselves with the explosives if the gates held fast.

Later, during the confession, Hussein Sharif, one of the terrorists arrested by the police, said to the Jordanians frozen in shock in front of their televisions: "I agreed to take part in this operation because I think it serves the cause of Islam."

Zarqawi had now become a major problem for the Jordanian services.

CHAPTER 10

Escape

On September 11, 2001, at 9:59 and 10:28 in the morning, the towers of the World Trade Center collapsed in on themselves, leaving 2,823 people injured or dead. On American soil, Al-Qaeda had committed the most important terrorist attack in history. The world was left speechless, as was the United States government. A coalition formed around the United States, and Operation Enduring Freedom got underway in the fall of 2001 in the mountains of Afghanistan.

The international coalition began a series of bombing campaigns in Afghanistan, followed by antiterrorist activities on the ground. These reprisals were only a partial success. Although Operation Enduring Freedom reached and destabilized Al-Qaeda, the group's core members, Osama Bin Laden and Ayman Al-Zawahiri, escaped the 30,000 American troops and 350 combat planes deployed in the area. But someone else, equally uncontrollable, escaped the United States efforts in Afghanistan: Abu Musab Al-Zarqawi.

After September 11 everything changed for the militants of Al-Qaeda. They would now be pursued by all the police forces of the world plus the United States Army. In reprisal for the attacks, the coalition bombed the group's landmarks, training camps, and hiding places. For days on end the mountains of Tora Bora were pounded by American planes. And so the Taliban and the upper echelon of Al-Qaeda fled, for the most part to Pakistan and the tribal regions of Waziristan.

During the offensive, a meeting was held at Kandahar, attended by Zarqawi, Abu Zubaydah, Saif Al-Adel, and Ramzi Binalshibh, who had coordinated the terrorist cell in Hamburg. Later, during his interrogation, Abu Zubaydah said he had wanted to spirit a group of twelve to fifteen fighters out of Afghanistan and bring them to Iraq. He added that the house in Kandahar where they met was hit by an American missile. Trapped under the rubble, Zarqawi escaped with some minor injuries.[65]

In an intercepted phone call on November 12, 2001, one of the heads of Zarqawi's network in Iran, Abu Ali, mentioned the bad health of "Habib" ("Beloved"), meaning Zarqawi. On that same day an associate of Zarqawi's named Ashraf Emad, who had already fled Afghanistan for Iran, related that Zarqawi had not yet slipped out of Afghanistan, and that he was lightly wounded in the legs and stomach but could still walk. Zarqawi confirmed the American losses in Afghanistan for his group of partisans based in Iran: at the beginning of November 2001 he counted eighty "pigs" (soldiers) and four "butterflies" (helicopters).

While other leaders began to flee through the western part of Afghanistan, Zarqawi's escape was organized by Iran. Since the end of 1999 the logistical support cell Tawhid had often been asked to intervene between Iran and Germany. Committed to Zarqawi's cause, they made every effort to transfer him, at least temporarily, to Iran.

A few days after September 11 one of the members of the German cell, Abu Ayyub, bought a satellite telephone for Zarqawi, and Tawhid soon made sure Zarqawi had everything he needed to survive in a hostile environment: false passports, night-vision equipment, and a radio. He now had to get to Tehran as quickly as possible to receive medical attention and, above all, to elude the coalition's antiterrorist operations.

Zarqawi decided to enter Iran through Zahedan in the far southern part of the country. There was no way to leave Herat and travel through Birjand and the border road of Qisla Islam: since the establishment of the training camp at Herat, his activities were known to Iranian security, and the Iranian authorities were on the lookout for members of Al-Qaeda leaving Afghanistan by that route. Savak also knew that his group controlled the Mashhad road in Iran, using it to move jihadists into Iraqi Kurdistan.

Zarqawi put the finishing touches on his escape plan, transferring $40,000 from Tehran to Germany in order to buy the false passports he would need to cross the border.

Phone taps set up by the German police revealed Zarqawi's new face. He spoke in a noticeably gentler way to those on whom he depended for survival and really seemed to be trying to become "Habib."

With the help of some supporters, Zarqawi left for Iran on December 12, 2001. One week later he crossed the border in the south and stopped in Zahedan,[66] phoning Germany to say that all was in order. Taking only a short rest, he set out again for Tehran, arriving in Mashhad, Iran, on January 5, 2002.

He was soon in the care of his group of partisans, who took him to a doctor. Zarqawi made a rapid recovery, and by mid-January he confirmed in conversations with Abu Ali of the Tawhid cell in Germany that he was cured. He would stay in Iran until April 4, 2002. There he made use of the telephone line of an individual named Rashid Haroun in Tehran. He also used satellite and cell phones, making sure to destroy all traces of his calls. Feeling spied on, under surveillance, he reported his concerns to his "brothers" in Germany. In phone conversations tapped by the police there, he explained that many of his associates were on lists of suspected persons, and he feared for himself.

On January 10, 2002, he was preparing to cross the mountains of Iraqi Kurdistan and told Abu Ali, who was still in Germany, that he needed a new Arabic mobile phone, lightweight lace-up shoes in size 42.5, boots in size 43, and a warm leather jacket with long sleeves. His finances were improving. On April 2 he told the German cell: "Almighty God has put me in a favorable financial situation."[67] He was able to cover the expenses of his escape and secure the approximately thirty passports that had been sent from Germany to Tehran for him and his associates.

But on April 23, 2002 the German cell was destroyed: the entire Tawhid group was dissolved by the BKA, the German criminal police.

This cell had been formed around Yasser Hassan (alias Mohammed Abu Dhess or Abu Ali), born on February 1, 1966 in Hasmija, Iraq. It also included the Jordanian of Palestinian origin Ashraf Al-Dagma, born on April 28, 1969; the Jordanian Ismail Shalabi, born on September 27, 1976; the Iraqi Zidan Emad Abdelhadie (alias Imad), born in Alhamza; the Kuwaiti Osama Ahmad, born on May 4, 1974, in Hawali; the Iraqi Thaer Mansur (alias Osman); and the Egyptian Sayed Agami Mohawal, born on February 25, 1964, in Cairo.

Tawhid was identified by the German police at the very moment of the September 11 attacks, just before Zarqawi escaped to Iran. The leader of the group, Abu Ali, met Zarqawi when he was passing through Iran and negotiated with him about details of several terrorist operations in Europe, particularly in Germany. During this meeting Zarqawi refused to let Abu Ali volunteer for a suicide mission in Germany. Whatever his other motives may have been, he still needed Abu Ali in order to survive in Iran.

The strategy of Zarqawi and the fighters around him was to divide into two groups that would set out from Iran in two different directions. The larger group was to go and fight in the mountains of Iraqi Kurdistan at the side of Ansar Al-Islam, while the others would join up with Tawhid and prepare attacks against "Jewish targets" in Germany. In his conversations with Abu Ali, to whom he revealed his plans, Zarqawi announced that his "brothers" were under surveillance by the Iranian services.

Zarqawi was just beginning to reorganize his activities in Iran when he was arrested in the company of his "brothers" by the Iranian security services. Little information has been leaked about the circumstances of this arrest and the imprisonment that followed. During the inquest on the German cell, Osama Bin Laden's former bodyguard, Shadi Abdalla, would confirm that Zarqawi was indeed held for a short time in Iranian prisons.[68] He would also tell the German police that Zarqawi had enjoyed the protection of the Iranian government. This information was later corroborated when Jordanian officials, visiting Iran in the summer of 2003, learned that Zarqawi had been incarcerated in Jordanian prisons in the spring of the preceding year and had been released because he held a valid Syrian passport. We may recall that it was from Syria that Zarqawi planned and financed the assassination of Laurence Foley.

In 2002 the American authorities had warned the Iranian regime about its excessively lax treatment of the escaping members of Al-Qaeda. Following Zarqawi's example, a significant number of jihadists had found temporary refuge in Iran. That country made a show of deporting several presumed members of Al-Qaeda, including Zarqawi's nephew Umar Jamil Al-Khalayleh. The expulsion came after a wave of arrests by the Iranian police in February and March 2002, at which time Zarqawi himself was arrested. Some 150 members of Al-Qaeda were imprisoned. Among them, according to several sources, was the Egyptian Saif Al-Adel, former colonel in the Egyptian special forces and a high official in the terrorist organization. Osama Bin Laden's own son, Saad Bin Laden, was also said to be in Iran at this time, though Saudi Arabia had tried in vain on a number of occasions to have him extradited.

A few weeks after his arrest Zarqawi was out of prison and immediately left for Syria via Iraq. In May 2002 his presence was noted in Baghdad, where he received medical treatment at Olympic Hospital.

According to information gathered by the United States government, he remained in Baghdad for nearly two months before returning to Syria.

If we are to believe the legal documents drawn up by the Jordanian authorities in connection with the Foley case, Zarqawi had been in Syria from May to September 2002 while he and his team were preparing the assassination of the diplomat on October 28 of that year. A European intelligence service looking into a series of telephone calls Zarqawi made to Europe attests to his presence on Syrian soil during the summer of 2002.

While in Syria, Zarqawi personally supervised the final details of the assassination by making clandestine trips to Jordan at a time when he had been sentenced to fifteen years in prison for his participation in the millennium plot. His first wife, Um Mohammed, would later state that she found her husband in the middle of a secret conversation in the house of Foley's killer.

Zarqawi's brief stay in Iraq in 2002 marks the beginning of a new era, that of the war in Iraq. In his speech before the Security Council of the United Nations on February 5, 2003, U.S. Secretary of State Colin Powell called Zarqawi the missing link between Al-Qaeda and the regime of Saddam Hussein. But this information was riddled with factual errors. Described by Powell as a Palestinian, Zarqawi is in fact a Jordanian. Supposedly in Iraq at the invitation of Saddam Hussein, he was in Syria at the time.

But, as events would prove, it is true that he represented a serious threat. From this time on, his repeated operations in Iraq and in the Middle East as a whole would make him, along with Osama Bin Laden, the most hunted terrorist on the planet.[69]

PART III

Zarqawi's Iraq

Sharpen your swords and burn the earth under the feet of the invaders.
—MESSAGE FROM ABU MUSAB AL-ZARQAWI,
APRIL 6, 2004

CHAPTER 11

Terrorist Iraq: From Myth to Reality

"I<small>RAQ</small> <small>TODAY</small> <small>HARBORS</small> <small>A</small> <small>DEADLY</small> <small>TERRORIST</small> <small>NETWORK</small> <small>HEADED</small> by Abu Musab Al-Zarqawi, associate and collaborator of Osama Bin Laden."[1] With these few words Colin Powell, speaking before the United Nations Security Council on February 5, 2003, intended to demonstrate the solid relationship between Iraq and the Bin Laden organization and justify a military action against the regime of Saddam Hussein. At that time the alleged presence of Zarqawi on Iraqi soil was a crucial element of the argument put forth by the United States.

Thus the old dogma of state terrorism was surfacing once again. Questioned by the Senate Armed Forces Committee of the United States Congress on March 19, 2002, in connection with the investigation into the attacks of September 11, George Tenet, director of the Central Intelligence Agency (CIA) at the time, had stated that it would be a mistake to discard the hypothesis of state terrorism, Iranian or Iraqi. This comment would have indicated a certain lack of perceptiveness on the part of the intelligence agency had it not, in reality, served to lend political legitimacy to the American offensive.

Bin Laden, who had been crossing national borders for years, represented precisely the opposite of state terrorism. This line of argument, moreover, would be defended by the CIA itself several months after Tenet's statement: in September 2002, in a report entitled "Iraqi Support for Terrorism," the agency indicated that, according to the Al-Qaeda leader Abu Zubaydah, it would have been extremely unlikely for Osama Bin Laden to enter into an alliance with Iraq.[2] Khaled Sheikh Mohammed, who planned the September 11 attacks, said the same after his arrest: Bin Laden did not stop at a purely ideological opposition. In the course of the 1990s he issued a fatwa calling for rebellion against Saddam Hussein and expressing hopes for his assassination.[3]

The most recent investigations and legal proceedings launched throughout the world against the Al-Qaeda networks reveal that Bin Laden and Saddam Hussein never formed an alliance of means and ends with a view toward waging a terrorist struggle in common. The notion that Al-Qaeda is an offshoot of Iraqi state terrorism is therefore false. On the other hand, these inquests do clearly show that the ideological and religious antagonism between the two sides has often diminished in the face of the logic of common interests. In short, the Bin Laden network and the regime of Saddam Hussein have formed only episodic and opportunistic relations as dictated by circumstances and their commitments at a given moment.

These ties were interpersonal at first. We know that a number of meetings were organized on the initiative of the head of Al-Qaeda and that these followed the same pattern: several Iraqi ambassadors in turn met with Bin Laden and active members of his network.

The initial contacts were made in Sudan in 1991 and 1996. According to the former director of the Iraqi nuclear program, Khidir Hamza, Bin Laden paid frequent visits to the Iraqi embassy in Khartoum in those years.[4] In December 1998, Hamza reports, he met with Farouk Hijazi, the Iraqi ambassador to Turkey and former head of special operations of the Iraqi intelligence services (Mukhabarat).

The meeting is said to have taken place in Kandahar, Afghanistan. After the attacks of September 11, Hijazi was deported from Turkey on the grounds of his closeness to terrorist groups.[5] According to Vincent Cannistraro, formerly an official in the antiterrorist section of the CIA, this information was confirmed by the reports of several intelligence services and was in fact divulged by people around Osama Bin Laden.[6]

A number of contacts were also established between Iraqi emissaries and active members of the terrorist group like Mohammed Atta, the operational head of the September 11 suicide commando, who was later proved to have met with an Iraqi diplomat in the Czech Republic in April 2001. Atta went to Prague on at least two occasions. According to the United States Immigration and Naturalization Service, the flight Atta took to Newark Airport in New Jersey when he entered the United States for the first time on June 3, 2000 had originated in Prague.[7]

On April 8, 2001, he met at the Iraqi embassy in Prague with Ahmed Khalil Ibrahim Samir Al-Ani, the vice consul, who also belonged to the Iraqi foreign intelligence service. The permanent representative of the Czech Republic to the United Nations, Hynek Kmonicek, and the Czech minister of the interior, Stanislav Gross, have confirmed this.[8] On April 19, 2001, Al-Ani was declared persona non grata on the grounds of "activities incompatible with his status as a diplomat" and was deported by the Czech authorities the following week.[9]

In addition, the Joint Inquiry Commission of the United States Congress on the Attacks of September 11, 2001 has established that in February 1999 the intelligence community obtained information to the effect that Iraq had trained a pilot for the purpose of suicide missions against the British and American forces in the Persian Gulf during the first conflict in Iraq,[10] a procedure reminiscent of the way in which the attacks of September 11 were carried out.

Other reports, to be sure without much conclusive value, have also revealed episodic relations between certain members of Al-Qaeda and Iraqi officials. Thus on June 26, 2002, Jose Luis Galan Gonzalez (alias Yussef Galan), a member of the Bin Laden network in Spain, received an invitation at his home address from the Iraqi ambassador in Madrid to a gathering on July 17 to celebrate the anniversary of the Iraqi revolution.[11]

Yussef Galan, who was arrested in Spain in April 2002 and was in preventive detention as of December 2004, is one of the rare terrorists of Spanish origin to have been brought in for questioning after September 11 in the context of Judge Baltasar Garzon's inquest into Al-Qaeda. His name once again came to the foreground after the attacks of March 11, 2004. Before converting to Islam and joining a military training camp in Indonesia, Galan had belonged for a time to the Basque organization Euskadi Ta Askatasuna (ETA).

The most marked convergence of interests between Al-Qaeda and Iraq appears when we focus on the economic and financial network constituted by Bin Laden when he moved to Sudan in 1991, welcomed by the religious leader Hassan Al-Turabi. The chemical industry was especially in favor of this rapprochement because Iraq, at this time, was working with Sudan to develop its arsenal and was trying to take advantage of the presence of terrorist organizations in the country. Former members of Al-Qaeda, testifying in 2001 during the trial of individuals involved in the 1998 attacks on the American embassies in Dar es Salaam and Nairobi, revealed that certain businesses owned by Osama Bin Laden were being managed by Iraqis at that time and employed people from that country. Thus several Iraqi engineers worked until 1998 for the Al-Hijrah construction firm, one of Bin Laden's properties. In the course of the same trial it was learned that the firm was headed by an Iraqi, Abu Ibrahim Al-Iraqi,[12] and no fewer than nine other Iraqis were identified as members affiliated with Al-Qaeda in Sudan.

At the same time, the directors of the Al-Shifa chemical manufacturing works, which also belonged to Bin Laden, were in increasing contact with the head of Iraq's program for chemical weapons and with Emad Al-Ani, one of the directors of the Iraqi firm Samarra Drug Industries, which, according to the Americans, was also helping to develop such weapons.[13] In this same period, traces of a component of gas VX, the formula for which was used exclusively by Iraq, were found in a sample taken by the CIA in the Al-Shifa works.

American sources indicated that, despite denials on the part of Sudan, there was clear and convincing evidence that chemical weapons were being manufactured at Al-Shifa,[14] and they had information pointing to the fact that Sudan had turned primarily to Iraq in its search for aid in developing its chemical weapons program.[15] The Al-Shifa works were finally destroyed by American forces on August 20, 1998 as part of the reprisals following the attacks on the embassies in Nairobi and Dar es Salaam.[16]

Iraq and Al-Qaeda also had in common their hostility toward the United States. In his declaration of war against the United States and the West dated August 23, 1996 and entitled "Message from Osama Bin Laden to his Muslim brothers throughout the world and especially in the Arab peninsula," the leader of Al-Qaeda made an unswerving commitment to the Iraqi people: "The children of Iraq are our children.... Our blood has flowed in Iraq." Likewise, in an interview with Robert Fisk in 1996, Bin Laden declared that "killing Iraqi schoolchildren is equivalent to a crusade against Islam,"[17] and in the same year he stated that his network now covered thirteen countries, including Iraq.[18]

On February 13, 2001, in the course of the trial of the people involved in the attacks on the American embassies in Africa, testimony by a former member of Al-Qaeda shed light on the position of the terrorist group with regard to Iraq. When the prosecutor asked him whether Al-Qaeda thought the United States would stop bombing Iraq if enough Americans were killed, he replied, "Yes, this is the conviction of Al-Qaeda."[19]

Certain statements from the Iraqi side also suggest that the regime of Saddam Hussein was no stranger to the attacks of September 11.

Thus, on that very day, the official Iraqi broadcasting channel commented on the attacks on the World Trade Center and the Pentagon in these terms:

> The American cowboy is reaping the fruits of his crimes against humanity. This is an accursed day in the history of America, which is tasting the bitter defeat of its crimes and its rejection of the will of the people to lead a free and decent life. The mass explosions over the center of American power, in particular the Pentagon, are a painful blow inflicted on American politicians so that they will cease their illegitimate hegemony and their attempts to impose their rules on people. It is not a coincidence that the World Trade Center was destroyed in suicide missions…. These operations express the rejection of the Americans' heedless policy. These events are the fruits of the new American order.[20]

Similarly, a poem recited in the presence of Saddam Hussein in a televised sequence on December 3, 2001 celebrated "the triumph over injustice" through the death of "six thousand infidels" and proclaimed that "Bin Laden has nothing to do with it"; it was due to "the luck of President Saddam."

Beyond such speeches there is a fact that has not been discussed since the end of the year 2001: Iraq was apparently a strategic fallback zone for the militants of the terrorist organization who were being hunted in Afghanistan before becoming an operational base after the overthrow of Saddam's regime.

The most disturbing revelation about the recent relations between Iraq and Al-Qaeda comes from the Kurdish Islamist organization Jund Al-Islam and its successor Ansar Al-Islam. Its principal director, Mullah Krekar, said to have taken refuge in Norway, declared in 2002 that he considered Bin Laden "the head of Islam." And then there is the role played in this movement by the very active Al-Qaeda member Abu Musab Al-Zarqawi.

A detailed examination of relations between Iraq and Al-Qaeda does, to be sure, indicate more than simple episodic contacts. In addition to their shared hatred for the United States, these two actors on the stage of the Middle East have found that their interests coincide from time to time. But it bears repeating that these episodes, though they have given the international community cause for grave concern, do not represent a lasting structural alliance between the two camps or an unnatural coalition between Saddam Hussein's dictatorship and Bin Laden's murderous movement.

CHAPTER 12

From the Taliban to Kurdistan

AFTER THE OVERTHROW OF THE TALIBAN REGIME, AL-QAEDA'S main protector, Osama Bin Laden and his chief lieutenants, aware that they would be unable to hold out for much longer against a military operation of this scope, began reconstituting their network outside Afghanistan. In addition to Pakistan, a fiefdom of the mujahidin Arabs who had come to fight in Afghanistan in the 1980s, Iraqi Kurdistan recommended itself as a rear base, a second front for the fighters of Al-Qaeda.

For decades the Islamist movements there had been fragmented, caught in a tug of war between rival leaders. The history of the Islamist movement in Kurdistan began in 1924, when this territory was conquered by the armies of Mustafa Kemal Atatürk. From 1952 on, the wish to preserve Kurdistan's Islamic roots encouraged the emergence of rather unstructured organizations under the influence of the Muslim Brotherhood. Then the Salafist movement, funded by the Saudis, established itself in the region at the end of the 1960s. But it was not until the late 1970s that a Salafist and jihadist current really took shape after the banning of the Muslim Brotherhood in 1971.[21]

Political life in Kurdistan centers around two movements, both of which were founded in the 1960s: Jalal Talabani's Patriotic Union of Kurdistan (PUK), founded in 1965 and supported by Iran, and the Democratic Party of Kurdistan (DPK), created in 1961 by Mullah Mustafa Barzani, father of the current director Massud Barzani and supported by Turkey.

One part of Kurdistan has enjoyed an autonomous status from the time of the 1974 Iraqi law establishing the Legislative Council of Iraqi Kurdistan; a quasi-independent "zone of protection" was created for the Kurds in 1991, after the first Gulf War.

In the 1970s the region was thrown into turmoil by two major events: the revolution in Iran and the occupation of Afghanistan by Soviet forces. It was in this context that the first armed Islamist group, the Islamic Army of Kurdistan, arose in 1980, followed by the Association of Islamic Jihad. The two groups merged in 1987 as part of the Islamic Movement of Iraqi Kurdistan under the direction of an Iraqi, Othman Abdul Aziz. There were a number of rebellions, especially one by the Al-Nahda (Rebirth) group in 1992 and, in 1994, one by the Islamic Union inspired by the Muslim Brotherhood.

In 1999 Aziz consolidated the Kurdish Islamist groups into a new organization, the Islamic Unity Movement. This reconciliation lasted only two years. In early 2001 several dissident groups emerged, some of which were influenced and supported by foreign countries. Thus Al-Tawhid Al-Islami (Islamic Unification) was created in April of that year, and Quwwat Suran rebelled that summer.

It was then that Zarqawi intervened. After being entrusted by Osama Bin Laden with responsibility for the camp at Herat, he is said to have set up an immigration pipeline to bring in Jordanian recruits, a channel passing through Iraq and Iran, in particular through Mashhad in the eastern part of Iran. In so doing, Zarqawi quickly became an essential intermediary in the region.

An event in 2003 sheds light on the formation of the alliance between Zarqawi and the Islamist groups of Kurdistan. The Americans arrested a 34-year-old Jordanian in Iraqi Kurdistan, a member of Zarqawi's network. Remanded to Jordan, Ahmad Mahmud Salih Al-Riyati gave up crucial information to the GID, revealing that from late 1999 on, Zarqawi had suggested that several terrorists who had come from Jordan, most of them members of Jaysh Mohammed and Bayt Al-Imam, as well as some Iraqis loyal to Mullah Krekar, be trained in the Al-Qaeda camps in Afghanistan. In this way, after several months a cosmopolitan group had formed, consisting of Iraqis, Jordanians, and Afghan and Chechen fighters living in Iraqi Kurdistan, Iran, and Afghanistan.

The members of this network were between 17 and 43 years of age.[22] They had available to them not only logistical and financial support from Al-Qaeda and the territorial base provided by the Islamists of Kurdistan, but, in a short time, also the support networks that were under Zarqawi's control and extended as far as Europe. In July 2001 several hundred Kurdish Islamists went to Afghanistan and received military training in Zarqawi's camp at Herat, not far from the Iranian border.

In August of that year a crucial meeting of Zarqawi's lieutenants took place in Tehran. Present were Al-Riyati, Khaled Al-Aruri, and Abdel Hadi Daghlas, along with Iraqi Islamists close to Mullah Krekar. Al-Aruri and Daghlas had begun their military careers with Zarqawi in Jordan, where, with their leader, they had been found guilty in connection with the Bayt Al-Imam case.

They now agreed in Zarqawi's name to establish a permanent base in Kurdistan, opening their own training camps in this area so as to facilitate the return of the Afghan Arabs and the recruitment of Jordanians. They also planned to train members of the network in the handling of chemical and bacteriological weapons.

Jund Al-Islam (Soldiers of Islam) was founded on September 1, 2001, at Tawileh, Iraq, by Abu Abdullah Al-Shafii, an Iraqi veteran of Afghanistan and Chechnya whose real name was Warya Salih Abdallah. The formation of this group of fighters owed nothing to chance.

According to a press release put out by the organization in September 2001, Al-Shafii had received the approval of Osama Bin Laden himself.

Jund Al-Islam arose from the merger of two Kurdish Islamist groups, both of which had been part of the Islamic Movement of Iraqi Kurdistan: Al-Tawhid, founded by Al-Shafii, and Quwwat Suran Al-Tawhid (Unity of All Believers), which up to then had been known as a Sunni Jordanian organization in Palestine. Osama Bin Laden is said to have given Jund Al-Islam $300,000 at this time[23] through two Al-Qaeda intermediaries in London, Abu Musab Al-Suri and Abu Basir.

Abu Basir, a Jordanian whose real name is Sheikh Abdallah Al-Munim Mustafa Abu Halimah, has published several works that have become a prime legal source for the fundamentalists, including *The Law on the Legality of Seizing Polytheistic Possessions, Laws on Atonement,* and *Idol.* He is also the author of *Good Answers to the Questions of Foreigners in Kurdistan.*[24] Together with the Sunni sheikhs Al-Maqdisi and Abu Qatada, Abu Basir is one of the most important ideologues of the culture of jihad. The works of these three men are referred to by the major Islamic fundamentalist movements throughout the world.

Nor was the other intermediary an unknown. Abu Musab Al-Suri, whose real name is Mustafa Setmariam Nasar, was born in Aleppo, Syria, in 1958. A naturalized citizen of Spain, he lived in that country for several years, maintaining regular contact with the members of the local cell of Al-Qaeda. The leader of that cell, Abu Dahdah, former editor in chief of the GIA newspaper *Al-Ansar* and member of the Muslim Brotherhood, moved to London in 1995, where he became the assistant to Abu Qatada, another figure we have met in connection with Al-Qaeda and the Zarqawi networks. In 1997 he moved with his family to Afghanistan, where he ran a training camp controlled by Bin Laden, who then put him in charge of collecting all the information available on enriched uranium and obtaining samples of it.[25]

According to the Spanish intelligence services, Al-Suri visited one of the members of the terrorist cell in Hamburg in 1996; from the same source we also learn that he met Osama Bin Laden in the company of Mohammed Bahaiah, the principal courier of Al-Qaeda in Spain and brother-in-law of one of its officials. According to the Italian intelligence services, Al-Suri returned to Iraq after the fall of the Taliban in Afghanistan to take part in the "resistance" alongside Zarqawi.[26]

The first press release from Jund Al-Islam was received on September 10, 2001, by the Arab newspaper *Al-Sharq Al-Awsat*, published in London. The group announced that for years it had been "dedicated to military training," and that the time had come "to declare jihad against the existing groups and parties in Iraqi Kurdistan, fighting them in order to make sure they do not seize areas under Islamic control." The press release added that the group had made contact with "several Islamic figures abroad before declaring jihad."[27]

Jund Al-Islam is based in Kurdistan around the villages of Tawilah and Biyara, in a border region of Iraq called "the Tora Bora of Kurdistan." The group basically consists of Arab Afghans who joined Al-Qaeda in the course of the 1990s. It seems to have been an offshoot of the Taliban movement from the outset, for these "Kurdish Taliban" fully adhere to the ideals of their Afghan comrades. Their main objective is to "implement Islamic law in daily life" by "destroying the laws of the democrats and conformists and any other law of the infidels."[28] Jund Al-Islam calls for the strict application of the Wahhabi doctrine prevailing in Saudi Arabia.

At the end of the year 2001 the Islamic Committee of Jund Al-Islam drew up a list of rules. In this farrago we read that "women must wear the veil when they go outside, and they are forbidden to travel alone to another city"; "photographs of women are forbidden everywhere: in shops, town centers, cars,…"; "it is forbidden to listen to music and songs, and it is forbidden to sell musical instruments"; "non-Islamic possessions like television and cable channels are forbidden."[29]

Jund Al-Islam made no secret of its alliance with the Arab jihadists or its sources of support. Thus its spokesman declared in 2001: "We have formed an alliance with our mujahidin brothers. We have been trained in religion and in handling weapons, and we agreed that the solution was to carry the banner of jihad once again," adding: "Thanks to our mujahidin brothers we have trained our children in the art of war."[30] The group even launched a newspaper with a revealing title: *Call to Jihad in Kurdistan.*

Most of the attacks against the Patriotic Union of Kurdistan for which Jund Al-Islam took credit beginning in September 2001 were carried out by the "Arab Afghans" who had fought in Afghanistan. The group's forces, approximately five hundred armed men, are said to have been joined by at least the same number of Al-Qaeda members at that time.[31]

Nor was this affiliation with Al-Qaeda concealed. For example, in a speech addressed to the mujahidin of the world and advocating jihad in Kurdistan, they stated:

Jund Al-Islam has completed its preparation in the handling of weapons and communications. During this time we have benefited from the ideas and experience of various intellectuals and military leaders. With the help of Allah we have finished our military, intellectual, and religious training. We are now ready to defend Islam and the Muslims against conservative rulers and their Jewish and Christian masters. This battle is directed against them in accordance with the will of Allah. And this battle will continue until Islam becomes the general law and the enemies of Islam have been punished at our hands.[32]

Jund Al-Islam said that it was "accompanied by the lord of Osama [Bin Laden]" and was "a friend to those who are close to Islam and an enemy of those who set themselves against Allah." The group officially claimed its relations with "Iran, Iraq, and Osama Bin Laden," who were called "enemies of the Americans."[33]

Yet no one seemed to be paying attention to this small group of Taliban in Kurdistan, minimizing their military successes and their political potential. Mullah Abdul Aziz, who had taken up the Islamist torch from his father, Othman Abdul Aziz, at the time of the latter's death in 1999, was firmly of this opinion. "We think that this movement and the ideas it is conveying have no future in Kurdistan," he said. "Its members are very few...and consist of young hoodlums." Jalal Talabani, leader of the Patriotic Union of Kurdistan, agreed: "The movement will not be able to find a base in Iraqi Kurdistan for waging a political battle."[34]

Far from the game of politics in Kurdistan, Jund Al-Islam differed from other forces present in the region by virtue of its military engagement and the surprising strength of its religious position and military victories. Some of the officials of the Islamic Movement of Kurdistan soon became aware of this. The dissenters came together at the initiative of a military leader who was still relatively unknown, Faraj Ahmad Najmuddin, alias Mullah Krekar, a former pupil in Pakistan of Abdallah Azzam, Osama Bin Laden's mentor.[35] Jund Al-Islam became the major center of attraction for Islamists in Iraqi Kurdistan in the fall of 2001.

CHAPTER 13

War Leader in Kurdistan

BORN IN 1956 IN IRAQI KURDISTAN, MULLAH KREKAR STUDIED sociology in Tehran for two years before settling in Karachi in 1985 to become a professor of jurisprudence and Islamic history at the University of Islamic Studies in that city. He would remain there until 1988. Married to a former Communist who converted to Islam, he took the names of his four children from the books of Sayyed Qutb, the spiritual father of the Egyptian Muslim Brotherhood.[36]

A bearded giant who looks like Rasputin, Mullah Krekar was described by his associates in Iraq as "a man thirsty for power" who issued brutal orders to his men. An excellent speaker, he could, according to one Kurdish leader, "bring his audience to tears" during his sermons at Friday prayers.[37]

Mullah Krekar is said to have established a housing center in Peshawar in 1988 for Kurdish fighters ready to leave for the Afghan front[38] and to have received military training at a camp run by Al-Qaeda in Afghanistan.[39] He has never confirmed this last point but admits that he met Bin Laden on the Afghan border in 1988.[40]

In June 1988 he joined the Islamic Movement of Iraqi Kurdistan

(IMK) and, in 1992, was named head of its military branch before taking charge of planning and development for the group in 1995. At that time he set up several military training camps in Kurdistan as well as a "military academy" to bring in new recruits. He was also developing IMK support networks in Europe, increasing the number of fundraising campaigns in the Netherlands, Norway, Great Britain, and Germany.[41]

This man, who likes to present himself as a Muslim intellectual (indeed, a poet), and who has in fact published over twenty works, is thus a real military leader, personally overseeing the training of Kurdish Islamists with a Kalashnikov rifle slung across his shoulder.

Unable to resign himself to the peace accord signed in 1997 between the IMK and Talabani's Patriotic Union of Kurdistan, Mullah Krekar decided in that same year to found the Islamic Union of Kurdistan alongside the IMK. The Islamic Union of Kurdistan was based in Irbil, a city located in the area controlled by the Democratic Party of Kurdistan under Massud Barzani, who was allied with Iran. He then settled in the village of Golpe, near Khurmal,[42] but kept close ties to the IMK and would never agree to condemn this movement.

In October 2001 intensive negotiations were carried out between the various Islamist groups in Kurdistan with a view toward uniting with Jund Al-Islam, negotiations that for the most part hit a snag when it came to the allocation of official roles and the delicate question of leadership. Jund Al-Islam was in the stronger position. An alliance with Jamaa Islamiyah failed at this time on account of the demands made by Jund Al-Islam, which wanted guarantees with regard to the security of its Arab Afghan fighters from abroad and refused to delegate military responsibilities to anyone but Afghan fighters.[43]

In November 2001 Mullah Krekar affirmed his sympathy for Jund Al-Islam, whose members he called "true mujahidin." In a speech before his associates, he also paid homage to Osama Bin Laden and made no secret of his wish to see the formation of a grand alliance of jihadist parties in Kurdistan.[44] The IMK then publicly stated its fear that Jund Al-Islam would try to profit by impeding the unification of the Islamist movements.[45] In December 2001 Mullah Krekar formed an alliance with Jund Al-Islam, the major group of Afghan Arabs in Kurdistan, which then became the primary Islamist military power in the region.

Thus in late 2001 there emerged a heterogeneous group formed by the merger of Jund Al-Islam and the dissident movements of IMK. This organization was headed by military leaders from Afghanistan, but its ideology was equally influenced by the Salafist current and the Muslim Brotherhood. Indeed, there was no ideological difference between the two groups, Jund and Ansar Al-Islam (Partisans of Islam, as the new organization was called), to the point where their Internet sites were practically identical in 2001; Mullah Krekar referred to either one of them when speaking of Ansar's doctrinal convictions.[46]

A document signed by Mullah Krekar and dated September 3, 2002 was seized by the police that same year in the baggage of the Ansar Al-Islam leader when he was arrested in Amsterdam. In it he harks back to the origins and aims of his organization: "[Ansar Al-Islam] is neither regional nor ethnic.... It is based on the laws of Islam and is preparing jihad.... Its goal is the return of the caliphate and it is working to that end in seventy-six regions of fifty-six nations."[47]

Like Jund Al-Islam, Ansar Al-Islam refers in its propaganda to the Muslim Brotherhood, especially to Hassan Al-Banna, founder of the Brotherhood, and to Yussef Al-Qardawi, one of its religious leaders. The movement also refers to Osama Bin Laden and his mentor, Abdallah Azzam, who was killed in 1989. In addition, Ansar Al-Islam disseminates the writings of "Professor" Omar Abdel Rahman, sentenced to life imprisonment in the United States for his role in the first attacks on the World Trade Center in 1993 and those of the Jordanian Abu Mohammed Al-Maqdisi, who was, as we recall, the mentor of Abu Musab Al-Zarqawi.[48]

On December 10, 2001, Mullah Krekar assumed the leadership of Ansar Al-Islam and its three jihadist components: Jund Al-Islam, the

Kurdish branch of Hamas, and the Al-Tawhid movement. The organization consisted of an emir (Mullah Krekar), along with two assistants, a military committee, a religious council, an Islamic court, and a security council.

Ansar Al-Islam soon acquired several training camps in the Biyara area, Sargat, and Khurmal, in particular camps that were intended for children and combined religious and military instruction. The organization used guerrilla warfare to combat the traditional groups in Kurdistan. Its members rarely employed modern means of communication, preferring human messengers.

Ansar Al-Islam took credit for a number of actions against its principal rival, Jalal Talabani's Patriotic Union of Kurdistan (PUK), including the attempted assassination of the Kurdish prime minister, Barham Salih, a PUK member, in April 2002, and the violent battles of December 2002 around Halabjah, in which over one hundred PUK members were killed. These actions would culminate in the destruction of the PUK headquarters on February 2, 2004 and a suicide attack that left over a hundred victims. But at the end of 2001 Ansar Al-Islam was essentially dedicated to gathering jihadist forces in flight from Afghanistan.

As early as 1997 Mullah Krekar was open about his friendship with the jihadists. He stated in an interview that it was "imperative to support the jihadist movements throughout the world, even if they do not support us."[49] He himself recruited far beyond the borders of Iraq; his fighters came from Morocco, Palestine, and Jordan. They were trained by Al-Qaeda in Afghanistan, and contact with Zarqawi was made only through one of his lieutenants, the Jordanian Abu Abdulrahman Al-Shami, who was eventually killed at the end of 2002 in fighting with the PUK.[50]

The organization's funding came from several sources. In addition to the initial contributions from Osama Bin Laden earmarked at the time for the formation of Jund Al-Islam,[51] Mullah Krekar's group was able to count on funds collected in Pakistan and Europe during campaigns on behalf of the Islamist cause in Kurdistan, especially those conducted in British and German mosques. Financial support also came from certain charitable organizations in the Persian Gulf states, such as the World Assembly of Muslim Youth, founded in Saudi Arabia and very quickly suspected of maintaining ties with terrorist organizations. Another Saudi group, the International Islamic Relief Organization (IIRO), a branch of the Muslim World League founded by the Muslim Brotherhood—more specifically, by Hassan Al-Banna's own son, Said Ramadan—is one of the most active supporters of the Kurdish Islamists. The IIRO is said to have built more than ten mosques in Kurdistan in the past five years, and, according to Mullah Sadeeq, formerly the financial officer of the Islamic Movement of Kurdistan, it has sent $20 million to the Kurdish Islamists since 1994.[52]

But Jund Al-Islam and its successor, Ansar Al-Islam, were also developing an embryonic local economy, in particular a network importing fuel and cement from Iran to be sold on the Iraqi market. The jihadists also collect taxes on merchandise crossing the border area under their control.[53] These important resources make Ansar Al-Islam a movement playing a major role on the military and political chessboard in the region, despite the fact that it is not actually recognized by neighboring countries.

Mullah Krekar's ties to Al-Qaeda and its leaders have been known for some time. Thus in 2000 he told a Kurdish daily newspaper that Bin Laden was "the crown atop the Islamic nation."[54] According to the testimony given to a European intelligence service by a former member of the terrorist network Ansar Al-Islam, Mullah Krekar also met Ayman Al-Zawahiri in Tehran in 2000.[55] Moreover, he admitted to having met Bin Laden and Al-Zawahiri in Afghanistan in 2002, calling the two men "true Muslim believers."[56] In 2003 he stated that Osama Bin Laden was "a generous man who has devoted his life and his money to the teachings of Allah."[57] This information is confirmed by Italian judicial sources, according to which

Mullah Krekar "admitted to Norwegian authorities that, during his trips to Pakistan, he met Osama Bin Laden, Abdallah Azzam, and Ayman Al-Zawahiri."[58] Ansar Al-Islam is even said to have given Osama Bin Laden the opportunity, on November 1, 2001, to tape a message to be broadcast by Al-Jazira.[59]

In an interview he granted to the Saudi daily *Al-Sharq Al-Awsat* Mullah Krekar related that his first meeting with Bin Laden in mid-1988 "took place in a villa in Hayatabad near Peshawar. The villa belonged to a Saudi prince, and Osama Bin Laden was accompanied by seven Saudi dignitaries." If we are to believe Mullah Krekar, it was not until an hour into the meeting that he realized that the man speaking to him in a "gentle" voice was none other than Bin Laden. The purpose of the meeting was "to obtain funds on behalf of the families of victims of Iraqi chemical bombing on the city of Halabjah in March 1988."[60]

Mullah Krekar also mentions that he gave the Saudi prince who was present at the meeting an album of photographs of the bombardments over Halabjah, and that he tried to persuade Sheikh Abdallah Azzam to take up the Kurdish cause. He reports that Azzam did indeed try to raise money in the Gulf States for the victims of Halabjah, but that this effort failed in view of Saddam Hussein's popularity in the Arab countries at that time.

Despite this series of statements, Mullah Krekar declared in 2002 that allegations of his links with Al-Qaeda were "totally unfounded."[61]

ACCORDING TO THE JORDANIAN INTELLIGENCE SERVICES, IN 2002 Abu Musab Al-Zarqawi met in person with Mullah Krekar and his associate Abu Abdullah Al-Shafii, the founder of Jund Al-Islam, in Kurdistan. The two leaders of Ansar Al-Islam formed an alliance on this occasion and decided to combine their resources, especially their weapons and explosives. Also present at this meeting were several Jordanian members of the Zarqawi network, including Isaf Abdallah Al-Nusur, Shihadah Naji Shihadah Al-Kilani, Muhammad Ratib Ibrahim Qutayshat, Mundhir Abdallah Al-Latif Yussef Shamma, and Umar Izz Al-Din Isam Al-Utaybi.

Thus beginning in the fall of 2002 Zarqawi's partisans had access to the arsenal and principal military bases of Ansar Al-Islam. In a text signed by his hand and dated September 3, 2002, Mullah Krekar took inventory of the arsenal at the disposal of Ansar Al-Islam: "We have a 155 mm cannon, approximately 1,000 bombs of Iranian manufacture that we bought at a low price, as well as other bombs recovered after the last conflict between Iraq and Iran.... We have also built tunnels and caves to protect ourselves from possible air raids... should there be attacks by the American-British coalition."[62]

Zarqawi's men were for the most part being trained in the camp at Khurmal, located on the Iranian border in the Halabjah area; in this same year the camp was transformed into a site for experimentation with and production of chemical weapons.[63] The military training was provided by the Jordanian Ahmad Mahmud Salih Al-Riyati, who would be arrested in March 2003 by American forces and handed over to the Jordanian authorities.[64] The chemical laboratory at the camp was under the supervision of Abdel Hadi Daghlas.[65]

In late 2002 Zarqawi and his partisans kept moving continually between Baghdad and the border area with Iran. This aroused the suspicion of the Iraqi authorities, who finally arrested three of Zarqawi's lieutenants between the end of 2002 and the beginning of 2003,[66] releasing only one of them before the onset of the American offensive.

Despite his closeness to the historical leaders of Al-Qaeda, Mullah Krekar soon saw his organization overwhelmed by the Arab Afghans. Its training camps gradually came under the control of Zarqawi's men, and its military commanders were replaced by Afghan fighters. Ansar Al-Islam was losing its character. Mullah Krekar asked for political asylum in Norway and was granted it in 1991 in the context of a contingent of United Nations refugees. On September 6 he was arrested in Tehran by the Iranian authorities and deported to the Netherlands six days later. Arriving in Amsterdam on September 13, he was arrested by the Dutch police.[67]

That same day the Dutch authorities received a request for international cooperation from Jordan, since a warrant for the arrest of Mullah Krekar had been issued there on the grounds of "conspiracy to commit murder."[68] The head of Ansar Al-Islam was also accused of having violated Jordanian narcotics laws.[69] This request was not honored, and Mullah Krekar was incarcerated in the Netherlands until January 13, 2003, at which time he was finally deported to Norway. There he was once again questioned and imprisoned for several months before being set free.[70]

At the time of Mullah Krekar's deportation to the Netherlands, the Dutch police seized a diary and telephone list establishing his relationship with Zarqawi, whose satellite phone number appeared under the name of "Rashid."[71] Since the end of 2001, Ansar Al-Islam has been under the de facto control of Zarqawi, who procures most of its financial and military resources as well as its recruits and supervisory staff.

In February 2003, Mullah Krekar was finally deposed by the fourteen members of Ansar Al-Islam's religious council. Headed by Al-Shafii, this council declared that he had strayed from "jihadist loyalty," the ideology and methods of the group.[72] In the same month Ansar Al-Islam was officially designated a terrorist entity by the United States.[73]

Though nowadays he disputes all allegations of links to terrorism, Mullah Krekar has not renounced jihad. Thus, asked in November 2003 about his possible return to Iraq, he stated that jihad is "a religious duty" and that he would rather "carry a Kalashnikov than become insignificant" in his Norwegian refuge.[74]

Be that as it may, on the eve of the American offensive in Iraq Ansar Al-Islam had over six hundred Arab fighters who had come from Afghanistan and were under the leadership of Abu Musab Al-Zarqawi.

CHAPTER 14

The Confusing Stakes in Iran

IN MARCH 2003 THE COALITION AGAINST ANSAR AL-ISLAM launched its offensive. Planes bombed its principal strongholds in Biyara and the villages around the valley of Halabjah. These air strikes were followed by the deployment of a hundred troops from the American special forces and nearly ten thousand Kurdish fighters. According to the Kurdish executive branch, the attack led to 180 deaths in the ranks of Ansar Al-Islam, and 150 men were taken prisoner.

Most of the members of Ansar Al-Islam then sought refuge in Iran or in the "Sunni Triangle" in the northwest of Baghdad. Its principal leaders, Abu Abdullah Al-Shafii, Ayub Afghani, and Abu Wael, were spotted in June 2003 in the border city of Sanandaj.[75] Kaywan Qader, recruited by Ansar Al-Islam at this time for a monthly salary of twenty-two dollars, reports that "after the onset of the American offensive in Iraq, we fled to Iran, where we stayed for nearly a month."[76]

Iran's concern regarding the Sunni Islamists of Kurdistan stemmed from the struggle for control of that part of Iraq, which for several years had been beyond the reach of the central Baathist power.

Iran's support for the Patriotic Union of Kurdistan (PUK) was not exclusive. For Tehran was quite subtly playing the Islamist card, and this clearly gave it a regional advantage. First of all, Iran had to deal with two regional conflicts on its borders: on one side Afghanistan was at war (and would remain so until the stabilization of the Taliban regime in 1996), and on the other side there was Kurdistan. Beginning in 1999 jihadist Islamists urged on by Osama Bin Laden and the Taliban exported their fight to the Kurdish border. Tehran opted for a benevolent neutrality. Second, Iran was keeping a careful eye on these Sunni Islamists, whose primary source of support was the Saudi regime. Finally, by entering into battle with the Baathist regime, the Islamists brought the PUK what it badly needed, namely a real military force that was trained, equipped, and led by men hardened by their Afghan experience.

Iran quickly tried to impose a modus vivendi between the various Islamist factions on the one hand and the PUK on the other, offering its mediation and, on a number of occasions, willingly receiving official delegates from Ansar Al-Islam, including Mullah Krekar, who had lived in Iran himself before becoming involved with the different jihadist movements.

Some have even gone as far as to suggest that Iran has played a crucial role in Ansar Al-Islam. Although this hypothesis remains unverified, it is supported by several troubling facts. For example, the Jund Al-Islam movement had adopted Farsi as its official language and published its news releases in that language. For its part, Tehran denies giving aid to Ansar Al-Islam and officially prohibited wounded members of the group from entering its territory after the American bombing in March 2003. But this public turnabout is recent and coincides with Washington's show of firmness toward the Iranian government.

Beginning in 1991, as a result of Iran's strategic choice to favor its territorial influence over Kurdistan to the detriment of diplomatic logic, the country was no longer content to offer temporary transit or clandestine aid to the Islamists but became a true sanctuary if not a rear base for certain terrorist networks.

On the strength of interrogations of several Al-Qaeda leaders, including Tawfiq bin Attash, the Independent Commission of Inquiry regarding September 11 has made it clear that Iran had hoped to get closer to Osama Bin Laden after the attack on the USS Cole in October 2000. The commission pointed out that Iran facilitated the movements of Al-Qaeda members passing through the country on the way to or from Afghanistan, adding that customs agents had been instructed not to affix their stamp to these men's passports but instead to an attached form, so that there would be no evidence that they had passed through Iran. This measure was of special advantage to the Saudi members of the terrorist network.[77]

The commission concluded that there was solid proof that Iran had facilitated this transit, including that of several of the future September 11 terrorists. And eight or ten of the terrorists implicated in those attacks did in fact pass through Iran between October 2000 and February 2001.[78]

Early in 2002, a few weeks after the onset of military operations against Afghanistan, U.S. Secretary of Defense Donald Rumsfeld stated that Iran had tolerated the presence on its soil of members of Al-Qaeda and the Taliban. The spokesman for the Iranian minister of foreign affairs, Hamid Reza Asefi, replied that Iran had "extradited to their countries of origin all foreigners linked or suspected of being linked to Al-Qaeda."[79]

On September 1, 2003, however, the Jordanian authorities let it be officially known that Iran had refused a request for the extradition of Abu Musab Al-Zarqawi, who was temporarily imprisoned by Tehran in 2002 during his flight to Iraqi Kurdistan. Iran's alleged reason was that Zarqawi was in possession of a Syrian passport and therefore could not be deported to Jordan.[80] In order to move about more easily, Zarqawi had a number of false passports: British, Lebanese, Jordanian, Iranian, Yemenite, and others.[81]

According to the German intelligence services, after he was wounded in the American offensive in Afghanistan Zarqawi found refuge in Mashhad, Iran, on January 5, 2002 and received medical care there. Zarqawi remained in Iran until April of that year, coordinating the retreat of the members of his network to Kurdistan. He is then said to have gone to Tehran and after that to Zahedan, in the south of the country. His imprisonment by the Jordanian authorities was of brief duration. He confirmed to one of his correspondents in Germany that several of his "brothers" had been arrested in Tehran, but his own assistant made it clear that for this entire period Zarqawi had been "under the protection of the Iranian regime and the Hekmatyar group."[82]

In addition, on the basis of the confessions of the Jordanian Ahmad Mahmud Salih Al-Riyati, arrested by the forces of the coalition in March 2003,[83] the Jordanian GID was able to confirm that in 2003 virtually all of the top officials of Zarqawi's network were in Iran.

In that same year the United States leveled a more direct and precise accusation against Iran. Donald Rumsfeld stated that Iran was harboring several Al-Qaeda leaders, and, under American pressure, Iran had to acknowledge in July 2003 that a number of members of the terrorist network had been arrested and that some of these had been deported to their countries of origin. The minister of intelligence, Ali Yunesi, explained that Iran had imprisoned "many other more or less important members of Osama Bin Laden's terrorist network."[84]

Several sources have confirmed the presence in Iran of Saif Al-Adel, one of the heads of Al-Qaeda, and Saad Bin Laden, one of Osama's sons, who is said to have been protected by an Iranian military unit. The Iranian government has strongly denied these accusations, even as it acknowledged the impossibility of controlling the integrity of the 1,900 kilometers of the borders separating Pakistan and Iran from Afghanistan and admitted that "certain elements of Al-Qaeda [may] have entered Iran."[85]

In October 2003 Iran submitted to the United Nations Committee on Sanctions a list of 225 suspects arrested and extradited since the time of the American offensive in Afghanistan, none of whom, however, was on the list of persons designated as terrorists and fugitives by the United Nations. The Iranian government stressed that in under two years more than 2,300 people had tried to enter Iran illegally before being escorted back to the Pakistani border.[86] Later, in early 2004, it showed its willingness to bring several Al-Qaeda members to justice despite demands for their extradition presented by several countries, including the United States. And in May 2004 the provisional administrator in Iraq, Paul Bremer, mentioned certain "disturbing" activities on the part of Iran in Iraq.

Situated at the crossroads of regional conflicts, Iran was trapped by the concessions it made to the Islamists of Afghanistan and Kurdistan. Thus, on the eve of the United States offensive in Iraq, it was to Tehran that the jihadists turned in their resolve to fight the American enemy.

CHAPTER 15

Tawhid wal Jihad

THE AMERICAN OFFENSIVE AGAINST IRAQ IN MARCH 2003 WAS A turning point for the Islamist movements of Kurdistan, which now revealed their intention and their true nature. In June the religious council of Ansar Al-Islam issued a press release calling for "all volunteers to join the ranks [of the group] to fight the Americans," warning that it would employ "the weapon of urban guerrilla warfare" to "confront the American infidels with the aim of destroying them throughout Iraq," and explaining that "the zones of entry and exit in the territory have been secured so as to ensure the flow of supplies for the fighters."[87] Ansar Al-Islam also launched an appeal for donations, the "backbone of jihad," as they called it. Recently subjected to the bombing, the organization had "lost its equipment," and "needed to buy weapons" and food for the "mujahidin" who had had to flee Kurdistan with their families.

In August Mullah Krekar declared that there was no difference between "the American occupation of Iraq and the Soviet occupation of Afghanistan in 1979," adding that there was "no doubt about the participation of members of Al-Qaeda in the training and organization of the jihadists of Kurdistan."[88] Ansar Al-Islam extended its presence on Iraqi soil right from the outset of the American offensive.

A new group, Ansar Al-Sunna, was formed in June 2003 under the direction of Abu Abdullah Hasan Ben Mahmoud, brother of Abu Abdallah Al-Shami, Zarqawi's lieutenant who was killed in Kurdistan in December 2001.[89] The group represented itself as "dissenting" from Ansar Al-Islam but continued to use it as a reference point.

In September 2003 Ansar Al-Sunna stated that "jihad in Iraq has become a duty for every Muslim."[90] It went on to call for "victory against the United States" and took credit for several attacks against the forces of the coalition, in particular the suicide mission directed against the Turkish embassy on October 14, 2003 and the assassination of several members of the Spanish intelligence services on November 29 of the same year.

Ansar Al-Islam took full part in the Islamist counteroffensive, as is clear from the publication on its Web site of the document in which the Abu Hafs Al-Masri Brigades took credit for the Madrid attacks of March 11, 2004. Ansar Al-Islam dedicated a page on the site to these events, presenting several photographs of the attack under the heading "The Battlefronts of the Crusade." In addition, a videotape containing threats, later recovered from the rubble of the apartment occupied by some of the Madrid terrorists, bore the mark of Ansar Al-Qaeda, a sign of the rapprochement in effect between the two groups.

Defeated by the massive American offensive launched in Kurdistan in March 2003, and despite the loss of approximately one third of its troops, Ansar Al-Islam reconstituted itself in Iraq and quickly resumed its operations. On September 5 the group declared that its members had managed to "take refuge in neighboring countries" (an implicit reference to Iran), where they had reorganized "with the help of our brothers who are the natural extension of our action" in order to redeploy their troops throughout Iraq.[91]

Tensions among the various armed forces in Kurdistan now

began to rise. Al-Shafii, who had succeeded Mullah Krekar as the head of Ansar Al-Islam in February 2003, issued a statement strongly critical of Jalal Talabani, secretary general of the PUK, whose forces had fought alongside the Americans in the attack on Ansar Al-Islam strongholds. He also denounced certain Kurdish Islamist groups, accusing them of having acted like "traitors" on that occasion.

For several weeks Ansar Al-Islam had been trying to gather the jihadist movements in Iraq under its own banner. Al-Shafii stated that the group's sphere of action, long confined "to a narrow and limited territory, [would henceforth] extend to the north and south of Iraq, from the east to the west of its borders," declaring that there was "a consensus among the mujahidin fighting in the country in favor of joining our cause." Al-Shafii indicated that the group might change its name in accordance with the alliances it was likely to make with other factions, adding that this name might soon be revealed. He also took credit for a suicide mission against the American forces but did not give any details.

Finally, Al-Shafii asked that "no religious Muslim issue fatwas forbidding the carrying out of operations against the Americans." Here he was referring to a fatwa sent some months previously by one of the religious consultants of Ansar Al-Islam, and of Zarqawi in particular, namely the Jordanian Abu Mohammed Al-Maqdisi. In April 2003 Maqdisi had distanced himself from the jihadist resistance in Iraq and condemned the sending of "Arab Afghans" to that country.[92] In a surprising break with his former writings, he criticized the sacrifice of young Muslims in wars "that have nothing to do with United States," stating that it is "forbidden for a Muslim to sacrifice his life to win a war between two infidels," these being the Americans and the regime of Saddam Hussein. He called for a stop to the "holocaust" of lives squandered on the battlefield, asking the Muslims: "Which Iraq are you talking about? The Baathist Iraq of Saddam Hussein,... the man who killed our clergy,... who exterminated the Muslims at Halabjah with his chemical gasses?... Where were you each time the United States supported Israel against our Muslim brothers in Palestine?...Where were you when the airplanes of the Crusaders bombed Kabul, Gardiz, Herat, and Kandahar?"

Maqdisi was in prison in Jordan at this time when the Americans were beginning their offensive against the Iraqi regime, and there is every reason to believe that his writing of this message was inspired by the GID; ten years earlier, he had been ready to use all military means, including chemical weapons, against the Jordanian government and American interests.

Another document, written by Maqdisi in the Jordanian prison in Kafkafa in 2004, reveals another facet of the man, surely a more authentic one. He did not hesitate to criticize certain of Zarqawi's operational choices: "Sometimes his decisions were not the right ones, for Zarqawi chose people without experience of jihad." Yet he supported Zarqawi's fight in Iraq: "I frankly confess that I am at the side of my brother Zarqawi against all his enemies....For what I know about Zarqawi is that he is ready to give his soul, his blood, his money, his life to help his brothers....May God keep him safe and strengthen him in the right path, thereby enabling him and those with him to help Al-Tawhid."[93]

As early as the end of March 2003 Ansar Al-Islam posted on its Web site images of the corpses of American soldiers and mutilated bodies taken from a propaganda tape distributed by an organ close to Al-Qaeda.

On March 24 Thabit Ben Qays, Al-Qaeda's new spokesman, called on Muslims "to take part in jihad against the United States in Iraq," although he refused to comment on the American bombing of the Ansar Al-Islam bases in Iraqi Kurdistan: "I have no intention of doing the Americans a favor in the service of propaganda that can be of only limited benefit to the actions successfully undertaken by the mujahidin against the forces of arrogance."[94] The message was clear nonetheless and was extensively repeated on Ansar Al-Islam's Web site.

It was on April 15, 2004 that Ansar Al-Islam finally joined the armed resistance against the United States in a statement calling on the Iraqis to respond to the American occupation with jihad and fight "the band of traitors and criminals" through martyrdom and "heroic operations" that would go down in history as "an eloquent and profound lesson" for all who are hostile to Islam and the Muslims. In the same statement the organization took credit for attacks against an army plane, Paul Bremer's convoy, and General Abizaid. The text concluded with a threat to utilize "all the weapons available to us, whether conventional, chemical, nuclear, or bacteriological" against the American enemy and issued this warning: "You are getting ready to live through darker days than September 11, 2001."[95]

As though further clarification were required, Ansar Al-Islam's spokesman added this: "We strongly support the heroes who are undertaking difficult missions, such as the members of the Al-Qaeda organization under the leadership of the venerable and courageous companion, the standard-bearer of jihad, the brave Osama Bin Laden." Ansar Al-Islam was now the new instrument of terror.

THERE ARE SEVERAL SIGNS OF THE INCREASING RAPPROCHEMENT between Zarqawi's own networks and those of Ansar Al-Islam beginning in the autumn of 2003. Thus the American forces arrested Husan Al-Yemeni, one of Zarqawi's assistants, when he was representing Ansar Al-Islam for the city of Fallouja. On January 22, 2004, Kurdish soldiers captured another of his partisans in Kurdistan; this was Hasan Guhl, a Pakistani veteran of Afghanistan close to Osama Bin Laden and Khaled Sheikh Mohammed, who planned the September 11 attacks. On October 2003 in Mossul, the Americans questioned Aso Hawleri, alias Asad Mohammed Hasan, who was number three in command in Ansar Al-Islam and close to Zarqawi. On May 30, 2004 Umar Bayzani, who had planned attacks against the United States in Iran, was also captured.[96]

In May 2004 the extremist Sunni movements in Iraq began their struggle for survival. Ansar Al-Islam, Ansar Al-Sunna, Salafiya Jihadiya, and the Abu Hafs Al-Masri Brigades were all candidates for the role of catalyst for the jihadist movement. As he had done in Kurdistan, Zarqawi exploited the dissension and fragmentation of these groups in order to establish himself as the unifier.

He decided to strike a great blow that would convince the different factions to rally behind him. On April 9, 2004, a 26-year-old American was kidnapped in the west of Baghdad and, on May 11, was executed by Zarqawi. The death of Nicholas Berg was the dire act that formed the basis of the jihadist union Zarqawi envisaged.

The videotape of the murder was disseminated on an Ansar Al-Islam Web site with the title, "Sheikh Abu Musab Zarqawi Slays an American Infidel." In a scenario that has been shown many times since then, Zarqawi and his accomplices stand, masked, behind a kneeling and bound hostage dressed in an orange jumpsuit like the ones worn by the prisoners at Guantanamo. Zarqawi or one of his accomplices then reads a text castigating the American enemy and calling on Muslims to join the ranks of resistance in Iran. The man who had never made war except in Zarqa declares to his coreligionists: "You are tired of the oratorical squabbling and public debates…. The time has now come to make jihad and brandish the sword that the prophet has sent us." Speaking of "vengeance," he concludes as follows: "You will see your warrior brothers hang the head of this infidel from one of the bridges in Baghdad, so that no one will forget the way we treat infidels. May he bear witness to the honor of the Muslims."[97] At that point the hostage is beheaded in an act of extreme savagery.

Thus began a long series of executions of hostages.

Two days later the group Al-Jamaa Al-Salafiya, headed by Abu Dajanah Al-Iraqi, announced its merger with a group recently founded by Zarqawi: Unity and Holy War, or Tawhid wal Jihad. In a communiqué cosigned by Zarqawi and Al-Iraqi on May 13, 2004, the two groups declared their agreement that "dispersion is a weakness and, over and above its legal obligation, unity is a duty imposed by circumstances.... The warriors of jihad and the knights of Islam... need to be united in the shadow of swords and the dust of battles." Both organizations stated that "their base is *tawhid* [unity], their path Sunni Salafism, and their means jihad." The members of Al-Jamaa Al-Salafiya dubbed Zarqawi their "leader within the group Tawhid wal Jihad." Borrowing from the American political vocabulary, the alliance was called the "ticket" for the victory of jihad.

Ansar Al-Sunna, for its part, carried out several joint operations with Zarqawi's group beginning in November.[98] It did not even need to formalize the fact that it was making its resources available to Zarqawi. Abu Abdallah Al-Shafii, whose name appeared in a list found in a training camp in Afghanistan when he was said to be the leader of the "Islamic Brigade of Iraqi Kurdistan," had sworn allegiance to Osama Bin Laden.[99]

Nor was it a coincidence that Zarqawi took the name of his new movement from the Tawhid group headed by Al-Shafii before he founded Jund Al-Islam and later Ansar Al-Islam with Mullah Krekar. But this choice really seems to be Zarqawi's homage to his mentor. For the name had already been in existence for four years: Maqdisi, who had apparently distanced himself from Zarqawi's fight the previous year, had called his Web site Tawhid wal Jihad.[100]

In any event, in May 2004 Zarqawi founded a true coalition of jihadist movements under the aegis of Tawhid wal Jihad. Some of these movements continued to exist under their original names, but all of them were controlled by Zarqawi from that point on. The principal groups are Ansar Al-Islam, Ansar Al-Sunna, Jaysh Mohammed, Al-Jamaa Salafiya, Takfir wal Hijra, and Jund Al-Sham.

CHAPTER 16

Terror

ZARQAWI IS NOT A GREAT STRATEGIST. HIS PROMINENCE IS DUE to his brute force against the American "invader." His coalition has no actual coherence other than its savagery, nor does it have a political point of view. It is the heterogeneous result of the coming together of "Arab Afghans" who fled Afghanistan, revanchist Jordanians, and criminals frustrated because they had not been able to fight in Afghanistan, Bosnia, or Chechnya.

The only religious authorities acknowledged by Tawhid wal Jihad are those from whom Muslim extremists draw inspiration, from Sayyed Qutb, formerly the religious leader of the Muslim Brotherhood, to Abu Qatada and Osama Bin Laden's mentor Abdallah Azzam. The group has a definite preference for martyrology and makes constant reference to "martyrs" such as Abu Hafs Al-Masri, also known as Mohammed Atef, the military leader of Al-Qaeda who was killed during the American offensive in Afghanistan and who gave his name to one of the jihadist groups active in Iraq, and Abdel Aziz Al-Muqrin, an Al-Qaeda leader in Saudi Arabia killed by the Saudi security services in June 2004.

According to a study prepared by the Iraqi intelligence services in 2004,[101] Tawhid wal Jihad consists of between 1,000 and 1,500 fighters from Iraq and other Muslim countries. The United States Army estimates the number of Islamist "resisters" active in Iraq as being between 8,000 and 12,000, nearly 20,000 if sympathizers are included.[102] Zarqawi's organization includes several specialists in explosives, missiles, and chemical weapons. His very narrow inner circle of colleagues has included the following:

Abu Anas Al-Shami, alias Omar Yussef Jumah: Al-Shami was one of the men closest to Zarqawi. A Jordanian cleric born in Amman in 1969, he was, like Zarqawi, a disciple of Abu Mohammed Al-Maqdisi. He grew up in Saudi Arabia, where his family had emigrated, and was a 1990 graduate of the University of Mecca before moving to Kuwait. In 1991, after the first Gulf War, Al-Shami returned to Jordan, where he became the imam in a mosque and later headed the Imam Al-Bukhari Center in Marqa.

In the mid-1990s he went to Bosnia-Herzegovina, officially as a missionary. Back in Jordan, he was one of the founders of the Islamist movement Jamaat Al-Sunnah wal Kitab. His mosque was closed by the Jordanian authorities. In 2003 his activities led to his being held for several days by the Jordanian police, after which he announced his departure for Saudi Arabia. His real destination was Iraq, where he was named the religious leader of Tawhid wal Jihad.

In April 2004 he published an Internet report, entitled "The Battle of Fallouja," on the battles that were raging in the Sunni Triangle with the Americans. "The religious council met at the request of our leader, Abu Musab Al-Zarqawi, to evaluate the situation," Al-Shami wrote. "After a year of fighting, jihad had still not emerged, our hiding places had been discovered, and several leaders had been arrested. We had to change our operational strategy, and so we decided to make Fallouja a safe refuge and an unassailable place."

On July 28, 2004, a radio message broadcast by Tawhid wal Jihad was attributed to Al-Shami. Pushing the strategy of chaos advocated by Zarqawi to its limit, he declared that "if the infidels take Muslims as protectors, and these Muslims refuse to fight, it is permitted to kill these Muslims." Thus he attacks the Shiites, "who have made an alliance with the infidels." Al-Shami's name appeared in the course of the trial of a Jordanian, Bilal Mansur Mahmoud Al-Hiyari, who was being prosecuted for having financed Al-Qaeda in the form of charitable donations. It was alleged that Al-Shami persuaded him to raise funds on behalf of the Iraqi resistance in March 2003. Hiyari went to Iraq, it was said, where Zarqawi suggested that he collect funds for him. Abu Anas Al-Shami was killed on September 20, 2004 by the forces of the coalition in Iraq.[103]

Khaled Mustafa Khalifa Al-Aruri, alias Abu Al-Qassam and Abu Ashraf: This 37-year-old Jordanian is undoubtedly Zarqawi's oldest friend; he is also his brother-in-law. Both men were found guilty and imprisoned together in Jordan in the context of the dissolution of the terrorist group Bayt Al-Imam in 1994. He followed Zarqawi to Afghanistan, then to Iran and Kurdistan, and is Zarqawi's man for special missions in Iraq and abroad.

Abdel Haadi Ahmad Mahmoud Daghlas, alias Abu Ubaydah and Abu Muhammad Al-Sham: Daghlas, too, helped Zarqawi found Bayt Al-Imam in 1994. He was one of the two men Zarqawi chose to go on terrorist suicide missions in Israel, but he was arrested by the Jordanian authorities in 1994. He ran the Herat camp in Afghanistan before following Zarqawi in his escape on September 12, 2004. Tawhid wal Jihad has published a press release announcing his death in Iraq.

Nidal Mohammad Al-Arabi, alias Abu Hamza Mohammad: This Jordanian joined the Afghan camps in 1999. After developing skill with explosives, he coordinated the preparation of most of the attacks using car bombs for which the organization has taken credit. He was killed by the American forces in 2003.

Abu Mohammed Al-Lubnani: Lubnani is a former Lebanese soldier and a specialist in explosives. He lived for a long time in Denmark before settling in Iraq in 2003.

Abu Ali Al-Iraqi: Al-Iraqi, who served in the Iraqi army, is a specialist in missiles.

Hassan Ibrahim: With the aid of two colleagues, Ibrahim coordinates the group's propaganda.

In addition to this nucleus of people close to Zarqawi, ten Jordanians with an average age of 30 belong to the upper echelons of Tawhid wal Jihad, Zarqawi's inner circle. They are Muwaffaq Ali Ahmad Al-Adwan, alias Abu Omar and Abu Anas Al-Jafarii; Jamal Rifat Ratib Al-Utaybi, alias Abu Abdallah and Jamal Awayis; Salah Al-Din Muhammad Tahir Al-Utaybi, alias Abdel Aziz Al-Anzi and Abu Jihad; Muhammad Ismail Nayif Al-Safadi, alias Abu Al-Harith; Sari Muhammad Hasan Shihab, alias Abu Safar and Suhayb; Maadh Issaf Abdallah Al-Nusur, alias Abu Al-Qaqa; Shihada Naji Shihadah Al-Kilani, alias Izz Al-Din; Muhammad Ratib Ibrahim Qutayshat, alias Khaid; Mundhir Abdel Latif Yussef Shamma, alias Abu Al-Harith and Mundhir Al-Tammuni; and Omar Izz Al-Din Issam Al-Utaybi, alias Al-Battar and Zakaria Omar Al-Barqawi.

Tawhid wal Jihad is organized in autonomous concentric circles. Communications with Zarqawi's inner circle pass through many intermediaries, which makes it extremely difficult to pinpoint its location and, *a fortiori*, where it has infiltrated. It is not unlikely, moreover, that Zarqawi directs the group's actions from a foreign country such as Iran or Syria, where he has been placed several times after the onset of the American offensive in Iraq.

Tawhid wal Jihad's primary zone of activity, the "Sunni Triangle," was divided into nine autonomous operational centers. The city of Fallouja, which serves as the movement's headquarters, has five hundred fighters under the command of Abu Nawras Al-Faluji. The Baghdad sector has fifty fighters headed by Umar Bazyani, who was recently captured by the Americans. The northern region is headed by Hussain Salim. The province of Anbaar has sixty fighters under Abu Azzam Abdallah. The commander of the city of Mossoul is Abu Talha, who supervises four hundred fighters. In addition, the Iraqi intelligence services estimate that fifty Tawhid wal Jihad fighters are in Samarra, eighty in the province of Diyala, and 150 in the city of Al-Qaim near the Syrian border. Each local or provincial command center is subdivided into detachments, as is the case at Fallouja.

In a letter sent from prison and dated 2004, Maqdisi made several recommendations to Zarqawi for a successful battle in Iraq: "I also advise you to take an Islamic group with an Iraqi commander who knows his people and how to speak to them."[104] Zarqawi apparently followed this advice, since one of his last lieutenants still present in Fallouja at the end of November 2004, during the American offensive, was the Iraqi Omar Hadid, a former member of Saddam Hussein's special guard.[105]

According to the American intelligence services, the "resisters" in Iraq have access to "unlimited" funding provided essentially by two sources: Saudi contributors and Islamic charitable organizations. For the most part the money is funneled through Syria.[106] Zarqawi's group also has its own financial networks; thus in 2004 the Jordanian services arrested a Jordanian recruited by Zarqawi to raise funds in the mosques for his organization in Iraq. The money collected by Bilal Mansur Al-Hiyari reached Zarqawi through the mediation of several messengers across Syria. Al-Hiyari even acknowledged

having collected $3,000 to buy an Opel car to be delivered to Zar-
qawi when he was in Iraq.[107]

Since January 2004 Zarqawi has been actively trying to rally
Muslim fighters to the cause of the "resistance." On January 5, in an
hour-long audio message broadcast in various media, he launched
an appeal to Muslims to join the jihad in Iraq, citing the most illus-
trious religious fundamentalists.[108]

The group's operations began after April 5, 2004, when the
United States Army began its attack on Fallouja. As early as April 9
the first American hostage was seized and executed. Starting in June
there would be other hostages: American, South Korean, and Turks.

On April 6, 2004, the day after the start of the American offensive
in Fallouja, Zarqawi published a long message explaining that he was
fighting against the Americans and their "collaborators," in particular the Kurds of the PUK and the Shiites. He took credit for several
actions, including attacks on the U.N. office in Baghdad and on the
coalition forces in Kerbala, Nasiriyah, and Baghdad. He also mentioned actions against the American intelligence services.[109]

The offensive of Zarqawi's group against the "collaborators" cul-
minated on October 23, 2004, with the murder of fifty Iraqi National
Guard recruits as they were leaving a training camp near Kirkuk. Zarqawi took credit for the action the very next day, stating that his group
had killed "corrupt men" and had managed to "steal two vehicles and
the salaries the soldiers had just received from their masters."[110]

Zarqawi knows that he will win this war primarily by mobilizing
public opinion in the West against the occupation. Thus civilians
have become the organization's main targets.

CHAPTER 17

The Hostage Strategy

ON SEPTEMBER 17, 2004, TWO LEBANESE MEN, CHARBEL HAJJ, age 31, and Aram Nalbandian, age 47, who worked for a cement importer, were in a car approaching the Sunni stronghold of Fallouja, fifty kilometers west of Baghdad, when they noticed a roadblock they thought had been set up by the Iraqi police. But they soon learned that the armed, masked men who signaled them to stop were not part of the regular forces. And there was a banner waving from the top of a makeshift pole: it showed a Kalashnikov and a forearm pointing toward heaven and resting on a Koran that dominated the globe, with this inscription, stark against a black background: Tawhid wal Jihad.

The men were stopped and asked for their papers. Because they were foreigners, Zarqawi's men informed them that they were going to be interrogated. They were blindfolded with a strip of cloth held in place by a metal wire, then driven to a house. There the kidnappers, still masked, gave them traditional garments including the baggy pants worn by Wahhabi Islamists. The men's boss tried to reach them from Baghdad on their cellphone. An Iraqi answered, and he immediately hung up, realizing that his two employees had just been abducted.

The interrogation went on for five days, during which the kidnappers tried to find out whether the two Lebanese men were collaborating in one way or another with the Americans. They had to give highly detailed accounts of their history, the company where they worked, the nationality of foreign employees there, the clients in Iraq, the areas to which they delivered, and the like. The hostages spoke of a real "war of nerves" in which they had to endure deprivations and were kept awake. The only way they could tell what time it was, Aram recalls, was by hearing the call to prayer issued from the mosques.[111]

When they were permitted to remove their blindfolds they found themselves facing masked men who told them they could take a shower every day and eat all they wanted. They were even given mattresses, pillows, and a fan. After five days they were transferred to another house, where they were no longer alone. There began an endless wait, punctuated by the screams of Iraqis being tortured in neighboring rooms and the voices of foreign hostages. Among these was an Egyptian less fortunate than they were, since he was eventually executed.

Finally persuaded that they were working for Iraq and not for the Americans, the kidnappers decided to release them and even suggested a farewell dinner. But their ordeal was not yet over. On October 12, 2004, United States forces bombed Fallouja, destroying several sites used by the Zarqawi network, including the house where the two men were kept hostage. They spent two hours beneath the rubble, one with a broken leg, the other with a fractured pelvis. They report that five fighters were killed in the raid and buried by their friends the same day without passing through the hospital morgue.

The two Lebanese hostages were finally freed the next day, at the end of twenty-seven days of detention and a brief hospitalization in Fallouja.[112] It is likely that a ransom was paid by their employer. The politics of the worst-case scenario, introduced in April 2004 by Zar-qawi's group in Iraq, rarely ends this way.

Another Lebanese hostage, Mohammed Ra'd, held at the same time, states that he was kept in a dark room whose floor was stained with dried blood. He relates that an Iraqi used to sharpen a knife with a large whetstone outside his cell. One day this man came to take him out of the cell, saying that he was going to show him "something that will be a lesson for all the Lebanese who try to cooperate with the American Army."[113] At this point two cars pulled up next to the house where he was being held. An Egyptian hostage was taken out of the trunk of one of the cars, dressed only in his undergarments, his entire body black and blue from beatings. Ra'd was put into an adjoining room behind a cameraman, a guard at his side. The Egyptian was clothed in a jumpsuit and made to kneel.

One of the kidnappers gave Ra'd a brief account of this Egyptian. This was the second time he had been abducted. On the first occasion he had publicly destroyed propaganda CDs in Fallouja; this time he was accused of providing women for the American soldiers.

The kidnappers then tied the Egyptian's hands behind his back and asked him to state his name, address, place of origin, and activities. After complying, he was about to apologize for his acts, but a man gave a sign to the "executioner" standing behind the hostage, who grabbed the man's tongue and cut it off, stating that the time for excuses was past. He then stuffed the Egyptian's mouth with cotton and read a statement in the form of a judicial sentence. The Egyptian was on the ground, with one of the kidnappers holding his feet. He was then beheaded.[114]

In October 2004 the United States military authorities held Zarqawi responsible for the deaths of 675 Iraqis and 40 foreigners, in addition to over 2,000 wounded since the beginning of the coalition's offensive.[115]

In a letter dated January 2004 and attributed to him, Zarqawi claimed credit for the bulk of the actions carried out against the coalition: "We have been the key for all the suicide missions that have taken place, except in the north. By the grace of God, I have conducted twenty-five operations up to now, in particular against...the Americans and their soldiers and the forces of the coalition."[116]

Altogether, the rebel Islamist groups active in Iraq kidnapped more than 150 foreigners in the course of 2004, including people of American, British, Lebanese, Jordanian, Egyptian, Turkish, Nepalese, South Korean, Pakistani, Italian, Bulgarian, and French nationality.

All this began, apparently, after the abduction on April 9, 2004 of Nicholas Berg, the 26-year-old American businessman. The kidnapping, claimed by Zarqawi's group, immediately aroused indignation throughout the world, but it nevertheless led to a wave of hostage takings in Iraq by the principal groups of Islamist "insurgents." Thus the Green Battalion took credit for a similar action a few days later, followed by the Islamic Army in Iraq, Ansar Al-Sunna, and the Abu Bakr Al-Sidiq Brigades.

Then there came a series of executions. Tawhid wal Jihad claimed nine executions in six months, including those of Nicholas Berg in May, the South Korean Kim Sun-il in June, the Bulgarians Georgi Lazov and Ivaylo Kepov in July, the Turks Murat Yuce and Durmus Kumdereli in August, the Americans Eugene "Jack" Armstrong and Jack Hensley in September, and the Englishman Kenneth Bigley in October.

When it comes to kidnapping and execution, Zarqawi's group differs from its Islamist competitors in several respects. First, although it advocates the politics of chaos in Iraq, it is very selective in its targets: it aims for the most part at Westerners and their "collaborators." In addition, it abducts mainly political and religious figures so as to arouse as much resentment in the media as possible. Thus Tawhid wal Jihad claimed credit for the assassination of Izzadin Saleem, the president of the council of the provisional Iraqi government, on May 22, 2004.

Though he accepts ransom payments in exchange for the release of certain hostages who are deemed "nonstrategic," what Zarqawi is seeking most of all is the media impact of the semipublic execution of Western hostages. His macabre scenarios make an impression because of the barbarity they display and the terror they inspire. This is just what Zarqawi is counting on. He is a master of the art of communication who has even established a "media department" within Tawhid wal Jihad under the direction of Abu Maysarah Al-Iraqi. Charged with writing and disseminating the movement's press releases, this department is said to have at least three staff members in Iraq. Its computer facilities are based in other countries and employ the most modern graphic and video techniques, combining audio and visual effects in a way that reinforces the impact of the executions.

The group has several media channels at its disposal. It has acquired a Web site for publicizing its messages and participates regularly in various Islamist discussion forums to spread its propaganda and kindle the exchange of ideas. In addition, several Arabic communications media in the Persian Gulf systematically relay the group's messages in their entirety.

Tawhid wal Jihad also knows how to defend its competitive advantage against other Islamist movements that are trying to benefit from Zarqawi's worldwide media coverage. Thus, when a new group called Tawhid Islamic Movement appeared in the summer of 2004, Zarqawi's media department gave out a press release on August 4, in which the organization informed "fighters not to confuse the Tawhid Islamic Movement with Tawhid wal Jihad, the name of the movement led by Sheikh Abu Musab Al-Zarqawi. Our brothers might have been fooled by the media that associated our banner with this name."[117]

Paradoxically, Zarqawi's group commits fewer terrorist acts than groups like the Islamic Army in Iraq, but his are the ones that are commented on throughout the world. Zarqawi is attentive to the regularity of the executions carried out by his movement—at least one each month since May 2004—and careful about their timing. In the same way he is very attentive to his group's general communications. The day after the onset of the American offensive in Fallouja in October 2004, Tawhid wal Jihad announced that it was joining Al-Qaeda so as to better coordinate the forces waging jihad in Iraq. This information served only to confirm the de facto situation, but the moment chosen for the announcement was important.

Zarqawi has tried several times in his writings and speeches to justify his barbaric acts, in particular after some religious Iraqis distanced themselves from his group or condemned it outright. He holds that these vile murders are authorized by the Koran and that the people he kills are not hostages but spies, "the sentence for the latter," he says, "being death."[118] He does, to be sure, admit that there can be differences of opinion regarding the way death is imposed, by fire or by the sword, and "takes into consideration the opinion of religious Sunnis with regard to knowing whether these killings are or are not permitted by religion, only when these clerics express their deep conviction and not when they speak in the name of a government or to satisfy it." Zarqawi says he is convinced that the killings in question are authorized, including when they involve the mutilation of bodies, since "God permits us to do the same thing to [the infidels] in return, with the same means they employ. If they kill our women, we will kill their women."

This fundamentally depraved conception of Islam is the fruit of a mind indoctrinated by the opinions it formulates, opinions that stem directly from those of the great theoreticians of modern jihad, notably Abu Mohammed Al-Maqdisi, Abu Qatada, and Yussef Al-Qardawi, all of whom Zarqawi has read, heard, and sometimes met, and to whom he constantly refers.

1. Family picture, with Zarqawi standing in front of his mother. (Private Collection)

2. Zarqawi's parents. (Private Collection)

3. School photo. (Private Collection)

4. Zarqawi before his departure for Afghanistan in 1989. (Private Collection)

5. Drawing Zarqawi made for his mother while in prison in Jordan. (©Gamma)

6. Identity photos.

7. Zarqawi during a ceremony in Afghanistan in 1991.

8. Zarqawi before the departure for Afghanistan. (Private Collection)

9/10. Zarqawi in prison in Jordan. (Private Collection)

11. Search warrant.

12. Suwaqah Prison, where Zarqawi was incarcerated from 1994 to 1999. (Private Collection)

13. Palestinian refugee camp in Zarqa and the Al-Falah Mosque. (Private Collection)

14. The cemetery below the house in which Zarqawi grew up. (Private Collection)

15. Family home in the Al-Ramzi district of Zarqa. (Private Collection)

16. Mullah Krekar, founder of Ansar Al-Islam.

17. Issam Mohammed Taher Al-Barqawi, alias Abu Mohammed Al-Maqdisi.

18. Mohammed Al-Khalayleh, Zarqawi's brother. (Private Collection)

19. Saleh Al-Hami, Zarqawi's brother-in-law. (© Lynsey Addario/Corbis)

20. Mustafa Setmariam Nasar, alias Abu Musab Al-Suri, Zarqawi's right-hand man in Iraq. (Private Collection)

21. Logo of Jund Al-Islam.

22. Logo of Ansar Al-Islam.

23. Logo of Tawhid Wal Jihad.

24. Camp in Khurmal, Iraqi Kurdistan.

25. Ansar Al-Islam fighters in a training camp.

26. Before the execution of Nicholas Berg.

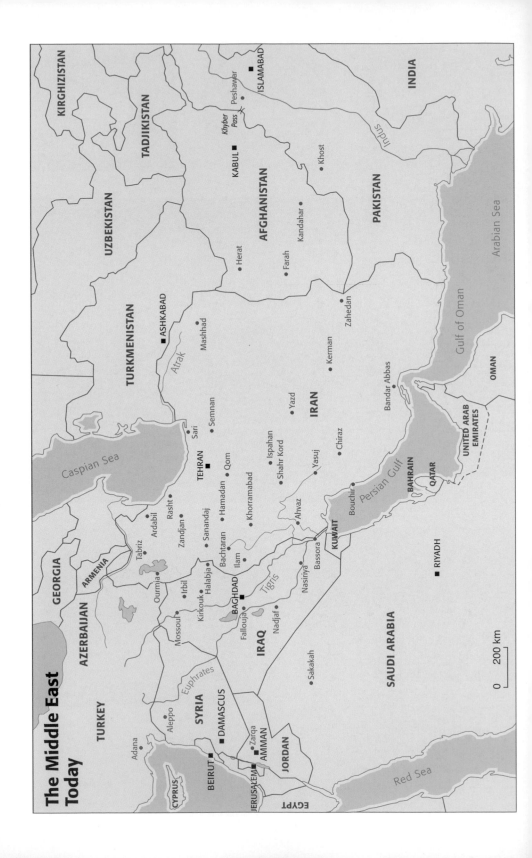

The Middle East Today

KIRGHIZISTAN

TADJIKISTAN

UZBEKISTAN

INDIA

■ ISLAMABAD

Peshawar

Khyber Pass

• Khost

■ KABUL

AFGHANISTAN

PAKISTAN

• Herat

• Farah

• Kandahar

Indus

Arabian Sea

TURKMENISTAN

■ ASHKABAD

• Mashhad

• Zahedan

Atrak

Gulf of Oman

• Kerman

OMAN

• Yazd

IRAN

• Bandar Abbas

• Semnan

• Chiraz

• Sari

UNITED ARAB EMIRATES

Caspian Sea

■ TEHRAN

• Qom

• Ispahan

• Yasuj

• Hamadan

• Shahr Kord

BAHRAIN

QATAR

• Rasht

• Khorramabad

• Ahvaz

Persian Gulf

• Ardabil

• Zandjan

• Sanandj

• Bachtaran

• Bouchir

• Tabriz

• Ilam

• Bassora

KUWAIT

Tigris

• Nasiriya

• Ourmia

• Irbil

• Halabja

• Kirkouk

■ BAGHDAD

• Najaf

• Mossoul

• Fallouja

• Sakakah

RIYADH ■

IRAQ

SAUDI ARABIA

GEORGIA

ARMENIA

AZERBAIJAN

Euphrates

SYRIA

TURKEY

• Aleppo

■ DAMASCUS

• Adana

• Zarqa

AMMAN ■

JORDAN

BEIRUT ■

JERUSALEM ■

CYPRUS

EGYPT

Red Sea

0   200 km

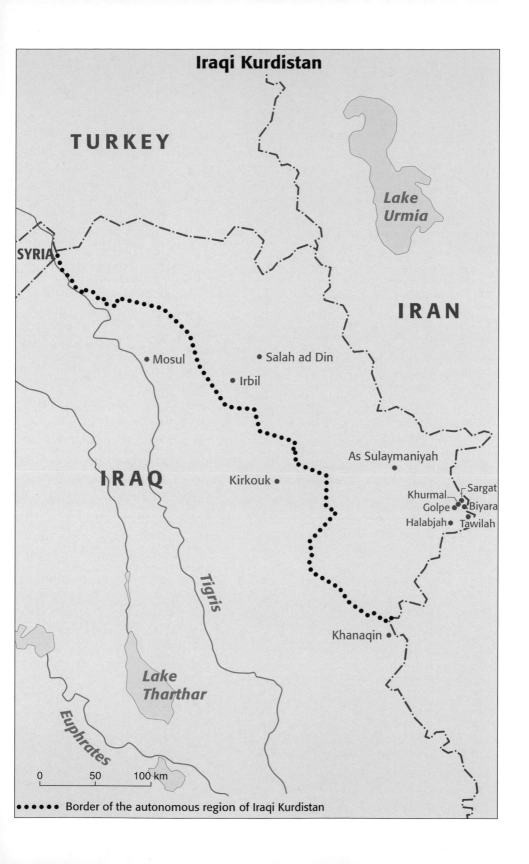

Iraqi Kurdistan

TURKEY

SYRIA

Lake Urmia

IRAN

• Mosul

• Salah ad Din

• Irbil

As Sulaymaniyah •

IRAQ

Kirkouk •

Khurmal ⌐Sargat
Golpe •• •Biyara
Halabjah• Tawilah

Tigris

Lake Tharthar

Khanaqin •

Euphrates

0	50	100 km

•••••• Border of the autonomous region of Iraqi Kurdistan

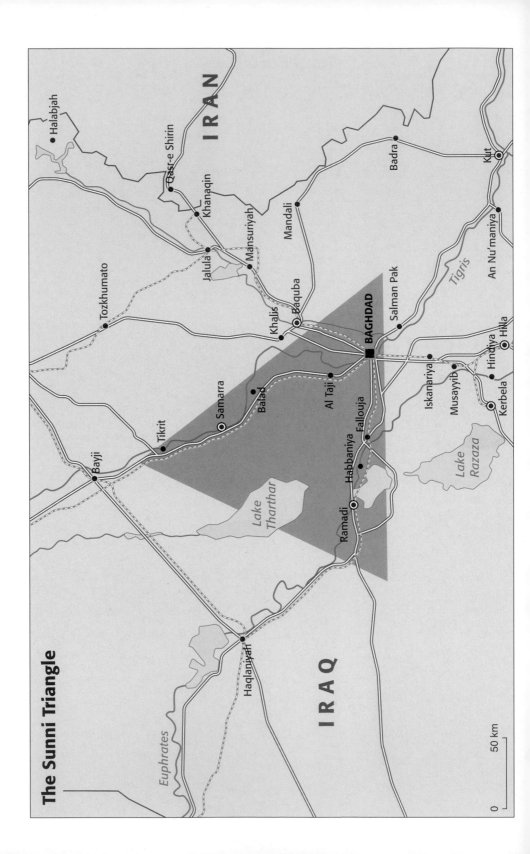

The Sunni Triangle

Halabjah

IRAN

Qasr-e Shirin

Khanaqin

Mansuriyah

Tozkhumato

Jalula

Mandali

Badra

Kut

An Nu'maniya

Baquba

Khalis

BAGHDAD

Salman Pak

Tigris

Hilla

Hindiya

Iskandariya

Musayyib

Kerbela

Samarra

Balad

Al Taji

Tikrit

Fallouja

Lake
Razaza

Bayji

Habbaniya

Lake
Tharthar

Ramadi

Haqlaniyah

IRAQ

Euphrates

0   50 km

CHAPTER 18

Al-Qaeda Yields

IRAQ HAS NEVER REALLY BEEN AT STAKE FOR AL-QAEDA. IN HIS first declaration of war against the United States and the West on August 23, 1996, entitled "Message from Osama Bin Laden to his Muslim brothers in the world and especially in the Arabian Peninsula," Bin Laden hardly mentions Iraq.

Islam is of course the dominant religion in Iraq, Christians representing less than five percent of the population. The Shiites are two thirds of the Muslim population, the Sunnis one third. These communities live together in relative calm, and the Sunnis are forced to keep a low profile vis-à-vis the Shiites so as to keep control of their strongholds.

The leaders of Al-Qaeda have always dealt carefully with Iran and its majority Shiite community. Thus, despite Iran's recent firmness with regard to Al-Qaeda's prisoners, neither Osama Bin Laden nor Ayman Al-Zawahiri has condemned the Iranians. Before the opening of the Iraqi front, Al-Qaeda had never attacked either the Iranian Shiites in Afghanistan, though they were close to the Northern Alliance, or the Saudi Shiites. Moreover, Bin Laden has never called for an attack on religious Shiites on Iraqi soil and has even denied the involvement of his organization in the assassination of Sheikh Bakir Al-Hakim, head of the Supreme Council of the Iraqi revolution in Iraq.

In contrast, Al-Qaeda's strategy of systematic opposition to the United States, particularly to the presence of Western troops in the Gulf, was part of its policy toward Iran, which could, if need be, provide a counterweight to the alliance formed between the Saudi regime and the United States. This strategy of peaceful coexistence, which was not a foregone conclusion given the historical opposition between Sunnis and Shiites, was a constraint on Al-Qaeda and its leaders until the time of the American offensive in Iraq.

Zarqawi, on the other hand, advocates a strategy of chaos in Iraq, rushing headlong into a denunciation of all the accomplices of U.S. "aggression," including the Kurds and the Shiites. In a letter attributed to him, seized on January 23, 2004 by the American forces in Iraq and made available by the Provisional Authority there (see Appendix VIII), Zarqawi called the Shiites "the greatest demon of humanity" because of their dealings with the American enemy. He compares them to a "malicious scorpion" that arrays itself in the garments of friendship so as to be in a better position to "stab in the back" the true representatives of Islam, the Sunnis. There are doubts about the authenticity of this letter, which is believed to be addressed to the heads of Al-Qaeda, but the simplistic conception of Islam that it expresses, especially the secular conflict between Shiites and Sunnis and the assertion that the former are trying to build a "new Iran" in Iraq, corroborates other statements made by Zarqawi and reveals his meager knowledge of religion.

In a taped message made public some months later, Zarqawi called the Shiites the "weak link" of the Islamic nation and the Americans a "Trojan horse" in Iraq.[119] This position is hard to reconcile with the ostensible neutrality of the leaders of Al-Qaeda toward the Shiite community. Nor must we overlook the fact that many of these leaders believe that Iraq is not the priority when it comes to taking action. Thus in October 2003, an Al-Qaeda official in Saudi Arabia explained, in the online magazine *Voice of Jihad*, Al-Qaeda's press organ in the Arabian Peninsula, that although he had received many suggestions to go to Iraq and considered that country a battle-front of jihad like others, one for which the organization had made many efforts, what mattered was the fight to drive the "infidels" from the holy land of Saudi Arabia.[120]

Under these circumstances Al-Qaeda's commitment to the cause of the Islamist resistance in Iraq has come about gradually and has been played out on two levels. It is largely the result of the positions taken by religious radicals calling for jihad in Iraq and later "authorizing" the activities of Zarqawi's group, including suicide missions, the taking of hostages, and executions. And the markedly large growth in the number of applicants for jihad since the summer of 2003 has given the leaders of Al-Qaeda less and less room to maneuver.

Beginning in 2002 there was an increasing call, especially among clergymen close to Al-Qaeda, for support of the jihad against the United States should there be an invasion of Iraq. Thus Abu Qatada replied as follows to a journalist asking him about the role jihadist groups might play in case of an American attack: "The growth of American tyranny... and its plan to attack Iraq and establish an 'Iraqi Karzai' will necessitate an even fiercer battle."[121]

In the course of 2003 Sheikh Yussef Al-Qardawi, religious leader of the Egyptian members of the Muslim Brotherhood who had taken refuge in Qatar, developed the concept of "resistance" to foreign aggression in Iraq. Sheikh Qardawi is one of the primary theoreticians of suicide missions before and after the attacks of September 11 in the United States. Beyond the ambiguous position of the disciples of the Muslim Brotherhood, his intentions are relatively clear on this subject. In February 2001 he told an Egyptian daily newspaper that "necessity justifies the prohibition [of suicide in the Koran]" and that "human bombs" are "a new weapon" whose sacrifice is tantamount to religious martyrdom.[122]

A few months later he was of the opinion that suicide missions were not the same as suicide and constituted "the noblest form of war."[123] Questioned in December 2001 after the attacks in the United States, Al-Qardawi had not changed his position, stating that "it is wrong and unjust to characterize suicide operations in this way, since they actually come under the heading of heroic action, and martyr attacks must under no circumstances be considered tantamount to suicide."[124]

Following strong protests from the West, Qardawi was silenced for awhile by the Qatar authorities, who suspended his Sunday religious program, "Sharia and Life," on the Al-Jazira network. But since the beginning of 2003 this Sunni has headed the group of clerics who gave a coherent form to the exacerbated opposition to the United States on the eve of the offensive in Iraq.

In late January 2003 Qardawi stated that "whoever is killed in a military operation intended to drive the American forces of occupation from the Gulf is a martyr," though he pointed out that "American civilians must be distinguished from their government and their army."[125] He gave a sermon on March 7 of that year, at the beginning of the American offensive, in which he said that jihad is an obligation in Islam and that Muslims have a duty "to resist and to drive out the unbelievers invading a Muslim country," denouncing all those who "cooperate" with the United States in Iraq.[126] In September 2003 resistance was no longer the only issue, since he begged God to "eliminate" the United States.[127]

The specter of a direct clash between Sunnis and Shiites, the main pitfall that the radicals close to Al-Qaeda in Iraq were trying to ward off because it would weaken them locally and marginalize them regionally, reemerged as a problem that the U.S. hoped to ignite so as to justify its presence in Iraq. Clerics affiliated with the terrorist organization then denounced what they regarded as a "plot" on the part of the United States to foment a war of religion between Sunnis and Shiites and divide the populace.[128]

Particularly after the arrest of Saddam Hussein, who had maintained the religious balance in Iraq, this crucial risk was a factor in the radicalization of the fundamentalists' position, according to which the United States was now the absolute "enemy" along with those who were "collaborating" with its war effort. Their position became more political in intent, with a number of clerics speaking of the "transgressions" and "lies" of the United States countered by "the courage of the men who face up to them," namely the resisters. The United States was condemned as fomenting the "division" of the Iraqi people and "invading" Arab countries in a vast "colonialist plot."[129]

The official support of radical Islamists for the Iraqi jihadists intensified in the course of the summer of 2004, as is shown by an important initiative—though one that went by with scant notice—emanating from ninety-three clerics. In an appeal published in London by *Al-Quds Al-Arabi* on August 23, the principal clerics from the Muslim Brotherhood, including the highest Egyptian official and Yussef Al-Qardawi, called for "supporting by all moral and material means the brave and honorable Islamic resistance" in Iraq against the "US-Zionist colonialist campaign."[130]

In early September Al-Qardawi dropped the veil. In a fatwa he authorized the abduction and killing of American civilians in order to "force the American Army to withdraw." In addition, he declared that from now on it was appropriate to combat "all Americans, including civilians" in Iraq, judging that any American soldier or civilian should be "considered an invader and fought against."[131] His conclusion was that "American civilians have come to Iraq to support the [military] occupation. Under these circumstances, therefore, the abduction and killing of Americans has become a religious obligation, since they must be forced to leave the country." But in a humane moment he added that "the mutilation of bodies is nevertheless prohibited by Islam."[132] In other words, killing is allowed, but it must be done the right way.

Though Al-Qaeda had not yet taken an official position on the "resistance" movement at this time, its traditional support networks and many of its members had already focused their activities on the new land of jihad.

In January 2004 Zarqawi seemed to ask for the aid and support of Al-Qaeda in the famous letter attributed to him by the United States government and made available by the Provisional Authority in Iraq. He wrote: "We need to create armies of mujahidin...to fight the enemy—the Americans, the police, the soldiers....We are continuing to train ourselves and strengthen our ranks. We will strike at them with suicide operations and car bombs." He went on to say quite clearly: "If you are of the same opinion, if you adopt it as your program,...and if you are convinced by the idea of fighting the infidels, we will be your soldiers, under your banner, obeying your orders and taking a public oath of allegiance to you."

There are several indications that the leaders of Al-Qaeda then changed their minds about jihad in Iraq. Among these signs is a letter published in the August–September 2004 issue of *Voice of Jihad*, in which Abd El-Rahman ibn Salem Al-Shamari was full of praise for the beheading of an Egyptian in Iraq. The lone wolf Zarqawi, whom the organization had been careful not to support up to that time, now became "the sheikh of killers." "O sheikh of killers Abu Musab Al-Zarqawi," Al-Shamari wrote, "continue to follow the right path, guided by Allah! Fight with the monotheists against the idolators, with the warriors of jihad against the collaborators, hypocrites, and rebels....Be merciless!" (pp. 36–38).[133]

The act that finally ensured the victory of Zarqawi's position was the public oath of allegiance sworn by Tawhid wal Jihad to Osama Bin Laden and made public on October 17, 2004. Signed "Abu Musab Al-Zarqawi, commander of the Tawhid wal Jihad movement" and placed on the group's Web site, it is unequivocal. Entitled "The Tawhid wal Jihad movement, its emir [Zarqawi], and its fighters have joined the cause of Al-Qaeda and sworn allegiance to Sheikh Osama Bin Laden."[134] The text states that Zarqawi had been in contact "with the brothers of Al-Qaeda for eight months," that they "exchanged points of view," and even that a "rupture" had intervened before contact was resumed.

Zarqawi's oath is presented as the symbol of a new rallying call: "O sheikh of the mujahidin, if you cross the sea, we shall cross it with you. If you give orders, we shall listen; if you forbid, we shall obey. You are the designated leader for the armies of Islam against all infidels, Crusaders, and apostates."

Beyond its lyricism, this announcement was primarily intended to reinforce Al-Qaeda's support, in the eyes of the fighters in Iraq and potential recruits, for the strategy implemented by Zarqawi. For in reality, as we know, Zarqawi's affiliation with Al-Qaeda goes back to 1999, and he had already sworn allegiance to Bin Laden in 2001. The October 17 announcement definitively marks Al-Qaeda's adherence to Zarqawi's orientations. The text implicitly confirms this in its assertion that "our brothers from Al-Qaeda have understood the strategy of the group Tawhid wal Jihad [in Iraq] and are satisfied with the methods we have employed," adding that Zarqawi's group is committed to "pursuing jihad." To give even further resonance to this commitment, on October 19 Zarqawi signed a document under the name of a new entity, the Al-Qaeda Committee for Jihad in Mesopotamia [Iraq].

The American offensive against Fallouja, essentially aimed at defeating the Zarqawi network, showed its limits in the face of an enemy who had undoubtedly left Iraq weeks earlier and was now calling for jihad in flaming press releases. Thus on November 12, 2004, Zarqawi exhorted the "courageous resisters of Fallouja."[135] In the name of Al-Qaeda Zarqawi left the field of battle and, like Osama Bin Laden and Ayman Al-Zawahiri, eluded capture.

The fate of Al-Qaeda was now more than ever tied to that of Abu Musab Al-Zarqawi.

PART IV

A Global Network

I am global, and no land is my country.
—ABU MUSAB AL-ZARQAWI, MAY 26, 2004

CHAPTER 19

From Kurdistan to Germany

ZARQAWI'S NETWORKS ARE WELL ESTABLISHED IN EUROPE. SHORTLY after the attacks of September 11, 2001, European investigators came to see the threat of Islamist terrorism in a new light, and these networks have become an important issue in the fight against terrorism. In Germany, Great Britain, France, Italy, and Spain, several cells have been dissolved because of ties to the terrorist activities of Abu Musab Al-Zarqawi and to the groups Tawhid and Ansar Al-Islam, which he controls, the former being an operational component of the latter.

The enemy has taken on a new face over time. The gradual withdrawal of Osama Bin Laden after the American bombings in Afghanistan has put the current spotlight on Zarqawi, and all the more so because he learns very fast. Whether it is a matter of reactivating a dormant cell in a foreign country or of publicizing his operations, he excels at applying Bin Laden's tried-and-true methods, methods that have proved their effectiveness from the time of Al-Qaeda's first strikes against the American embassies in Kenya and Tanzania in 1998.

For the hundreds of jihadists trained and financed by Al-Qaeda to commit terrorist attacks, the weakening of the organization's command echelon, most of whose members have fled or been arrested, is a hard blow. The successive arrests of Abu Zubaydah, Ramzi Binalshibh, and Khaled Sheikh Mohammed have considerably undermined the command structure of Al-Qaeda, and many of the rank and file have felt constrained to break all ties with the leadership.

With more discretion than Osama Bin Laden but almost as much charisma, Zarqawi reappeared in the Middle East after his escape from Afghanistan. Strengthened by the presence at his side of a solid group of the faithful and by the freedom of movement available to him in the region, he has taken his place in the community of post-September II jihadists as the new man to follow.

For many of those who fled Afghanistan, Zarqawi was not an unknown. He belonged to the second circle of Osama Bin Laden's lieutenants, and his career in Al-Qaeda between 2000 and 2001 was quite familiar to the other fighters. On the basis of his past links to the organization and his directorship of the camp at Herat, he was able to gain influence over the historical figures of the Al-Qaeda networks. Over the course of time he even became one of the few commanders who could implement large-scale operations, and in this way he established himself as the organization's de facto head of operations.

The power of Zarqawi's networks has a variety of components that, taken together, perfectly embody the Islamist terrorist threat in Europe. First there is the relationship, chaotic but sustained, between Zarqawi and Abu Mohammed Al-Maqdisi, which has been of great value in unlocking doors for Zarqawi, in particular that of his representative in Europe, the Jordanian Abu Qatada, who has since been incarcerated in Belmarsh Prison, England. Abu Qatada and his lieutenant, Abu Doha, have been mentioned several times in connection with the investigation into Zarqawi's German networks.

A second element is Ansar Al-Islam and its political arm, the Islamic Movement of Iraqi Kurdistan, recently dubbed the Hezbollah of Kurdistan. Advocating the creation of an Islamic state, a caliphate, in Iraqi Kurdistan, the militants of Ansar Al-Islam have acquired a large support network in Europe and run several religious centers in European capitals, including those of Germany and Italy. The centers are used by Zarqawi for recruiting new partisans to carry out terrorist operations in Iraq and Europe. Among these networks are the Tawhid cell in Germany, Ansar Al-Islam's support cell in Italy, and the amorphous group of Moroccan Salafists in Spain, as well as groups that have different origins but pursue the same goal: exporting jihad into Iraq on behalf of Zarqawi.

Zarqawi himself has been the focus of the most recent and complex European investigations. Apart from the Jordanian GID, the German intelligence services, Bundesnachrichtendienst (BND), are surely those that know him best. For several months in 2002, they even managed to wiretap and tape several members of Tawhid based in Germany, which enabled the officials of the BND to analyze with great precision Zarqawi's behavior at various periods of his flight from Afghanistan. Anxious one moment, cordial with his associates the next, he presented another facet of his personality. Some six hundred pages of proceedings, interrogations, and wiretapped conversations collected in connection with the Tawhid case show that Zarqawi is not only the cold monster who beheads hostages in Iraq; when it comes to saving his own skin, he knows how to be conciliatory and seductive even as he remains a solid leader of men. A terrorist, yes; a suicide bomber, no.

Hans Josef Beth, head of counterterrorism in the German intelligence services, emphasized Zarqawi's "highly active" role in the Tawhid cell. After that group was dissolved, Beth stated that "Al-Tawhid is an extremely disturbing Islamist cell. It drew support from several cells in Europe, and especially in Germany. Al-Tawhid is a component of Al-Qaeda. Its spiritual leader is Abu Qatada, known for his extremist theories."[1]

The uncovering of Tawhid is of major importance for the German and European counterterrorism effort. Only a few weeks after the formidable Hamburg cell responsible for the attacks of

September 11 was revealed—too late, to be sure—it turned out that yet another terrorist group had enabled a significant number of Al-Qaeda members, including Zarqawi, to escape the Americans in Iraq and continue the jihad.

The story unfolded mainly between Tehran and Wilhelmstrasse in Beckum, Westphalia, home of the group's leader, Mohammed Abu Dhess, alias Abu Ali. Other German cities, for example Leipzig, also harbored several "sleepers." A total of nearly thirty individuals coming from Jordan, Iraq, Iran, and Yemen were apprehended by the German police in the course of the investigation. The case was entrusted to the public prosecutor Kay Nehm, who had previously distinguished himself in the investigation of the Hamburg cell. The Tawhid network had woven its web across national borders. Branches would be found in Denmark, Iran, and Great Britain.

As is often the case in matters of terrorism, the people arrested were known to the police or the courts. Some had even been convicted before. Such was the case with Thaer Mansur, sought by the Italian police for his involvement in an earlier Al-Qaeda cell in Milan.[2] Another man, Sayed Agami Mohawal, born in Cairo on February 25, 1964, had been sentenced in Egypt to ten years in prison for belonging to a fundamentalist terrorist group and illegally carrying firearms.[3]

Still another, Ashraf Al-Dagma, was also known to the German security services. This 34-year-old Palestinian was not especially excited about analyzing religious texts when, allegedly hunted by the Palestinian intelligence services, he found refuge in Berlin in 1994. Little by little the German police recorded his first criminal act, selling cocaine at the Zoo subway station. He was arrested and sentenced to two years in prison followed by probation. Al-Dagma then discovered very rigorous Islamic commentators and began to frequent small, radical religious circles. Eventually arrested in April 2003 for involvement in a terrorist plot and possessing a false Portuguese passport in the name of Conti Sanchez,[4] he was one of the most active members of the Tawhid cell.[5]

Taking skillful advantage of laws on the right of asylum, these terrorists first obtained the status of political refugees and then ended up in extremist groups based in Germany itself.

The investigation actually got underway with the placement of taps on the seventeen portable telephones of a single man, Mohammed Abu Dhess, alias Abu Ali. A native of Jordan, Abu Ali is a strapping man over six feet tall. A jack-of-all-trades in his forties, a former basketball player, and a crooner in the plush palaces of Amman, once he emigrated to Germany he revealed another facet of his personality, a darker one, that of an experienced trafficker. Zarqawi's main partner in Germany, he was already known for his wheeling and dealing in Palestinian circles. Abu Ali also took part in several important operations involving arms trafficking for the Islamist cause. The German Federal Office for the Protection of the Constitution (BFV), in charge of security, admitted in 2001 that they had had him under surveillance since 1997. Abu Ali's name regularly appeared in connection with large-scale trafficking.

His experience in this field was useful to Zarqawi, who was trying every means of escaping the strikes of the coalition in Afghanistan. Thus he contacted Abu Ali in Germany, for whom it was an honor to help a highly placed leader of Al-Qaeda. On several occasions Zarqawi categorically refused to let his principal German contact conduct a suicide mission, despite the latter's insistent demands. Abu Ali had even told his mother that he was going on such a mission, asking her to pray that he would die as a martyr.[6] But to no avail; as the tapes show, Zarqawi was firmly opposed: "If we lose you now, we lose an ally," he explained. Abu Ali had deep respect for Zarqawi and liked to call him *Habib* ("Beloved") on the phone. The two men put the finishing touches on the operational functioning of the Tawhid cell at a secret meeting held in Iran, which clearly shows how important Mohammed Abu Dhess was in this organization.[7]

On the basis of this privileged relationship with Zarqawi, Abu Ali ran the cell from Essen, in the Ruhr region. He gave orders, criticized, advised, and even punished. Although he was very involved in the carrying out of operations, the German intelligence services decided not to arrest him immediately so that they could continue to gather information. They hoped to learn more about Zarqawi, this new key figure of jihad. But, of course, they reinforced their surveillance apparatus around the group.

Within a short time the Tawhid cell was organized at Zarqawi's personal instigation. Various members of the group in Germany went to Afghanistan with Zarqawi and his closest associates to get ID photos that they then sent on to Essen in Germany and Horsholm in Denmark, where a clandestine workshop for false official documents was run by Shaker Yussuf El Abassi, alias Abu Yussuf, who forged passports using stolen documents. These were then sent back to Afghanistan. In only three months' time nearly three hundred passports left this workshop, a number of which were collected by Zarqawi in Afghanistan.

Conversations between Zarqawi and Abu Ali became more frequent. Abu Ali gave increasingly precise details about his actions to the sheikh (the "chief"), who was satisfied with them. Although the two men spoke in code, on the basis of the experience gained in connection with the Hamburg cell the German investigators soon deciphered the meaning of each expression. Thus Abu Ali spoke of "black pills," meaning explosives, or "Russian apples," meaning hand grenades, or "little girls," meaning false driver's licenses.[8]

In the terrorists' language, the "university" meant prison, which suggests that the fundamentalists used their years of incarceration to improve their knowledge of applied terrorism. A "dancer" was a passport, an "acorn" a piece of ammunition. Everyone complied, or almost everyone. When one of the members of the group went astray and committed a lapse in his use of the code, Abu Ali would correct him in strong terms, shouting, "The dogs are listening!" All this time the German counterterrorism services were carefully taping each conversation.

In any event, Zarqawi was content with the way the Tawhid group was working. He was especially pleased with the new passport Abu Ali got him: "The dancer was from Morocco," he crowed.

Week after week Tawhid intended to diversify its activities and proceed to action on Zarqawi's behalf. Mounting terrorist operations had, after all, been the initial goal of the Tawhid cell when it was founded by Abu Ali and Shadi Abdalla in the late 1990s and the beginning of the new millennium.

The cofounder of the group, the Jordanian Shadi Abdalla, revealed to the investigators that Tawhid's strategic objective was to strike at Jordan according to a plan hatched by Zarqawi. More realistic were the terrorists' immediate plans to commit an attack in Germany using a pistol outfitted with a silencer in a crowded square and then to set off grenades near Berlin's Jewish Museum with the aim of "killing as many people as possible." The attacks were supposed to be carried out by Shadi Abdalla, an imposing 26-year-old Jordanian who was, along with Ashraf Al-Dagma and Ismail Shalabi, a former member of the guard close to Osama Bin Laden. The roles assigned to Shadi Abdalla in Germany included identifying potential targets and, above all, procuring the arms necessary for pursuing the operations.

In March 2002, when Zarqawi was getting ready to leave Iran and was awaiting news of his associates, Shadi Abdalla wanted to speed up the course of history. He tried to get a pistol equipped with a silencer ("mute" in the transcription)[9] and a battery of grenades. Yet the weapons did not arrive at their destination, for Shadi Abdalla,[10] Mohammed Abu Dhess, Ismail Shalabi, and Jamel Mustafa[11] were arrested on April 23, 2002. The series of attacks planned by the Tawhid cell had failed.

The ten members of the German cell were arrested one by one. Although Shadi Muhammad Mustafa Abdalla cooperated closely with the German judiciary in order to mitigate his sentence, he was nevertheless sentenced in November 2003 to four years in prison. His profile as a high-level terrorist was of great interest to the German and American investigators. Like Zarqawi, he had left for Pakistan in 1999. The two men met in May 2000 and shared their resentment of the Jordanian monarchy. Shadi Abdalla was then placed under the protection of the son-in-law of Osama Bin Laden, Abdullah Al-Halabi, whom he met during a pilgrimage to Mecca. In 1995 he was granted political asylum by the German government. On Zarqawi's orders he went to Germany in May 2001, where he helped Abu Dhess set up the Tawhid group.

The goal of this cell at the time was to strike at Jewish targets in Germany. It was also charged with perpetuating the culture promulgated at the Herat camp: "Tawhid wal Jihad," a sign at the entrance to the camp had proclaimed. In taking the camp's watchword as its own, the German group laid de facto claim to Zarqawi's Salafist ideology. Like Al-Qaeda, the Tawhid movement was clearly trying to make a place for itself in the history of jihad.

Every Islamist terrorist wanted to accomplish his own September 11. The advancement of a terrorist group often comes through the recognition of its leader, and, in fact, Zarqawi's ambition is to equal, indeed to surpass, Osama Bin Laden—this despite the oath of allegiance to Bin Laden. Shadi Abdalla summed up his analysis before his German judges as follows: "An attack in Germany would have made Al-Tawhid famous.... This would have led to the same results as September 11."[12] Such a plan reinforces the idea that the invocation of religion is just a pretext for committing terrorist acts of increasing violence. No terrorist is engrossed in God, especially not Zarqawi, for whom the Koran is just an instrument of power.

Shadi Abdalla imparted more and more revelations to the police, who took careful note of each detail. Leaving Germany in 1999, he said, he returned in 2001 on a mission of collecting money. He explained exactly how he and Abu Ali had established a system for raising funds in the various German and European mosques in order to finance the Zarqawi networks.[13]

From his base in Germany, Shadi Abdalla remained in permanent and close contact with Zarqawi. Ultimately, in the emergency situation of escape from the American bombing in Afghanistan, Tawhid was used as a base of logistical support.

Intelligence emerging from the investigation suggests that this cell, initially conceived for such logistical support, was gradually transformed into an operational terrorist group. Information given to the German police by Shadi Abdalla has helped in taking the measure of the vast support network put in place by Zarqawi.

The offshoots of this group extended to Hamburg, Berlin, and Wiesbaden. Operational terrorists also provided assistance from the United Kingdom and the Czech Republic. Under the iron rule of the confirmed trafficker Abu Ali, the entire group was trained in circuits of clandestine finances, sending money into Afghanistan via commercial firms or nongovernmental organizations such as the Wafa Organization, later placed on the list of "terrorist" organizations by the United States. According to Shadi Abdalla, half of the money arriving in Afghanistan from Germany was attributed to Al-Qaeda, the other half coming from Zarqawi and the Taliban. He stated that Zarqawi always balked at handing out these subsidies[14] and confirmed that Abu Ali was in charge of the overall collection of funds in Germany.

Shortly after the discovery of Tawhid, the German antiterrorist investigatory services recognized the growing role of Islamist cells in their country. Some 180 investigations of groups or individuals more or less closely linked to the Islamist threat are currently in progress. After the arrests in connection with Tawhid, officials of the German criminal police (BKA) publicly declared that Germany had become "a rest area, a fallback position, and a place of preparation" for Islamist terrorists.[15] This statement is especially true in the case of the Zarqawi group.

Throughout his interrogation Shadi Abdalla characterized the Tawhid cell as an autonomous, clandestine entity initially created by

Al-Qaeda and later taken over by Zarqawi for his own purposes. "The aim of this group is to strike at the Jordanian government and fight the Jews," he told the German investigators. In his testimony Abdalla also described in detail the close relationship between Zarqawi and Abu Qatada, who was then living in London. He stated that Zarqawi "could do nothing without the prior agreement of the cleric Abu Qatada."[16]

Abu Qatada Al-Filistini (whose real name is Umar Mahmud Uthman or Omar Mahmoud Othman) did indeed have a real influence on the decisions and orientations of Zarqawi within Tawhid. Very close to Zarqawi's mentor Abu Mohammed Al-Maqdisi,[17] Abu Qatada was granted political asylum in Great Britain in 1993. Judiciary proceedings taking place in Spain, Germany, and France have been able to establish Abu Qatada's preeminence in the European sphere of Al-Qaeda, where he was considered to be Bin Laden's representative. Videotapes of his sermons were found in the personal effects of the September 11 terrorists.

As we have seen, he also had extremely close ideological and operational ties to Abu Musab Al-Zarqawi. Along with Zarqawi, he had been sentenced by the Jordanian courts for his involvement in preparing the millennium plot. Then there was his long-standing and solid friendship with Maqdisi. Finally, if we are to believe Shadi Abdalla's confessions before the German courts, he was the intermediary in Europe for the operations carried out by the Zarqawi networks.

Because of these various incriminating factors, Abu Qatada was arrested by the British authorities in October 2002. In March 2004 his request for release was rejected, since the judges considered him "a truly dangerous individual" who was "heavily implicated in the terrorist operations of the Al-Qaeda group."[18]

CHAPTER 20

The Group of "Italians"

THE DISCOVERY AND DISMANTLING OF THE TAWHID CELL IN
Germany gave an idea of the extent of Zarqawi's networks in Europe. This intuition was confirmed by the antiterrorist Italian magistrate Stefano Dambruoso. With the help of the Italian antiterrorist police, DIGOS (division for general investigations and special operations), several members of the terrorist group Ansar Al-Islam were soon arrested on Italian soil after the "Bazaar" operation. Other members of the Italian group were later arrested in Germany.

On the model of Tawhid, the group of "Italians" took as its aim facilitating the illegal entry of fighters in Iraqi Kurdistan and providing logistical support for Zarqawi and his partisans. In 2002 and 2003 the investigation conducted by the Italian services revealed the machinery of a complex terrorist organization. According to the ruling of the Milan tribunal, pronounced on November 21, 2003,

> the accused constituted on Italian soil a terrorist cell of Ansar Al-Islam, whose acknowledged leader is Mullah Krekar. This group was also linked to the terrorist organization Al-Tawhid, headed by

Emir Abu Musab Al-Zarqawi, who is at the present time still an important member of Al-Qaeda. The aim of this organization was to find false documents, to recruit several persons for logistical support and possibly to send them to training camps located for the most part in Iraq, and to raise funds necessary for the accomplishment of the aims of the organization.[19]

Just as the suspects were about to flee to Syria, the Italian authorities in Parma arrested Mohammed Tahir Hammid and Mostafa Amin Mohammed, two 27-year-old Iraqi Kurds. The Milan police also arrested the number two man in the organization, the Egyptian Radi El Ayashi, alias Mera'i, age 27, and the Somali Cabdullah Mohammed Ciise, an active member of Al-Qaeda. Two days later, in Cremona, DIGOS arrested the Tunisian Murad Trabelsi, imam of the mosque in that city, and 26-year-old Hamrawi Ben Mouldi.[20]

These men wanted to transport fighters from Italy via Turkey and Syria to swell the ranks of Ansar Al-Islam in Iraqi Kurdistan. The group was to take part in these operations on behalf of Zarqawi and a high official of Ansar Al-Islam named Muhammad Majid, a 32-year-old Kurd who preferred to be called Mullah Fouad and who coordinated the actions of the group between Kurdistan and Syria until March 2003.[21]

The organization's intermediary on the ground, Mullah Fouad, welcomed newcomers. In several conversations taped by the Italian police, he mentioned his need for people to carry out suicide missions. These conversations were in code: "I'm looking for people coming from Japan," Mullah Fouad said to the Somali Ciise, who remained in Italy. The death machine went into overdrive during a conversation between Mullah Fouad and the head of Ansar Al-Islam in Germany, Abderrazak Mahjoub: Fouad asked Mahjoub to send sick and weakened people to Iraq for suicide missions.

. . .

OPERATION BAZAAR, CARRIED OUT IN ITALY, WAS OF GREAT INterest to the entire intelligence community in Europe, for it appears that cells traditionally affiliated with Al-Qaeda were transformed into a network for assisting the armed Islamists in Iraqi Kurdistan. This was the new face of Al-Qaeda revealed by the Italian investigators.

The cells acted autonomously and horizontally, with almost no hierarchical links. Each group obeyed the leadership of one of its members, but operated without a precise organizational flowchart. The pyramidal command structure of Al-Qaeda had become obsolete since the onset of counterterrorist operations in Afghanistan. From now on, each cell would act independently, as in a network of franchises. For the "Italians," the model was Ansar Al-Islam, the group controlled by Zarqawi.

Shortly before the American strikes in Iraqi Kurdistan DIGOS picked up the trail of a militant who had slipped out of Italy. This was Nureddin Drissi, alias Abu Ali, former librarian at the mosque in Cremona, who no longer lived in that peaceful Italian city but in Khurmal in the mountains of Iraqi Kurdistan, the epicenter of Ansar Al-Islam. With his wife and two children he had left a few months earlier for this region at war, passing through Damascus before taking refuge in Iran.

In March 2003 this enclosed, remote region on the border of Iran and Iraq became Zarqawi's favorite terrain. The Jordanian had surreptitiously placed his right-hand men there and was gradually infiltrating the Islamist movements of Kurdistan from his own camp at Herat, in Afghanistan.

Nureddin Drissi, the former librarian, was in Khurmal at the time, not far from the city of Sargat, where Zarqawi had opened his training camps specially devoted to the handling of chemical and bacteriological weapons. Drissi used a satellite phone to call his partner in Italy, the imam of the Cremona mosque Murad Trabelsi, to say that he was worried about the level of the new recruits and hoped to have experienced fighters at his side. The conversations between the two men were taped by the Italian police. Drissi kept informed about the training of the young recruits summoned to Iraq to fire on the Americans.

Several of these "fighters" were of North African origin. After emigrating to Italy, these men, often Tunisians, then branched off toward the new lands of jihad. Whereas Chechnya had been the favored destination for the young radicals at the end of the 1990s, Iraq was one of the top places on the list of hot zones at the beginning of the 2000s. And the Italian foreign services established that several Italians of Tunisian origin took part in combat operations before, during, and after the war in Iraq alongside the organization Ansar Al-Islam.

For months on end the DIGOS investigators had suspected the existence of clandestine channels illegally transporting fighters to Iraq. The investigators—not only Italians but also members of various Western services—also spoke of an attempted redeployment of Al-Qaeda in Iraqi Kurdistan. In this poor, mountainous region, they said, the Islamists hoped to repeat the Afghan experience: a caliphate, terrorist training camps, the wearing of the burkha, public executions, and Islamic law by way of a constitution. Everything was being done by the militants to make Ansar Al-Islam a new Al-Qaeda. And the group was extending its networks into the very heart of Europe, mainly in Germany and Italy.

The Italian cell of Ansar Al-Islam did indeed come to the assistance of this massive redeployment of Al-Qaeda. It participated directly by sending some forty radical Islamists to Kurdistan. Some of these men were trained there and, once skilled in terrorist techniques, returned to Italy. Others repeatedly attacked the troops of the Italian Army in Iraq. But the young recruits, like the Tawhid cell, were primarily "dedicated to logistical support, financing, and provision of false passports."[22]

This logistical schema reveals the key role played by Syria when the jihadists were passing through on the way to Kurdistan. In the reverse direction, too, it seems that a number of them found refuge in

Damascus or Aleppo after the American strikes. The Italian counterterrorist investigatory services emphasized "the pivotal role of Syria in the transport of recruits between Europe and Ansar" and found that Zarqawi and Ansar Al-Islam definitely "benefited from a logistical structure in Syria."[23]

These conclusions by the Italian courts in connection with the case of Ansar Al-Islam corroborate the Jordanian legal documents already cited, according to which Zarqawi stayed in Syria on a number of occasions after his escape from Afghanistan. And there is reason to think that he enjoyed stable protection in Syria: the ties uniting Zarqawi to Iraqi Kurdistan pass through Syria, more precisely through Damascus and Aleppo.

In Italy the members of Ansar Al-Islam were coordinating operations. And, as with Tawhid, the militants of the group were providing unfailing support for the Islamists on the ground. Mohammed Tahir Hammid and Mohammed Mostafa Amin, the two young Kurds living on the outskirts of Parma, stepped up their attempts to recruit fighters in the streets and near places of worship. Hammid, called in for questioning by the Italian police in October 2003, stated that he had started out as an active member of the Islamic Movement of Kurdistan, one of the organizations that merged with Ansar Al-Islam. He reported that he had trained in the Khurmal camp before joining the information and propaganda section of Ansar Al-Islam, and that Mullah Krekar, whom he had known since 1993, was the principal leader of that group.[24]

Moreover, the telephone numbers of the two young recruiters turned up in 2003 on Mullah Krekar's personal phone list. Krekar was then arrested in Amsterdam before being extradited to Norway. During a phone call taped on January 18, 2003 by the Italian police, the number two man in Ansar Al-Islam's recruitment network, the Egyptian Radi El Ayashi, alias Mera'i, expressed his concern about the imprisonment of Mullah Krekar.

On March 9 of that year Mera'i was visited by a contact who

invited him to join Mullah Fouad in Syria. The contact in question was a certain Ibrahim, alias Abu Abdu, who used a portable Swiss telephone with a prepaid card, a phone that was one of those personally used by Zarqawi, as the investigation revealed, to communicate with Salem Saeed Ben Suweid, the murderer of Laurence Foley, and with his "Italian" recruiters. Up to October 2004, the prepaid, anonymous telephone cards bought in Switzerland were used by many high-level terrorists, including the mastermind of the September 11 attacks, Khaled Sheikh Mohammed.

The agents of DIGOS continued their investigations on the ground, assisted by the American authorities in tracking "illegal fighters." On January 18, 2003, in the court of Milan, the police questioned Mera'i. In the listings for his Thuraya satellite phone, the investigators deciphered the telephone numbers of Zarqawi's lieutenants in Iraq.

In the electronic phone list of one of Ayashi's partners, Sali Abdullah Ali, were the name, address, and phone number of Abu Ashraf, one of the lieutenants close to Zarqawi. Abu Ashraf, whose real name was Khalid Mustafa Khalifa Al-Aruri, had been one of Zarqawi's major partners in the terrorist organization Bayt Al-Imam,[25] and up to 2003 he was at Zarqawi's side in the important position of quartermaster in charge of running the camps, particularly in Iraqi Kurdistan.

The European investigations also revealed several close ties between Tawhid and the Italian cell of Ansar Al-Islam. Furthermore, the head of the German network, Mohammed Abu Dhess (Abu Ali), called Zarqawi on a satellite phone whose number was also used by the man called Remadna Abdelhlim, a member of the Italian group. There were frequent communications between the German and Italian cells. This same Abu Ali, who phoned Zarqawi regularly during the latter's escape to Iran, was also in contact with other members of the Italian cell of Ansar Al-Islam, including Maewad Sayed and Thaer Mansur.

Another Ansar Al-Islam recruiter was soon arrested, this time in Hamburg, on November 23, 2003, on the basis of an Italian request for information. He was a 30-year-old Algerian named Abderrazak Mahjoub, alias the Sheikh, who was also sought by the Spanish courts in connection with an investigation into certain planned attacks on the Costa del Sol.[26] He had been arrested for the first time by the Spanish police in July 2003 and released several weeks later. According to the charges brought by the Spanish antiterrorist judge Baltasar Garzon, Mahjoub had gone to Damascus in March 2003 on the way to Iraq, where he planned to welcome others.[27]

Mahjoub was arrested in Hamburg at the request of the Italian authorities. The DIGOS investigators suspected him of being one of the European pivots of Zarqawi's network in Iraq, recruiting young radical candidates for suicide missions in that country. He worked for Zarqawi together with two other Tunisians questioned in Milan, Buyahia Maher Abdelaziz and Husni Jama. German investigators learned after the fact that Mahjoub also had connections to the September 11 terrorists based in Hamburg. He was finally extradited to Italy on March 19, 2004.

According to German officials Mahjoub was responsible for the recruitment of around a hundred jihadists in Germany. Some of these fundamentalists, the officials report, joined Zarqawi's forces in Fallouja and around Baghdad. Others were said to have taken part in violent attacks on Italian troops, and still others to have helped to set up the booby-trapped truck that exploded in Nasariyah in November 2002, killing nineteen Italian soldiers. And an Italian of Moroccan origin, Kamal Morshidi, was involved in the rocket attack on the Hotel Rashid in Baghdad in October 2003 while U.S. Assistant Secretary of Defense Paul Wolfowitz was staying there. The "Italians" who left to fight in Iraq readily attacked the soldiers who were part of the contingent coming from their own country.

The Italian network dismantled in the course of 2003 was supported by an innovative organization: the operatives of Al-Qaeda joined with those of Ansar Al-Islam to increase the number of recruits and financial resources and extend their logistical networks. The two groups sustained each other. The presence of the Somali Cadbullah Mohammed Ciise in the Italian cell of Ansar Al-Islam is quite significant in this context. Before his arrest in Milan in April 2003, Ciise was known to the antiterrorist services as an important emissary of Al-Qaeda. Italian and Israeli investigators suspected him of having financed, via Dubai, the attack of November 28, 2002 on the Hotel Paradise in Mombasa, Kenya, which left eight people dead. In his conversations Ciise often referred to Mullah Fouad, "a high official of Ansar Al-Islam stationed in Syria, as the gatekeeper of Iraq."[28]

In a general sense the Ansar Al-Islam cell in Italy had the human and logistical means to implement its policy. In terms of men, forty-eight jihadists ultimately left Italy to join Ansar Al-Islam. In terms of logistics, their contribution was likewise significant. The members of Ansar Al-Islam in Italy invested in several satellite telephones, which are markedly more expensive than traditional mobile phones, and they traveled a great deal, both in Italy and abroad. This moving around had a price. In addition, the group took advantage of several "guest houses" in Syria where new recruits were received. But at the same time it is hard to believe that the logistics put in place between Italy and Iraq were not supported by a structured organization.

CHAPTER 21

Threats of Chemical Weapons in Europe

ON JULY 10, 2002, SEVEN MONTHS BEFORE COLIN POWELL DREW the world's attention to Zarqawi and his sidekicks, the Turkish authorities were made aware of the arrival in their country of an envelope containing a biological poison. The highly toxic substance had been sent from abroad to an individual calling himself Musab. A group of terrorists was supposed to receive the envelope and use the product within twenty days (after which it would lose its harmful properties) against the Russian and American embassies in Turkey.

The American embassy in Ankara alerted the heads of Turkish security to the imminence of an attack of this type. Two names were put forth by the local branch of the CIA: Abu Atiyya and Abu Taysir, two close associates of Zarqawi's operating in the northern Caucasus. The CIA's message was immediately transmitted to the police, who stepped up their vigilance. The threat did not come to pass. But had the terrorists succeeded in placing the substance on doorknobs and in stadiums and trains, they could have caused contamination on a large scale.

At this time, that is, in the summer of 2002, the government of

Georgia, headed by Eduard Shevardnadze, did not deny the presence of Al-Qaeda cells in the Caucasus. Under pressure from the American authorities the Georgian regime promised to arrest the terrorist groups that had found refuge there, notably in the gorges of Pankisi. According to internal sources in the Russian intelligence agency, the FSS (Federal Security Service) did not look askance at the American antiterrorist operations taking place right in the middle of Georgia.[29] In the end it was the security forces of Azerbaijan that captured Adnan Mohammed Sadiq, alias Abu Atiyya, in August 2003. Shortly thereafter he was extradited to Jordan, his country of origin.[30]

After the September 11 attacks and Operation Enduring Freedom in Afghanistan, several hundred Taliban and Al-Qaeda members are said to have fled the bombing. Some went through the Khyber Pass to the tribal areas of Waziristan, while others, like Zarqawi, went to Iran with a view to reaching Iraq, and still others headed for the various provinces of the Caucasus, traveling through Turkmenistan or Uzbekistan.

Even before September 11, 2001, Al-Qaeda had made the same arrangements in the Caucasus as in Iraqi Kurdistan. Certain enclosed areas in the grip of armed Islamist guerrillas could serve as fallback positions for Al-Qaeda fighters. This was the case in Chechnya, Dagestan, and Georgia. And Abu Atiyya was among Al-Qaeda's principal lieutenants in Georgia from 1999 on. He had had to flee Chechnya after the violent terrorist actions of that year. Like Abu Zubaydah, Zarqawi's head of operations, and Zarqawi, Abu Atiyya is a Jordanian. Married to a Chechen woman, he settled in the Caucasus and represented Zarqawi's interests in that crisis zone. A veteran of the war in Chechnya, where he lost a leg, he was especially skilled in the use of toxic gases.[31] Soon he was receiving new recruits from Europe and training them in the handling of explosives and chemical agents. In many cases these recruits returned to their countries of origin and formed terrorist cells under Abu Atiyya's direct leadership.

Abu Atiyya was also close to a man named Yussuf Amerat, alias Abu Hafs, head of operations for the rebel leader Emir Khattab. Just as Zarqawi placed his pawns in Kurdistan, Abu Atiyya got involved with the armed Islamist movements in the northern Caucasus.

It was in this region, especially in the Pankisi gorges near the mountainside village of Omalo, that the Frenchmen Merouane Benhamed, Menad Benchellali, and Noureddine Merabet learned to handle chemical weapons. They spent weeks refining their combat techniques in the company of Chechen rebels and Al-Qaeda officials, including Abu Atiyya. Benchellali soon found himself to be a born chemist, and he specialized in this "subject matter." The area was unsuited to the manufacture of very elaborate products, but the recruits were trained in spreading cyanide derivatives through water mains. In the jihadists' personal effects French investigators would later find methylene blue, considered an antidote to cyanide.

In December 2002 the French counterintelligence agency DST called in for questioning several individuals of Algerian origin from the suburbs of Paris, first in La Corneuve and then in Romainville. In the first home search the investigators found vials of chemicals, two gas cylinders, and protective clothing used by those handling chemicals. They also found equipment, in working order, for triggering explosives.

The ministry of the interior stated that "the electronic systems that had been manufactured were in working order and permitted explosive devices to be set off by remote control using portable phones."[32] This was how the attacks in Madrid on March 2004 would be launched.

Shortly after the arrest at La Corneuve of the chief suspect, Merouane Benhamed, the DST questioned Menad Benchellali[33] in a building on Rue David-Rosenfeld in Romainville, department of Seine-Saint-Denis. Extremely important pieces of evidence were seized, indicating that the group was manufacturing chemical weapons. According to the press release from the French ministry of the interior, the search revealed the presence of products for "the manufacture of explosives and toxic gases of the cyanide type."[34]

The members of this Chechen ring apparently intended to strike at the Russian embassy in Paris in reprisal for the disappearance of Emir Khattab and the attacks by the Russian authorities against Chechen terrorists when hostages were taken in the Dubrovka Theater in Moscow on October 24, 2002.

The men called in for questioning had a home laboratory for the production of chemical agents. Menad Benchellali, brother of Mourad Benchellali, one of the detainees in Guantanamo, and son of Chellali Benchellali, the radical imam from Vénissieux, was planning attacks from his apartment. The majority of these terrorists were in contact with a recruiter from Al-Qaeda, Rashid Bukhalfa, alias Abu Doha, born on November 29, 1969 in Constantine, Algeria. Abu Doha was also close to Abu Musab Al-Zarqawi. He is awaiting extradition to the United States, where he is suspected of having taken part in the attempted attack on the Los Angeles airport in December 1999.

These young Islamists are known to have spent time in Afghanistan and then in Chechnya. The investigation into the Chechen ring took a special interest in the Benchellali family. The father, Chellali Benchellali, had been arrested upon his return from the jihad in Bosnia and found to be in possession of a firearm. The French minister of the interior at the time, Nicolas Sarkozy, declared soon thereafter that one of the arrested men, the elder son Menad Benchellali, had been trained in the handling of chemicals.[35] Two of Benchellali's associates admitted that they had planned chemical attacks against the Russian embassy in Paris using ricin and botulin, two highly toxic substances. The French investigators from DST were of the opinion that the Vénissieux group was clearly linked both to the Chechens and to Zarqawi.

It was established that in the time between his return from Georgia and his arrest in Romainville, Menad Benchellali had set up a home laboratory for the production of ricin in the family apartment in Vénissieux. Thus, right in the heart of the Minguettes district, he and his associates had been handling highly toxic chemicals for weeks, storing them in jars of Nivea cream. His father eventually admitted that he was aware of what his son was doing in his room. On several occasions officials of the French counterterrorist effort spoke of the involvement, at least indirect, of Zarqawi in the planning of these attacks.

The French antiterrorist judge Jean-Louis Bruguière stated in 2004 that the intervention of the DST foiled "an attempt at a major attack likely [to have affected] the Parisian subway system and other targets with a new chemical weapon," causing in France "more casualties than in Madrid" on March 11, 2004.[36]

But Zarqawi's name also came up in connection with another threatened chemical attack, this time aimed at Great Britain. The scenario was roughly the same as the preceding one. On January 5, 2003, a few days after the arrests in France, acting on information supplied by the French authorities the British police arrested six men of North African origin in Wood Green, in the northern part of London. Four of them were arrested by Scotland Yard for manufacturing chemicals in connection with a terrorist venture. They were Mustafa Taleb, 33; Mouloud Feddag, 18; Sidali Feddag, 17; and Samir Feddag, 26.[37] British police scientists found traces of ricin in the apartment. This poison entered history in 1978 with the assassination of the Bulgarian dissident Georgi Markov, killed on Waterloo Bridge by an injection of ricin from a needle hidden in an umbrella. The legend of the "Bulgarian umbrella" was born. But, given the right mode of dispersion, this chemical can also kill on a large scale.

The men of Algerian origin arrested in the Wood Green apartment were planning attacks on civilian targets in the United Kingdom. According to sources close to the British investigation, they had apparently been sent there by Abu Attiya for the purpose of carrying out chemical attacks. This hypothesis is corroborated by the statements and conclusions of the German investigation of the Tawhid cell. On several occasions the German investigators emphasized that Zarqawi's structure was being shifted to the United Kingdom.

One of the most important axes of the Zarqawi network in Great Britain is the Luton refugee center on the outskirts of London. The British investigators seized five hundred kilograms of ammonium nitrate between Luton and London in a raid in April 2004. British sources were also of the opinion that the men planning to use this significant amount of the explosive were in contact with associates of Zarqawi in Pakistan.

CHAPTER 22

A Shadow Over Madrid

AT EXACTLY 7:30 AM ON THURSDAY, MARCH 11, 2004, FOUR BOMBS exploded near Atocha Station in Madrid, explosions aimed at the city's main railway platforms in rush hour: Atocha, El Pozo, and Santa Eugenia. Thousands of residents of Madrid who live in the suburbs take the train each morning to get to the city center. The explosions ripped apart railway cars and left hundreds of victims. Madrid awoke to find itself in a bloody war zone.

This was the most violent terrorist attack in modern Spanish history. By the end of the day the authorities had counted 192 dead and 1,400 wounded. Ten explosive devices, weighing a total of 150 kilos, had been placed by the terrorists in three different trains. Three bombs were defused.

Once past the initial moments of alarm, the government of José Maria Aznar strongly accused the Basque terrorist group ETA of responsibility for the attacks. In reply, the president of the Basque government, Juan José Ibarrextxe, stated that those who committed the attacks were "animals, not Basques."[38] At 2:10 PM on March 12, it was the turn of Arnaldo Otegi, political leader of the Basque separatists, to assure Spain that ETA had "nothing to do with the attacks."[39] That evening the ministry of the interior admitted that it was following another track: in a panel truck abandoned in front of the Alcala de Henares station seven detonators had been found along with a tape recording of verses from the Koran.

The investigation by antiterrorist forces began amid a major political crisis in the Spanish government. Aznar was unable to withstand the general elections held on March 14, just three days after the attacks. Some of the Spanish voters were critical of the government's policy of intervention in the war in Iraq, which might have been a factor in the explosions. Others suspected the government of having tried to manipulate the election by holding ETA responsible.

Speaking before the parliamentary commission of inquiry, Judge Baltasar Garzon, chief magistrate in charge of cases of terrorism, stated on July 15, 2004 that Spanish participation in the war in Iraq was "an important contextual element" in the March 11 attacks.[40]

In a forty-two-page booklet issued by Al-Qaeda, dated December 2003 and entitled "Iraq in Jihad: Hopes and Risks," the organization emphasized Spain's engagement in Iraq and its own wish to strike at Spain in reprisal: "We believe that the Spanish government will be unable to endure two, or at most three, strikes before withdrawing from Iraq under popular pressure." The text continues: "Should armed forces remain after these strikes,...the victory of the Socialist Party...would guarantee the retreat of Spanish troops."[41] Given the realities, these statements sound like a strange premonition.

The authors of the booklet describe Spain as the "first domino," the other game pieces being Poland and Italy, the two main allies of the United States in Iraq. Beyond its astonishing predictions, the text indicates Al-Qaeda's growing professionalism in the conduct of its operations. The mujahidin are asked to act not in a disorderly, hasty fashion but with "preparation and planning," which are the elements underlying "the success of any project." The Madrid attacks, of course, were the result of highly detailed preparation.

Credit for the attacks was claimed by the Abu Hafs Al-Masri Brigade in a communiqué published by Ansar Al-Islam, a movement that, as we know, was under Zarqawi's control. Ansar Al-Islam even devoted a special page on its Web site to these events; entitled "The Fronts of the Crusade," the article contains several photographs of the attacks. A videotape of threats later found in the rubble of the apartment occupied by some of the members of the Madrid network is marked "Ansar Al-Qaeda," a sign of the close relationship between the two organizations.

The withdrawal of Spanish troops from Iraq in no way shook the determination of the terrorists in Spain, as is shown by the dismantling on October 18, 2004 of a cell planning an attack on the Spanish high court. On March 11 Al-Qaeda, through its affiliates, considered Spain the prime mover of the fight against terrorism in the world.

The railway attacks had taken place at 7:30 AM. At 10:50 AM an anonymous resident of Madrid called the police station of Alcala de Henares to note the suspicious presence of a small van. At 2:15 PM, investigators discovered the seven detonators and the tape of the Koran in the vehicle, which was soon transferred to the headquarters of the antiterrorist police for analysis. March 11 ended in uncertainty, and the police continued their investigation under popular and political pressure.

That night the investigators worked tirelessly on the various clues. The police station of Vallecas in suburban Madrid announced the discovery of an explosive charge hidden in a gym bag. It was not until Saturday, March 13, that the investigators arrested three Moroccans, Jamal Zougam, his brother Mohammed Shawi,[42] and Mohammed Bekkali, all of whom worked in a store selling mobile phones. Two Spaniards of Indian origin, Suresh Kumar and Vinay Kohly,[43] were also apprehended for selling telephone cards to Zougam and Shawi. All these suspects were identified by analysis of the electronic chip found in the device that did not explode. The principal suspect lived 200 meters away from the site of the attacks.

Investigators were interested in the agendas of the two main suspects, Zougam, born in Tangiers in 1973, and Shawi, born there in 1969. Witnesses reported having seen them taking backpacks out of the van parked at Alcala de Henares. One witness was "struck by the fact that they were wearing ski hoods although the weather report wasn't right for that type of garment."[44]

Zougam is said to have been one of the men who placed the bombs in the different train compartments. He was not unknown to the Spanish antiterrorism services. In the context of the largest investigation ever conducted on the Al-Qaeda networks in Spain, Operation Datil, begun in 1997 and headed by Baltasar Garzon, Zougam had already appeared as one of the associates of the top Al-Qaeda official in the country, a Spaniard of Syrian origin named Abu Dahdah (Imad Eddin Barakat Yarkas). Abu Dahdah had been incarcerated ever since the September 11 attacks for his major role in carrying out terrorist operations in Spain.[45]

The Spanish police had taped several of Jamal Zougam's phone conversations with Abu Dahdah. In a conversation on August 14, 2001 Zougam said, "Friday I went to see Fizazi, and I told him that if he needed money we and our brothers could help him."[46] Zougam and Fizazi were said to have met in the Beni Makada Mosque in Tangiers.

Mohammed Fizazi, the mastermind of the bloody attacks in Casablanca on May 16, 2003, was an occasional preacher at the Al-Quds Mosque in Hamburg attended by Mohammed Atta, the September 11 terrorist.[47] The Moroccan police held Fizazi responsible for the terrorist movements in that country, Salafiya Jihadia and Assirat Al-Mustaqim, the two organizations involved in the Casablanca attacks. Today he is serving a thirty-year sentence without the possibility of parole in a Moroccan prison.

The investigators then discovered the "Tangiers ring" of Islamist terrorists inspired by Salafism, a group that took advantage of the porosity of the borders between Morocco and Spain. In this connection the arrest of Abdelaziz Benyaich was decisive. Called in for questioning on June 14, 2003 with regard to his role in the Casablanca attacks, Benyaich was also implicated in the Madrid explosions a few months later; a member of a famous brotherhood of jihadists, he took part in supervising Jamal Zougam. According to the German intelligence services, he was in contact with Khaled Al-Aruri, Zarqawi's right-hand man.[48]

Zougam's brother, Mohammed Shawi, was also named in conversations of Al-Qaeda members taped by the Spanish police in 2001. Thus, during a discussion between Abu Dahdah, the Al-Qaeda leader in Spain, and Abdulak Al-Magrebi, an operational terrorist, Magrebi said, "We have to get in contact with Jamal [Zougam] and his brother Mohammed Shawi of Tangiers," adding, "I'm going to go to Tangiers, because [the two brothers] are close to Saïd Shedadi." A former mujahid back from the war in Bosnia-Herzegovina, Shedadi was later convicted in Spain for his participation in Al-Qaeda.

Well before the September 11 attacks, Zougam and Shawi were known to the Spanish intelligence services. Zougam's name appeared on the lists of at least three intelligence services. The French DST knew that he had been part of the file on "Afghan rings,"[49] the Spanish CNI (National Intelligence Service) had identified him as being affiliated with an Al-Qaeda cell in Spain, and the Moroccan DST had him on file as a high-risk individual after the Casablanca attacks.

On the operational level Jamal Zougam, the prime suspect in the Madrid explosions, had close ties to Amer Azizi, one of Al-Qaeda's top officials in Europe who was found guilty by Judge Garzon in 2003 of belonging to the Al-Qaeda cell in Spain. The Spanish police had found Azizi's name, address, and telephone number in a search of Zougam's apartment conducted in 2001 at the request of the French courts.[50] Azizi escaped the police and fled to Iran, where he joined up with Zarqawi's group.[51]

Before Azizi and Zarqawi met in Iran, the former to elude the Spanish courts, the latter the American bombings, the two men had an acquaintance in common, a Moroccan named Abdulatif Mourafik, alias Malek Al-Magrebi.[52] According to the Spanish courts, Mourafik was a close associate of Zarqawi's in Afghanistan. After Mourafik's identifying information was found in his apartment, Azizi was considered by the Spanish security forces to be one of the originators of the attacks of March 11, 2004.

In contrast to the situations in Germany and Italy, where Zarqawi played an active and decisive role, he was linked only indirectly with the group responsible for the Madrid attacks. We know that he was in contact with Azizi and that the latter knew Jamal Zougam. These ties were brought to light by the judicial documents gathered by Judge Garzon in connection with his investigation of Al-Qaeda.

Under strong popular and political pressure, the Spanish investigators followed the various paths leading to the attacks. With Azizi on the run, they had to go forward with the first men questioned on March 13, 2004, namely Zougam and Shawi.

While the interrogations of Zougam were in progress, the police rounded up several individuals, some of whom had come up in the initial investigations in 2001 concerning Al-Qaeda in Spain. In that year Spanish officials, acting at the request of the French courts, had searched the Madrid apartment of Jamal Zougam. Identifying information was found for a large number of Al-Qaeda operatives in addition to Azizi and Abou Dahdah, including the visiting card of a member of the terrorist network Ansar Al-Islam, Abu Mumen Al-Kurdi, who lived in Sweden and was close to Mullah Krekar, the deposed founder of the Kurdish Islamist movement.

On this occasion the police also seized a videotape relating the battles and operations of Ansar Al-Islam. According to the police, this propaganda video was intended to facilitate funding of the operations of this movement, which would later be run by Zarqawi. The video also gave identifying information for military leaders in Norway who were also presumed to be part of the group, namely Mullah Krekar and his brother Abu Faruk. On several occasions the police also taped contacts between an important Al-Qaeda official in

Spain, Abdallah Khayata Kattan, and the Norwegian leaders of Ansar Al-Islam. A former mujahid in the war in Bosnia, Kattan is said to have gone to Norway to meet Mullah Krekar and suggest that he send men from the ranks of Ansar Al-Islam to Iraqi Kurdistan.[53]

Another major factor strengthened the investigators' conviction that Zarqawi was implicated. They learned that in 1997 Abu Dahdah, head of the Spanish cell of Al-Qaeda, had sent almost $11,000 to Abu Mohammed Al-Maqdisi when he was incarcerated with Zarqawi in Suwaqah, Jordan. Abu Dahdah had sent the money with the help of the fundamentalist preacher Abu Qatada in Great Britain, the intermediary chosen for the occasion.[54] Abu Dahdah subsequently tried to get into direct contact with Maqdisi on a number of occasions and even made plans to visit him in prison.[55]

Finally, on September 11, 2004, six months after the railway attack, the Spanish police completed their marathon investigation. Of sixty-seven people questioned, only nineteen were held in detention. The investigators ultimately identified the coordinator of the operation, Serhan Ben Abdelmajid Fakhet, alias the Tunisian, born on July 10, 1968 in Tunis. Along with six accomplices, he had committed suicide on April 3 in Leganes, in the southern part of Madrid, just before the police stormed their quarters.

The Spanish inquest was over. Yet the identity of the "brain" behind the March 11 attacks is still uncertain. Several names have been mentioned by the Spanish services and specialists in counterterrorism. Two in particular recur often: Rabei Osman Ahmed El-Sayed, 32, called "Mohammed the Egyptian," and especially Mustafa Setmariam Nasar, alias Abu Musab Al-Suri.[56]

It is all the more important to clarify the role of the Syrian Mustafa Setmariam Nasar in the Madrid attacks because the trail leads directly to Zarqawi.

Nasar is known to his friends as Abu Musab Al-Suri or Abu El

Abed. Born on November 26, 1958 in Aleppo, Al-Suri is without a doubt one of the Salafist terrorists representing the highest potential for harm in the Middle East. He became a Spanish citizen in 1993 upon marrying a Spanish woman, with whom he would have two children. Two years later, on June 26, 1995, he fled Spain when an informer told him that the Spanish intelligence services were investigating him. He took refuge in London, where he managed *Al-Ansar*, the press organ of the Algerian GIA, whose editor-in-chief was none other than Abu Qatada. According to the French authorities, Al-Suri was also one of the principal editors of the extremist newspaper *El Fajr* and the founder of the Islamic information service based in London.[57]

Al-Suri was briefly held by the British authorities after the Paris attacks of 1995. Upon his release he remained in very close contact with the extremist diaspora, in particular with Riad Oklah, alias Abu Nabil, a top official in Jordan of the Syrian terrorist group Taliah Al-Muqatila. He was also very close to Abu Dahdah.

But Al-Suri's power chiefly lies in the major role he plays in the jihadist networks in his country of origin. Known to the various European security services, Al-Suri soon decided to take his family to the Afghanistan of the Taliban. According to information gathered by the Spanish police, from 1988 on he ran a training camp under the direction of Osama Bin Laden.[58] With the luster conferred by his association with Bin Laden, and increased by his appointment to the religious council of Al-Qaeda shortly after his arrival in Afghanistan, Al-Suri became the icon of the Syrians who had joined the ranks of the terrorist organization.

All other things being equal, Al-Suri occupied the same position in the eyes of the Syrians in Al-Qaeda at that time as Zarqawi did in the eyes of the Jordanian jihadists. Because of their charisma and the effectiveness of their networks in their respective countries, Zarqawi and Al-Suri are two key men for the Islamist fighters in the Middle East. From his quarters in Afghanistan Abu Musab Al-Suri continues to maintain close relations with the Spanish Al-Qaeda cell, which regularly sends young Syrians to his camp for training in the handling of weapons. The chief financial officer of Al-Qaeda in Spain, the Syrian Mohammed Ghaleb Kalaje Zouaydi,[59] supplies the necessary funds.

Even if he does not have the same notoriety as Zarqawi, many antiterrorist analysts are aware of his strong potential for action. And the Spanish authorities are now of the opinion that, because he sent one of his men to Madrid just before the explosions, he had an active role in the conception of the attacks of March 11.

CHAPTER 23

Syria: The Rear Base

IN APRIL 2002 YASSER FATEH IBRAHIM FREIHAT WAS AWAKENED in his hotel room in Damascus, the Syrian capital, by Zarqawi's lieutenant Mohammed Ahmad Tyura. Hotel Al-Marjah, on Martyrs Square, was not chosen at random. It is a safe place, located just opposite the ministry of the interior.

Tayourah drove the 28-year-old Jordanian to "one of the military barracks"[60] of Damascus. Freihat, the accomplice of the murderer of Laurence Foley, spent a week there. Under the supervision of three soldiers, he was trained in the handling of the pistol, the M16, and the Kalashnikov. He also learned to use grenades, and, most important of all, to manufacture bombs with ammonium nitrate. It was the head of the "Foley commando unit" who had insisted that Freihat get this training. A few weeks later, two other members of the commando unit, Mohammad Daamas and Neaman El-Harach, were trained under the same circumstances.

According to charges brought by Jordan, Zarqawi lived in Syria between May and September 2002, enjoying free access to the "military barracks" charged with the training of his recruits, using a Syrian passport, and traveling relatively freely from Syria to Jordan and Iraq. Moreover, the Jordanian investigation revealed that the Foley operation had been planned almost in its entirety by Zarqawi and his closest collaborators from their quarters in Damascus. And it was Syria that provided the weapons used for the Foley murder, weapons sent by Tyura, Zarqawi's Syrian agent, including the 7-mm pistol used in the crime itself. In the arsenal assembled by Zarqawi for the occasion, the Jordanian police found several Kalashnikovs, tear-gas bombs, and even bullet-proof vests. Syria also provided some of the funds Zarqawi made available to the killers.

These revelations are much more serious than the accusations leveled against the regime of Saddam Hussein, but they have been wrapped in silence until now. Only Jordan, echoing the United States, has expressed reservations about Syria's willingness to fight against the spread of terrorism in the region.

Shortly before his trip to Syria in August 2004, Jordanian Prime Minister Faisal Al-Fayez stated: "The lack of control on the part of Syria over the border has evolved in a disturbing way over the past months, to the point where the situation is becoming unacceptable."[61] He also asserted that since the preceding March the Jordanian authorities had foiled "several attempts at infiltration by extremists transporting explosives and weapons." And the recent attempts to attack Jordan had, in fact, been largely organized from Syria.

In short, Amman implicitly accused Damascus of offering asylum to the associates of Abu Musab Al-Zarqawi, notably to the Syrian national Sulayman Khalid Darwish, alias Abu Al-Ghadiyah, who was suspected of having recruited five Syrians for Zarqawi with the intention of committing the chemical attack of April 2004 on the headquarters of the Jordanian intelligence services.

Syria was Zarqawi's logistical and operational rear base in late 2001 and early 2002, after his escape from Afghanistan. The crossroads of the region, it has the advantage of opening onto Iraq and being a bridge to Jordan, Zarqawi's favored target at that time.

After the onset of the coalition's offensive in Iraq, Syria became the principal gateway to Iraq for the jihadists. On July 29, 2003 General Richard B. Myers, chairman of the joint chiefs of staff of the United States Army, reported that most of the fighters infiltrating into Iraq from abroad were coming from Syria, and that at least eighty of them had had several months of training in a Syrian camp.[62] What is more, he said, the Syrian government was supporting the Islamist rebellion in Iraq.

This aspect of Syrian regional politics came up for discussion in a meeting at the military post of Al-Kaim, on the border between Iraq and Syria, between the commander of the American forces in Iraq, General Ricardo Sanchez, and General Maher El Assad, commander of the Syrian Republican Guard and younger brother of the president. During this meeting the American general showed his counterpart Syrian passports that had been found on Islamist fighters who had been killed or arrested. In addition, he said, several Syrian prisoners confirmed in the course of their interrogations that they had received logistical support from Syrian military security under the direction of General Assef Shawkat.[63]

General John Abizaid, commander in chief of the American forces in the Persian Gulf, expressed the opinion in August 2003 that the primary danger in Iraq lay in the influx of fighters coming from abroad via Syria.[64] On August 21, 2003 Israel's ambassador to the United Nations stated that the booby-trapped truck used in the attack on U.N. headquarters in Baghdad came from Syria.[65] In September 2003, six months after the start of the coalition's military operations in Iraq, the American administrator Paul Bremer, reporting that 248 foreign fighters, including 123 Syrians, had been taken prisoner, noted that most of the foreigners had entered through Syria.[66]

The testimony of a former mujahid who left to fight in Iraq in response to Zarqawi's appeal is especially revealing with regard to the Syrian channel. The recruits, he said, received a military kit costing $200 and containing an automatic weapon, a grenade launcher, and ten grenades. An Iraqi smuggler, who received between $500 and $1,000 per person, would then collect the men in Syria and take them to join the rebels. All this, he stated, took place with the full knowledge of the Syrian authorities.[67]

IN REALITY IT WOULD TAKE YEARS FOR THE WESTERN INTELLIgence services to become aware of Syria's pivotal role. The country has come to be known as the Pakistan of Iraq because of its benevolent attitude toward Islamist terrorists and the protection it offers them.

Thus as early as 2001 the Italian intelligence services, DIGOS, dismantled a support structure of the Islamist Kurdish movement Ansar Al-Islam, emphasizing Syria's role as intermediary in the transporting of fighters and money to Iraq. Their documents, covering thousands of hours of taped telephone conversations along with the interrogation of suspects and their differences of opinion, reveal that Syria "is a unifying force in the transporting of recruits between Europe and Ansar Al-Islam." According to the antiterrorist magistrates, the Italian network of Ansar Al-Islam, under Zarqawi's control, had "the advantage of a logistical structure in Syria."[68]

According to the investigators, nearly forty recruits passed through Syria to Iraq, as did sums of money. Mullah Fouad plays an essential role in this trafficking. He is even considered to be "the guardian of access" to Syria for the volunteers heading for Iraq. Based near Damascus, he and his lieutenants send orders to their Italian recruitment cell.[69]

Still in Italy, but in connection with a related case, the magistrates established in 2001 that the head of an Al-Qaeda cell in Milan, Abdelkader Mahmoud Es Sayed Ben Khemais, was in close contact with the Syrian government. In a phone conversation intercepted in 2000, he referred to that government as "true heroes" and told one of his accomplices about a conversation he had with the Syrian minister of defense, Mustapha Tlass, about the aims of "his organization." Tlass was said to have provided Ben Khemais with the telephone numbers of Hamas and Islamic Jihad, adding: "Talk with them, call them; they know you."[70]

Mustapha Tlass occupied a central position in the Syrian regime. The powerful minister of defense for over thirty years, he had control over the army and the intelligence services until his resignation in May 2004. His convictions were known for a long time. In October 2001, at a meeting with a British delegation, he is said to have stated that the attacks of September 11 were the work of a "Jewish conspiracy" and that Mossad, the Israeli intelligence service, had even alerted thousands of Jews working in the World Trade Center of the impending attack.[71]

The involvement of the Syrian security apparatus in the active networks of radical Islamism is also mentioned in several other international investigations. Nevertheless, on May 25, 2003 Syrian president Bashar El-Assad expressed his doubts about the very existence of Al-Qaeda in an interview with the Kuwaiti newspaper *Al-Anba*: "Is there really an entity called Al-Qaeda? Was it in Afghanistan? Does it still exist?... [W]e are talking about a certain ideological sphere of influence. The problem is the ideology and not the organizations."[72]

Questioned by the Moroccan security services in connection with the investigation into the Casablanca attacks of May 2003, the Frenchman Robert Richard Antoine Pierre stated that earlier in that year a channel had been organized in Morocco to send mujahidin to Iraq via Libya and Syria. He claimed that he had finally abandoned the idea of going there in order to carry out attacks in France, in particular against "nuclear installations and synagogues."[73]

Baltasar Garzon is responsible for the dismantling in 2001 of what was surely the largest Al-Qaeda cell in Europe, composed mainly of Syrian nationals. In the course of this process three letters were seized at the home of one of the members of the cell, Ghasoub Al-Abrash Ghalyoun.[74] Written and signed by him, they were addressed to the head of the Syrian intelligence services. In one of these letters he described his military training in Iraq. In another, drawn up in the form of a report on his activities, he wrote that "upon request" he would also send a report to the head of intelligence in the city of Homs.[75] It is quite clear from this correspondence that Ghalyoun was acting with the agreement of the Syrian authorities, if not in concert with them, and that at the very least they were perfectly aware of his situation and his intentions. In the course of the investigation it was revealed that Abu Dahdah, head of the Spanish Al-Qaeda cell, had belonged to the Syrian Islamist organization Taliah Al-Muqatila. Although the members of this organization had originally been opposed to the Syrian regime, they were pardoned by Bashar El-Assad.[76]

Certain members of the Syrian intelligence services are also believed to have been closely associated with the Hamburg cell that provided the kamikazes of September 11, to the point where Manfred Murck, assistant director of the BFV, the German service for domestic intelligence, spoke of a "Syrian connection" during the investigation of this cell.[77]

At the center of the investigation was a textile import-export company called Tatex Trading GmbH, founded in 1978 in Rethwisch, Germany.[78] This firm was created by Abdul Matin Tatari, a German of Syrian origin in his 60s, who later established another company, Tatari Design. Tatex Trading had two shareholders, one of whom was Mohamad Majed Said, whose career was of the highest interest to the German services. For Said had been the former director of the Syrian intelligence services from 1987 to 1994, and in 2001 he was a member of the Syrian National Security Council, the country's chief security agency.[79]

Starting in late 2001, the German investigators discovered the extent of the ties among these companies, the Syrian intelligence services, and the Hamburg cell.

Tatari Design and Tatex Trading were officially suspected by the German judicial authorities on the grounds that they served as a cover for forging documents and laundering money for the militant Islamists in Germany. The federal prosecutor in charge of terrorism, Kay Nehm, pointed out that the Tatari family was "suspected of having contributed to the jihad of violent Islamist militants." It was clearly stated that the Tataris had engaged in money laundering in order to provide identity papers and visas for operational members of Al-Qaeda.[80]

On September 10, 2002, two houses and three offices belonging to the Tataris were searched. The family was questioned for several hours and made its initial confessions. In 2003 a judicial inquiry was opened against Abdul Matin Tatari in Hamburg.

The police learned that one of the Tatari sons, a student at the Hamburg Technical University, had signed the petition of Mohammed Atta, one of the September 11 terrorists, calling for the formation of an "Islamic studies" group in the university. They also learned that Mohammed Hadi Tatari, the older son, had often visited Atta, in the Hamburg apartment occupied at the time by several of the future kamikazes, as well as Marwan Al-Shehhi, the hijacker of United Airlines flight 175, which struck the second tower at the World Trade Center, and had attended the wedding of Mounir El Motassadeq, who was also found guilty in connection with the September 11 attacks.

The father, Abdul Matin Tatari, admitted that he had employed two Syrians from Aleppo who turned out to be close to the Hamburg cell. They were Mohammed Haydar Zammar, considered to be one of the recruiters for Al-Qaeda, and Mamoun Darkazanli, whose company is suspected of having given financial assistance to the September 11 terrorists.

The German investigators also discovered that it was none other than Mohammed Haydar Zammar who had recruited Mohammed Atta. In a phone conversation intercepted by the police, Tatari referred to his employee as "a friend and a brother."[81] Both men were members of the Muslim Brotherhood.[82]

By the end of their inquest into Tatex and the role of Mohamad Majed Said, the German investigators were convinced that the Syrian authorities must have been in contact with the terrorist cell in Hamburg.

As early as 2001, during the trial of the defendants found guilty of the 1998 attacks on the American embassies in Africa, a witness for the United States government, Jamal Ahmed Al-Fadl, had revealed the existence of an organization affiliated with Al-Qaeda in Syria, Jamaat E Jihad Al-Suri, under the direction of a certain Abu Musab Al-Suri, whom we met in the preceding chapter. Al-Fadl remembered Al-Suri as having blond hair, a rather unusual feature for an Islamist fighter.[83] Al-Suri was Mustafa Setmariam Nasar, convicted in Spain by Judge Baltasar Garzon. A high official in Al-Qaeda, he had "directed a training camp in Afghanistan"[84] and, in 1996, had gone to Hamburg to meet a certain Darkazanli, the former employee of Tatari.

There are many examples of the involvement of Syrian terrorists in the channels of Al-Qaeda. In particular, several "Syrian connections" to Al-Qaeda in Germany and Spain have come to light in connection with the September 11 attacks. These involvements developed after the American intervention in Iraq, and it now appears that Syria is at the crossroads of various jihadist groups in the Middle East.

After forty years of troubled relations with the harshest Islamist movements, it would be highly surprising if the Syrian government were really outflanked by the extremist threat. After all, the fifteen security services in that country are considered the best informed in that part of the world. Each of these services has a broad mandate and direct access to the offices of the president. Moreover, the methodical and systematic coverage of the entire country by the security services is such as to preclude the existence of "gray zones" escaping central control. On the contrary, there is every reason to believe that by facilitating the transit of fighters from abroad and sending fighters from Syria itself, the government is trying to control the guerrilla warfare in Iraq.

In response to the urgent requests of the United States for more effective monitoring of the border between Syria and Iraq, Damascus has finally agreed in principle to joint Syrian-American patrols. Yet there continues to be a massive influx of Sunni fighters into Iraq across the Syrian border, which seems incomprehensible in view of the redeployment along the Iraqi border of thousands of Syrian soldiers formerly stationed in Lebanon.

There can be no doubt that in the light of the Iraqi conflict the Syrian regime has revealed its true nature.

CHAPTER 24

France in the Islamist Trap

ON AUGUST 30, 2004, FRENCH DIPLOMATS TURNED TO YUSSEF Al-Qardawi in an attempt to persuade him to issue a public condemnation of the kidnapping of two hostages, Christian Chesnot and Georges Malbrunot. On this occasion the theoretician of suicide missions was promoted to the rank of "the great conscience of Islam," in the words of the French minister of foreign affairs.[85] No doubt it was felt that the easiest way to influence the terrorists was to appeal to one of their spiritual guides.

No one denounced the duplicity of the French Islamists, who publicly supported the initiatives of the government to obtain the release of the hostages and even sent a delegation to Iraq, while at the same time the religious leader of the Union of Islamic Organizations of France, Faisal Mawlawi, surreptitiously cosigned a manifesto in the Arab press calling for "support by all moral and material means the courageous and honorable Islamic resistance" in Iraq against the "colonialist, U.S.-Zionist" campaign.[86]

It is futile to try to make sense of French policy with regard to Islamism. Nicolas Sarkozy, minister of the interior at the time, made the lot of Muslim women the symbol of an archaic and increasingly radical Islam in his public interrogation of Tariq Ramadan. But six months earlier the minister of foreign affairs had sought the support of one of the most extremist of Muslim clerics, Yussef Al-Qardawi, a man who provided theoretical justifications for the inferiority of women in Islam, a man who was one of the rare Muslim clerics to justify the attacks of September 11, and, finally, a man who is one of the top leaders of the Muslim Brotherhood.[87]

France seems to be caught in the trap of double dealing, the favorite dialectical weapon of the Muslim Brotherhood, instead of denouncing or simply analyzing its real objectives. A founding document of this fraternity explains that it is appropriate to adapt one's positions to the country in which one finds oneself, so as to "infiltrate the organs of influence" and "have a decisive say in political decisions."[88] They could not have imagined a better set of circumstances. Here they were, after their public recognition, political and diplomatic actors on the stage of a naive France that had no confidence in itself and no longer dared to denounce extremists.

The process of recognizing Islam in France is based on the idea that this will inevitably lead to the political integration of the Islamists and hence to their moderation. The strategy has turned against its originators today and has caught France in the trap of its contradictions. For how can one explain the country's claim that it is fighting Islamist terrorism at the same time that it refrains from fighting what is, in essence, radical Islam? In privileging, indeed legitimizing, the radical Islamist current, France is also weakening its moderate Muslims and thus playing the game of those very extremists.

Isn't this the logic that led the French minister of foreign affairs, Michel Barnier, to ask on September 27, 2004 that the International Conference on Iraq bring together "all [Iraqi] political powers, including those that have chosen the path of armed resistance"?[89] Was French diplomacy, in its angelic purity, going to offer Zarqawi a seat at the negotiating table?

This clumsy message, uttered under complex, chaotic conditions going beyond the canons of traditional diplomacy, was perceived by some as a form of recognition of the armed resistance in Iraq. In any case, this is how Hezbollah described it the following week on its official television channel, Al-Manar: "We are able to announce that the brave, honorable, and respectable resistance in Iraq has won international recognition. France, one of the five permanent members of the United Nations Security Council, has asked for the participation of the forces of resistance [in the International Conference on Iraq]. This is a recognition of the legitimacy of the resistance and of the fact that it is advancing on the right path."[90]

By an odd coincidence, on November 16, 2004 the CSA (Conseil supérieur de l'audiovisuel), which oversees broadcasting in France, authorized Al-Manar to use the airwaves, which led to an uproar; this channel is known for its anti-Semitism and its support for Islamist extremists of all stripes. Ever since the American offensive in Iraq, Al-Manar has redoubled its efforts to condemn the "invaders" and claim the legitimacy of the use of force "by every means."[91] However this debate is resolved, the Islamists will not fail to see in the initial decision yet another sign of French procrastination, if not confusion.

FRANCE HAS BEEN BLINDED BY THE IRAQI CONFLICT IT LEGITImately opposed. Today it refuses to admit that since the spring of 2003 the second war in Iraq has turned into a confrontation against Islamist terrorism, and that because Iraq has become the Islamists' preferred battleground, a crucial fight is underway there against the terrorist networks. Thus Iraq has become a distorting prism for France, the sole analytical grid for the Muslim world and what is at stake for it. The need to combat the terrorist scourge has come under the same suspicion of American hegemonism as the questionable political objectives cited to justify the invasion of the country. And it is not a certainty that France will win the peace there.

France has not been spared the threat of Islamist terrorism. In June 2004 several Islamists were arrested in the Paris area. Members or organizers of a Salafist mosque in Levalois-Perret who had been under surveillance for some months, they were believed to have set up a recruitment channel to send jihadists to Iraq. On June 15 searches resulted in the seizure of several pieces of evidence: software for forging official documents, two weapons, false papers, and Islamist documentation including tape recordings of Abu Qatada and tracts calling for jihad.

The most damning pieces of evidence were a message sent by a Frenchman in Iraq on June 11, 2004, on a portable telephone belonging to a member of the charitable association Iqra, which ran the Salafist mosque. The message was explicit: "The group has arrived. I'll contact you if I need help." The group in question, three members of which were identified, consisted of Frenchmen and Tunisians.[92]

The second piece of evidence was a power of attorney given by the International Islamic Relief Organization (IIRO) to one of the members of Iqra, authorizing him to raise funds in its name.[93] While in police custody two suspects admitted that they had transferred money abroad and sent recruits to Iraq. The judge, however, considered the evidence insufficient to uphold the determination that the suspects were part of a terrorist undertaking. Some of them were held to be mere beneficiaries of the charity; others were examined under caution on the grounds that they possessed false documents and irregular residence permits, and were then set free.[94]

This case, at first treated as a local matter, nonetheless had a significant international dimension. And the public prosecutor's department in Paris signaled its difference of opinion by appealing the decision, surprising to say the least, of the antiterrorist magistrate.

A CIA report of 1996 had already noted that the IIRO was linked to Ramzi Yussef, convicted in the United States of having taken part in the first attack on the World Trade Center in 1993, and to Osama Bin Laden, described at the time as "a rich Saudi currently living in Sudan who supports various extremist Islamic groups."[95]

As for Iqra, although the investigators were unable to establish its link with the worldwide organization Iqra International, there are institutional connections between it and the IIRO. The president of Iqra International, a former Saudi minister of information, also heads IIRO's committee on investments.[96]

Finally, on September 20, 2004 the office of the public prosecutor in Paris opened a judicial inquiry into the "Iraqi connections," largely on the basis of a note from the DST, the French counter-intelligence agency, dating from August and establishing the suspicious departure of ten Frenchmen of Tunisian origin for jihad in Iraq by way of Syria. In addition, the note reported that two Frenchmen had been held for questioning on the border between Syria and Iraq before being sent back to Turkey.[97]

Ever since the first months of the American offensive, reports from the United States intelligence services have noted an increase in the threat and an influx of candidates for jihad. In November 2003 the bureau chief of the CIA said he believed the situation in Iraq was getting worse for several reasons, including the flood of Iraqi and foreign recruits for guerrilla warfare, the stockpiles of weapons available to the rebels, and their improving organization and coordination. The CIA identified fifteen groups that were actively involved in armed resistance.[98]

In June 2004 internal sources in the CIA indicated that for several months there had been increasing "evidence of the support by several charitable organizations for the Iraqi insurgents." According to an agent of the CIA's antiterrorist center, the funds identified up to that time came largely from Pakistan and Europe and reached Iraq via these nongovernmental organizations (NGOs) in a regular manner. The CIA considered that it was now confronted by a "phenomenon similar in nature and importance" to the one observed in the early 1980s in Afghanistan, when many Islamic NGOs lent their support to the Arab mujahidin.[99] The provisional government of Iraq has noticed the same phenomenon: "Terrorists have been pouring into Iraq from several countries.... They come from Afghanistan, Pakistan, Europe, Morocco, [and] Syria."[100]

On October 22, 2004 it was learned that a 19-year-old Frenchman, Redouane El Hakim, had died in combat in Iraq in the ranks of the Islamist "resistance." He had gone to that country earlier in the year by way of Syria, which he left ostensibly to pursue his studies, accompanied by his brother Boubaker. The latter's name had appeared in the police inquiry into the mosque in Levallois-Perret.[101] Since that time no fewer than five Frenchmen fighting on the side of the Islamists have been killed in Iraq.

A Successor to Bin Laden

ZARQAWI MIGHT ALMOST BE SAID TO REPRESENT THE ANTITHESIS of Osama Bin Laden in that their origins, careers, education, and worldviews are very different. Yet it must be noted that, thanks to the second war in Iraq, what Bin Laden had been able to win on the ideological terrain Zarqawi has reshaped through the use of weapons, so much so that today, and perhaps permanently, he has eclipsed Bin Laden's leadership of the partisans of a radical and aggressive Islam.

The violence of his actions is what has won Zarqawi his position of power among the Islamist militants and clerics and enabled him to develop and consolidate his networks, notably by taking over from Al-Qaeda the leadership of a number of movements and cells traditionally affiliated with Bin Laden's organization. The Zarqawi effect even extends to the religions sphere: a number of radical Islamists now position themselves in accordance with the Jordanian's most recent activities in Iraq.

Yet Zarqawi is neither a myth created out of whole cloth by the Americans, as is sometimes said, nor the "ghost of Superman" that Mullah Krekar, the former head of Ansar Al-Islam, saw in him. For the fighters, Zarqawi is above all a military commander, a leader of men, and this is why they have accepted him. For the radical clerics, he is the man who perpetuates the "spirit of jihad" incarnated up to now by Bin Laden.

We know that this reference to jihad is the source of Al-Qaeda. This is evidenced by several hundred historical documents seized in March 2002 at the offices of a nongovernmental organization directed by the former head of logistics for the group. To this day these archives are the most important collection of documents ever seized. They shed remarkable light on the genesis of the organization.

Al-Qaeda was born in the Afghan conflict in 1988 as part of the huge wave of enthusiasm following the victory of the Arab fighters over the "impious" enemy. Today this war is still a legend for thousands of jihadists. Its battles have attained mythological status in the collective memory of the mujahidin, a set of signs from heaven confirming the justice of their fight.

The doctrinal foundation of the movement was presented in April 1988 in the magazine of the mujahidin of Afghanistan, *Al-Jihad*. Abdallah Azzam, mentor of Osama Bin Laden and founder of the first organization recruiting mujahidin for the Afghan front, wrote an article calling for a "solid base" (Al-Qaeda Al-Sulbah) from which those who took part in this war could "maintain the spirit of jihad."[1] According to the minutes of a meeting prior to its creation, Al-Qaeda is a group whose mission is to "keep alive the spirit of jihad" among Muslims, and among Arabs in particular, so as to "open new paths for jihad and maintain contact" among them.[2]

Osama Bin Laden then expressed the idea of pursuing jihad at a meeting held on August 11, 1988, with Abu Al-Ridha. This was the occasion of the first mention known up to now of Al-Qaeda, called *Qaeda* ("base") in the transcript of the meeting. Bin Laden explained that the period of war "has been a period of education, consolidation, and training for the brothers who have come to fight," and that it also "demonstrated the existence of the Islamic world." He continued as follows: "In undertaking this mission, in the darkest hours we have known and in so little time, we have benefited greatly from the Saudi people, we have been able to offer the mujahidin a political force, take advantage of a large number of donations, and restore power. The time has come to organize."

The meeting ended with an "initial estimate" of the number of members of the organization: "In six months of Al-Qaeda's existence, 314 brothers will be ready and trained."[3]

On August 20, 1988 there was a decisive meeting of the top nine leaders of the future Al-Qaeda, including "Sheikh Osama," Osama Bin Laden himself. The meeting ratified Bin Laden's separation from his mentor, Sheikh Abdallah Azzam, and established the foundations of the organization. According to the minutes, Osama Bin Laden believed that Maktab Al-Khidamat, the organization founded by Azzam, was "badly run and ineffective." Al-Qaeda was to be "an organized Islamic faction" whose aim was "to spread the voice of God, to make his religion victorious." The participants even determined the conditions for belonging to the group: candidates would have to "become members without a time limit," be "attentive and devoted," have "good manners," be "sponsored," and "obey the regulations and instructions."[4]

The meeting also decided on the oath that each new member would have to take: "The oath of God is mine, to listen to and obey the superiors, who are carrying out this work with energy, vision, difficulty or ease for the man who is superior to him, so that the voice of God may be strongest and his religion victorious." Another document indicates that as a result of this meeting "Al-Qaeda activity began on September 10, 1988" with "a group of fifteen brothers, nine of whom are in charge of administration." On September 20 Al-Qaeda already included "thirty brothers fulfilling the necessary conditions."[5]

The universalist, militaristic, and nihilist ambition of the group soon became apparent in certain propaganda organs such as the magazines *Al-Jihad* and *Al-Bunyan Al-Marsus*, in which Zarqawi would take part in 1999. They were printed in Pakistan at the time. In

July 1989 an editorial signed by a member of Al-Qaeda clearly showed the path of jihad: "It is the duty of all Muslims to raise the challenge of jihad until we have reached America and liberated it."[6]

Al-Qaeda was born and bred on jihad. This is what enabled it to unify the Islamists after 1996, and especially after 1998, with the formation of a "front" against the Jews and the Crusaders. Thus the "initiatory" jihad in Afghanistan was pursued in Bosnia and Chechnya with other means, other military leaders, and other soldiers, but it remained the foundation of the terrorist organization.

The offensive of the American coalition in Iraq, however, was what made it possible for Zarqawi to emerge as the new representative of the jihadist current. As such he is ready to ensure the ideological survival of Al-Qaeda, as is proved by the adherence of the organization to its own aims. Without this conflict he would never have been anything but one of Bin Laden's commandants among others.

Yes, jihad is definitely the impulse behind the Islamist terrorist movements inspired by Afghanistan. Without this ideological and military base they would become terrorist groups lacking true religious underpinnings and destined to lose their credit and recruits in short order.

The future and outcome of the war against terrorism depend on our ability to understand it so as not to fertilize other areas favorable to jihad and in so doing make the dominant warlord on the scene into a spiritual leader. Today jihad is Zarqawi's greatest strength. Tomorrow it may be his Achilles heel.

Chronology

1987

Sentenced to two months in prison for deliberate violence but avoids serving time by paying a heavy fine.

1988

Marries his first wife, Intisar Baqr Al-Umari.

FEBRUARY 15, 1989

The last Soviet soldier leaves Afghanistan.

SPRING 1989

Goes to Pakistan, then to Khost in Afghanistan.

1989

Meeting with Issam Mohammed Taher Al-Barqawi (alias Abu Mohammed Al-Maqdisi) in Peshawar, Pakistan.

Correspondent for the jihadist magazine *Al Bunyan Al-Marsus*.

Meets Saleh Al-Hami.

1991

His sister marries Saleh Al-Hami in Pakistan.

1991–1992

Takes part in battles between rival Islamist factions in Afghanistan, principally at the side of the Islamist leader Gulbuddin Hekmatyar.

1992

Military training in the terrorist camp in Sada, Afghanistan.

MID-1993

Returns to Zarqa, where he manages a video-rental store for several months.

1993

Renews his relationship with Maqdisi.

MARCH 29, 1994

Arrested along with his associates in connection with the Bayt Al-Imam affair. Imprisoned in Suwaqah.

1994

Death of Fadil Nazzal Mohammed Al-Khalayleh, Zarqawi's father.

NOVEMBER 27, 1996

Sentenced to fifteen years in prison by the Jordanian courts. Incarcerated in Suwaqah, then in Jafar.

MARCH 18, 1999

Decree of amnesty pronounced by King Abdallah of Jordan.

MARCH 29, 1999

Leaves prison.

SUMMER 1999

Leaves for Hayatabad, Pakistan, ostensibly to sell honey there.

Meets his second wife, Asra Yasin Mohammed Jarad.

OCTOBER 1999

The government of Benazir Bhutto purges the Arab militants. After a brief imprisonment, leaves Pakistan for Afghanistan.

LATE 1999

Settles in Kabul. Recruits several Jordanians in Afghanistan to carry out a series of attacks in Jordan.

EARLY 2000

Takes over the direction of an Al-Qaeda training camp near the city of Herat.

Establishes the Al-Tawhid cell in Germany.

OCTOBER 2000

Convicted in absentia in Jordan for his participation in the millennium plot in Amman.

BEGINNING OF 2001

Takes an oath of allegiance to Osama Bin Laden.

MID-2001

Goes to Kandahar, where he receives $35,000 from Al-Qaeda to recruit Jordanians and organize attacks on Israel. The terrorists in charge of the operation will be arrested in February 2002 in Turkey.

FALL 2001

Beginning of Operation Enduring Freedom in Afghanistan by a coalition headed by the United States in retaliation for the attacks of September 11.

DECEMBER 10, 2001

Mullah Krekar assumes the leadership of Ansar Al-Islam.

DECEMBER 12, 2001

A telephone tap indicates that Zarqawi was wounded in the stomach and leg during a bombing raid by the Americans. He flees Afghanistan for Iran.

JANUARY 5, 2002

Arrives in Mashhad, Iran.

MID-JANUARY 2002

A telephone tap indicates that he is well again.

FEBRUARY 11, 2002

Sentenced by the Jordanian Security Court to fifteen years in prison for his participation in plans for the millennium attacks.

EARLY 2002

Transfers $40,000 from Iran to Germany for the purchase of false passports.

APRIL 2, 2002

A telephone tap indicates that his financial situation is good.

APRIL 4, 2002

Leaves Iran for Iraq.

APRIL 23, 2002

His support cell in Germany is dismantled.

MAY–JUNE 2002

Spotted in Baghdad and Northern Iraq.

EARLY JULY 2002

Meets Mullah Krekar and seals their alliance.

JULY–SEPTEMBER 2002

Settles in Damascus, Syria.

SEPTEMBER 9, 2002

Leaves Syria briefly for a clandestine trip to Jordan.

LATE SEPTEMBER 2002

Travels to Baghdad.

OCTOBER 28, 2002

Assassination of the American diplomat Laurence Foley in Amman, an operation conceived and planned by Zarqawi.

DECEMBER 2002

Abu Zubaydah reveals Zarqawi's involvement in the attempted chemical attacks in Europe.

FEBRUARY 5, 2003

Speech of U.S. Secretary of State Colin Powell before the United Nations Security Council describing Zarqawi as the link between Al-Qaeda and the regime of Saddam Hussein.

MARCH 20, 2003

Onset of the offensive of the coalition in Iraq.

MARCH 2003

Dismantling of a support network of Ansar Al-Islam in Italy. Telephone taps reveal a channel for moving fighters to Syria.

JULY 2003

Iran states that it has imprisoned significant numbers of Al-Qaeda members.

AUGUST 7, 2003

An attack on the Jordanian embassy in Iraq, attributed to Zarqawi, leaves fourteen dead and forty wounded.

JANUARY 23, 2004

In a letter seized by the United States and attributed to him, Zarqawi takes credit for most of the actions carried out against the coalition since March 2003.

JANUARY–APRIL 2004

Two audiotapes by Zarqawi are made public in which he appeals to Muslims to join the jihad in Iraq.

FEBRUARY 29, 2004

Death of Zarqawi's mother, Um Sayel.

MARCH 11, 2004

Attacks in Madrid.

APRIL 6, 2004

Sentenced to death by hanging by the Jordanian Security Court for his participation in the murder of Laurence Foley.

APRIL 2004

First Western hostages are taken in Iraq.

APRIL 20, 2004

Arrest of members of a group, controlled by Zarqawi, planning a chemical attack in Amman.

MAY 2004

Founding of the terrorist group Tawhid wal Jihad.

MAY 11, 2004

Execution of the American Nicholas Berg by Zarqawi's group.

MAY 18, 2004

Zarqawi takes credit for the assassination of Izzadin Saleem, president of the council of the government of Iraq.

JUNE–OCTOBER 2004

Zarqawi's group executes several Western hostages in Iraq.

OCTOBER 2004

The United States holds Zarqawi responsible for the deaths of 675 Iraqis and 40 foreigners.

OCTOBER 17, 2004

Repeats his oath of allegiance to Osama Bin Laden.

His group takes the name Al-Qaeda Committee for Jihad in Mesopotamia.

NOVEMBER 8, 2004

Beginning of the coalition's offensive against the Sunni stronghold of Fallouja.

Appendices

I

Warning Sent to Zarqawi by the Municipality of Zarqa in 1987

(Photocopy of the Original)

بسم الله الرحمن الرحيم

Zarka Municipality

Tel: 3982131 Fax: 3982455
PO.Box: 14
E-mail admin@zm.gov.jo

بـلـديـة الـزرقـاء

هاتف ٣٩٨٢١٣١-٣٩٨٢١٣٢-٣٩٨٢١٣٢

فاكس ٣٩٨٢٤٥٥-ص.ب. ١٤.

البريد الإلكتروني : admin@zm.gov.jo

الرقم : ....

التاريخ : ..../......../......

الموافق : ..../......../.........

انذار

العامل :- احمد فضيل الخلايلة

قسم الصيانة

نظرا لعدم انتظامكم في العمل الموكل اليكم ضمن قسم الصيانة وتكرار التغيـب دون اذن مسبق فانني انذركم انذارا ثانيا والالتزام بالعمل دون اية مبررات غير مقبولة والـــرر حسـم ثلاثة ايام من اجركم .

نسخة / مدير شؤون الموظفين

نسخة / مدير الصيانة

نسخة / للمدير المالي

رئيس بلدية الزرقاء

ياسر العسري

Source: Municipality of Zarqa, 1987. Author's archives.

I
———————————

Warning Sent to Zarqawi by the
Municipality of Zarqa in 1987
(Translation of the Original)

(HASHEMITE KINGDOM OF JORDAN)

Municipality of Zarqa
Tel: 3982131 Fax: 3982455
P.O. Box 14
Email: admin@zm.gov.jo

Municipality of Zarqa
Tel: 3982131 Fax: 3982455
P.O. Box 14
Email: admin@zm.gov.jo
No. 3M/Warning 19/06/1987

Warning

To Employee Ahmad Fadil Al-Khalayleh from the Office of Maintenance of the City of Zarqa.

We have determined that you are not serious in the exercise of your job
that we have entrusted to you at the Office of Maintenance. You have
been absent on several occasions without authorization. For this reason
I am sending you this second warning and ask that you be serious in
your job without unjustified excuses, and I have decided to deduct three
days' pay from your salary.

cc: Director of Human Resources
cc: Director of the Office of Maintenance
cc. Financial Director
cc. File

[signature]
Yasseer Al-Omari
President of the Municipality of Zarqa

II

Zarqawi Agrees to
Renounce Violence in 1987
(Photocopy of the Original)

بسم الله الرحمن الرحيم

Zarka Municipality

Tel: 3982131 Fax: 3982455
PO.Box: 14
E-mail admin@zm.gov.jo

بـلـديـة الـزرقــاء
هاتف ٢٩٨٢١٣١-٣٩٨٢١٣٢-٣٩٨٢١٣٢
فاكس ٣٩٨٢٤٥٥-ص.ب. ١٤.
البريد الإلكتروني : admin@zm.gov.jo

الرقم : بـ/د/م/جح/م.ا.د./شأ.م
التاريخ :٦١/ح/١ـم.../٨٥٨٧/
الموافق : ....../....../.........

انذار

لعامل :- احمد فضيل الخلايلة

قسم الصيانة

نظرا لعدم انتظامكم في العمل الموكل اليكم ضمن قسم الصيانة وتكــرار التغيــب دون اذن
مسبق فانني انذركم الذارا ثانيا والالتزام بالعمل دون اية مبررات غير مقبولة والقــرر حســم
ثلاثة ايام من اجركم .

نسخة / مدير شؤون الموظفين،
نسخة / مدير الصيانة
نسخة / للمدير المالي

رئيس بلدية الزرقاء
باسر العسري

Source: Municipality of Zarqa, 1987. Author's archives.

II

Zarqawi Agrees to Renounce Violence in 1987
(Translation of the Original)

HASHEMITE KINGDOM OF JORDAN

Hashemite Kingdom of Jordan
Zarqa District
Zarqa

Declaration

We the undersigned agree to respect the laws, and should that not be the case we agree to pay a fine of 1,000 Jordanian dinars or see to it that the indicated guarantors do so:

Mohamad Saleh Awad [signature]
Saleh Khaled Zawahiri [signature]
Ahmad Fadil Nazzal (Al-Khalayleh) [signature]
Walid Salim Sarsur [signature]

January 7, 1987

Guarantors:

Nabil Al-Hani Tamimi
Mohammed Salah Al-Harama

Deputy Mayor [signature]

(official stamp required)

III

Transcript of the Examination of Zarqawi by the Jordanian Court in 1994, Signed and Authenticated by Him
(Photocopy of the Original)

ما بعد

نأخذ ما بذ وكذلك محو الرواشده وكذلك عامر السراج، وبعرض لحمايته
يعرض عليه الشباب المذكورين على المشتكى عليه خصام بالمعاد لدورى الرشد
علينا حيث ألقى لمعة دروس من منزل المذكور يزيد والحين بعض
الدروس من منزل عامر قبل، وكانت جميع دروسه عن العقيده والبواطه
وكانت تعتمد هذه الدروس على أبدعها العقيده نتفرق بلاية إمام
هي تعاهيد الروبيبيه وقد تعرف به دخول ذلك الى أسم من محاورين
ما أنزل الدعمقدر كأمر لعقده تقابل ((ومن لم يحكم بما أنزل يعتبر
أنزل منا ولئن يحكم الكافرون)) ولقد صيد الذ محاد ولصفاتي
ولقد صيد الأولوبيه وكنا نتعرض حين جلساتنا لدروس التي
كانه تلقيها المشتكى عليه لعام ناس بالكلام في الوقت الحاضر كونهم لا
يكلفونه بما أنزل بنهم كفرة . وفي بداية عام ١٩٩٤ ذهبت مع
كل من سه المدعو المشتكى عليه لعصام محمد طاهر والمدعو خالد العدوري بالمدعو
يولى بو البراء الى عصام حيث كان يعيش بضاحي الباكما
مدرسى الى منزله في منطقة بالعقر بالكول . وكانت زيارات دورية لم نظم
منها لأنه أمرت نتظيم وكانه يفه لزيارة سه أصل أفكر حوا ز
ألاأنه لم يستطع بيعه . وبعد مغادرتى سه ميش رحمن لمذيرات
وحضورى في الباكما من أنه حمل بنا شته أكياته وأنه نتعتلى
السلام رباني حيو من المسى والبندفيه وقد رافقنى في لدة الزيارة
المشتكى عليه لعصام محمد طاهر عمداً صديقى منا حمد
المشتكى عليه   محمد طاهر

طلبنا مساعدة لجنة براءات العامة . قلت أنا أعتقد أنه يستطيع أن ينسب
لدائرة لجنة براءات العامة و ساعدهم بحل لأربعة عقوبتهم بالسلام إذا
حاولوا المعتقلين كما حدث بشان بأنه لم يسلم نفسه و أذا حاول آزا
المعتقله بأنه سيقاوم بمقدمت شوارع برشاش لدائرة بملته
من لمركز شمال بمبلغ ثمانية دينار ـ و ذلك مسه أصل مشاورة رجال
المخابرات في جال المعتقل رأى سم الرشاش الذي أستعرضته أمي
قابلة و كذلك شرته في زه عادته لنفس السلاح و لذي (٣٥) طلقت
عائده لرشاش من شهيم أن نتظيم الى حركة بيعه بالأعلا بدرلم
تشكل تنظيم وأثار المشكل عليه عصام محمد طاهر وأسم انفجركاته
كرم النتظيمات وحصون شهر ثانية بنائي لأبن أهلي ميلام
١٩٩٢ زا بني المشكل عليه عصام محمد طاهر ورحاني الكبيسة و عدتم
ذهبنا لزيارة أخرى أحينانة صاحب شركة تجارية وأستقبل الأولاد
و ذكر في بانه كوزته سنة شمال دقسمه القام مزودية وتاخذوا
من الكميت و بعد ذلك عرضت عليه أن سه بعطينات أباه للغفيرا
في منزل بتوقفه على ذلك و بعد يومين من ذلك بقد ذهبت و كانه
يمضني المذكور ضاده لصادري اكس منزل المستكن عليه عصام بطاهر
ست وأص أحضر الغنادس بالغام وبالبعض شنة أحد الماكس
هينشي وكان بداخله الغنادير بالغام المسا بالها أعلاه .
وبتدتها يعيحا على رسلمني أباها وبعد ذلك عدت الى سنز لي
في حجين زلصب جدا لراي منزله و بدفعته بالغام بالغنادي جرزن
لمرج أ سم بلمن لغريبا وبعد ذلك أستقر مني من لغنابل بالغام
نغلت له بأنني لم أجد مكانه جيد لأخفاء الغنادس بالغام فقدها
طلمون واعادوتها الميح و بالبعض شنة أحذت الغنادس بالغام
المركة

المشار علي
(٣ رمضان ١١)

ما بعد   ١٩٥

ما عدسنا للمستمع عليه عصام محمد طاهر وكان يبعتقد المذكور خالد
العازرين ومنه سلطته أ ياضا بأ بستشار يستبدلين جيتبعها
كوزين من أجل أ ستقلها من محله تنائيه داخل لنراطي
المحله صد الكراء الصهيونى . بالفعل ومحصد المشاور الحله ي
السراح المحله للمدد سها بد طالب أبزه ولمركز عبد الهادي دخلس
ودرس سير أجل وضعها بالقرب من الحدود إبذرائته لإسرائيله
وكنت أحمز على مصعد لاس وأ عمدنا كذلن سها أجل الحله صورة
بتردي رصد عباءه عسم تقيفني خلاسته كون دتم وضعها بالإضافه
للفتاتع لميقو علميسه وزلى سها أجل دحقها بن تكاسترتيب مبالحدود
صز ودته لإسرائيله من أجل تنفيذ العليه ازني نهض اليوم للملكي
من اعمار العيق ورهم الخط مقد المتقرى المرفوع بد الهادي دخلس
دلم نقيم بستنفذ العمليه وأ هذت أنكر بالهروب من لحدود
مفوضت علىي المذكو محمد حسه الجمادي والذي لك يلطمني بربته لزمار
بالقرب من سيد الحسين أ بد ميلى الى شخى لاس أ بد ميلاي
عمى فرسيله بعرف سخا مقيم بتزوير جوا باشر سعا منقته من فرقه
لهذا منك لاس بالفعل بنت أ بلغني بأ بد زلى استخى بيرمجوب كنيه
مجا من أجن تزوير جوا زستوري حبا لي سنه دنا ـ وغوازته على
زلى وأ بطشه صح سنجه وسلغ ما نه دنا رلعيد أستورى
تفرست أ حقرب جوا سخا سفيذ بلجس أ كيفي أ حمد عبد الله لي بوي
وأ بت لصه لملعقه عله صدرى الشخه رمحمد الرحمي (ل٢٥٧٢٢)
وصعم لعروض على ا الأبه ، وهذا كريل أ بين الحواز ويبيز بالحروف
مخافقا من قنه لنقه و طلته منم أحفت ـ صدرب رقعه ومنه
المستمرعلي   العبد للعام

نى/ا

ما بعد   طه؟

دينا ـ لقي شخص وقت تسليم صدرهم الشخصية والنقود للدكتور
محمد رحمه الحياوي وتام لعيدنى دلعديررا سموا لنفسي
غام ب صف ـ جوا ز ب سعر مزورن لحلا به صدقة فريه مشكي
عليه وعام دائمنو طالدا العادري دبعي جوا ز لفو لعزوز لزب
يمن لعود الشقه الند ه كى أ لصا ا به لتي لعض علیه وتم حف
مجوزني كما جري لقتشى منزلي وتم منط جوا ز لسق لمزوروتم
منط رمسانى أم بعد ضايف هيث تم منفظه في منزل مشوى
هيث محنة با ضانة در به لحم شقيقى دخت بالرباط علي لمنا
وتم ا حضا نة وعه بلي نه مزسر وتمن ٦٠ طلقت عما ع و لم
وجيه مخزرين لوس آ سود إنا بالسنه للقنبلتن العي لحنا
سمو ز ئي منىد با لطار حما للعدر سليا به خري وتم طغلان في منزل
لسميه سليا به العدر نقا بلاين من سقة واديا كهر ما ا با سد ث
لحما زنه الفنا بلي لالنام وكذلي حما زنه لسلا ميوس رضع نلوي
وكذلي نفعلي في نزور جوا ا المنر وهته اعادني ا صادريا
لمنع شخي لعند بلا هنا بى ما سى حريسة ٩٤/٨/٣١

المستلم علیه   ١٩٩٤/٨/٣١
المنكر

Source: Confessions of Abu Musab Al-Zarqawi, State Security Court of the Hashemite
Kingdom of Jordan, Decision 95/300, August 31, 1994. Author's archives.

III

Minutes of the Examination of Zarqawi by the Jordanian Courts, 1994
(Translation of the Original)

HASHEMITE KINGDOM OF JORDAN
SECURITY COURT
DECISION 95/300

Ahmad Fadel Nazzal Al-Khalayleh, from Ramzi Street, Zarqa (near the Al-Falah Mosque), age 28, educated and married. Arrested on March 29, 1994, imprisoned since that time.

Ahmad Fadel was transferred from Zarqa. He lives there in the Ramzi district (near the Al-Falah Mosque). He is 28 years old. He is a Muslim. He has taken part in an illegal organization. He possessed bombs without authorization in addition to carrying arms. He also offended verbally against the honor of the king. He engaged in the falsification of passports and used them himself, in contravention of Law 63 of 1961.

Uncoerced declarations by the accused:

In 1989 I went to Pakistan, and during my stay I made the acquaintance of Issam Mohammed Taher [Abu Mohammed Al-Maqdisi]. I remained there until I returned to Jordan in 1993. I received training in a military training camp (Sada). I was trained in handling Kalashnikovs, RPGs, and Hown cannons in order to take part in the jihad in Afghanistan. I returned to Jordan in mid-1993. I learned that Abu Mohammed Al-Maqdisi had also returned. I paid him a visit and reminisced about our time in Pakistan. Our relationship grew stronger. I had friends to whom I introduced him. They were in Zarqa. They were religious extremists. One of them was Sherif (also called Abu Ashraf). There was also Sulaiman Taleb Hamza, Khaled Al-Aruri, Nasser Fayez, my brother, Nafez Fayez, Mohammed Rawajde, Amer Sarraj, and Nazri Tahayinah.

We took part in religious instruction at Sherif's house. There were also many lessons at the home of Nasser Fayez. The courses had to do with religion. The courses had to do with the need to judge and conduct life as in the Koran. The king and the Arab and Muslim presidents do not respect these precepts. These courses took place at the home of Issam Mohammed Taher. In 1994 I went with Issam Mohammed Taher; Khaled Al-Aruri; and Mustapha, Taher's brother-in-law, to visit Fayez (Abu Al-Barrar) in the city of Ma'an. Fayez lived with us in Pakistan.

When I visited Abdul Majid Al-Majali my friend Khaled Al-Aruri was with me. We visited him at Al-Qasr in the Al-Karak region. It was a courtesy visit. We did not talk about religion, jihad, or organizations. On this visit I also intended to take back a K7 camera I had given him to sell but that he was not able to sell.

I knew that the secret services were watching me. I visited Yanal Ramzi because during my stay in Pakistan I had heard that he had opinions close to mine, and that he had weapons, and that he was a professional marksman with the pistol and rifle. He was with me on a visit to Issam Mohammed Taher.

The intelligence services summoned me. I refused to go. I would have done anything not to go and to resist if they decided to bring me in. When I knew I was summoned I bought a submachine gun in Yanal, I forget the make, and paid 800 dinars for it. I did this with the aim of resisting if the police came to my house. The make of the submachine gun was M15. I had three rounds for this weapon and thirty-five cartridges.

I do not belong to Bayt Al-Imam. Issam Mohammed Taher and I were against the Americans because they rejected Islam, and in the month of December 1993 Issam Mohammed Taher came to see me and invited me to his house. We went together to meet a friend who had a local business. On the way Issam told me that he had six bombs and five individual mines that he had bought in Kuwait. I asked him to give them to me so I could hide them, and he agreed. Two days later I went with Khaled Al-Aruri to Issam Mohammed Taher's house to get the bombs and the mines. And he really did have a bag containing the bombs and mines I mentioned. I then returned home, and Khaled went back to his house, and I kept the bombs and mines at my house for about two weeks. Then Issam spoke to me and asked questions about the bombs. I told him I hadn't found a good place to hide them. Issam asked me to return them, which I did. Khaled Al-Aruri was with me. I gave everything back to Issam, with the exception of two bombs I kept for use in a suicide operation in the territories occupied by the Zionists. We began to prepare this operation with the two suicide bombers, Suleiman Taleb Hamzi and Abdel Hadi Daghlas. The bombs were to be placed near the border between Israel and Jordan. For this operation we prepared two Kalashnikov weapons to put them with Suleiman Taleb Hamzi near the border to carry out the operation. But the day after the preparation Abdel Hadi Daghlas was arrested, and we could not continue the operation. I began thinking about fleeing Jordan, then someone called Mahmoud Hassan Hajawi, who lives in Zarqa near the Hussein Mosque, asked me to go see someone he knew well and who knew someone in his family who makes false passports. He agreed to Hajawi's request that he help me. Hajawi had asked me for a photo and 100 dinars. I paid him and gave him a photo. About a week later he gave me the false passport in the name of Ali Ahmad Abdullah Majali and the photo was mine. The number of the passport was D725303. I suggested this to Issam and Khaled Al-Aruri and they agreed and I asked each of them for a photo and 100 dinars. I gave it all to the same person named Mahmoud Hassan Hajawi. A week later I gave the false passports to Issam and Khaled Al-Aruri, but the police found everything and searched my house and found my false passport and the M15 submachine gun in my brother's house where I had hidden it without his knowledge. They found it with the three rounds and sixty-five nine-millimeter cartridges and two black rounds, and as for the two bombs I kept I gave them back to Suleiman Hamza. They found them at the house of Suleiman's brother-in-law, whose name is Noman who lives in the Wadi Hajar district. I am guilty of having possessed bombs and mines and having weapons without official permission and having a false passport and making false passports for friends. I confirm and sign.

Signed: Ahmad Fadel
August 31, 1994

IV

Death Sentence of Abu Musab Al-Zarqawi
Pronounced by the Jordanian Court
(Photocopy of the Original)

العقوبـــــة

نطقاً على ما جاء في قرار التجريم فان المحكمة تقرر بالاجماع ما يلي

٨. بالنسبة للمجرم الثامن احمد فضيل نزال الخلايله الملقب / ابو مصعب { الفار من وجه العدالة } : -

الحكم عليه بالاعدام شنقاً عملاً باحكام المادتين {١٤٧ و١٤٨/٤} من قانون العقوبات رقم ١٦ لسنة ١٩٦٠ وتعديلاته .

قراراً صدر بالاجماع وجاهياً بحق المجرمين الاول والثاني والثالث والسادس والمتهم الرابع وغيابياً بحق المجرمين الرابع والخامس والسابع والثامن والتاسع والعاشر باسم حضرة صاحب الجلالة الملك عبد الله الثاني بن الحسين المعظم قابلاً للتمييز وافهم علناً بتاريخ ٤/٦ / ٢٠٠٤ .

الرئيس
العقيد القاضي العسكري
فراز البقــور

عضو
المقدم القاضي العسكري
احمد عياش العمور

عضو
القاضـــي
توفيق القيسي
١ ع١٠/م/ز
٢٠٠٤/٤/٦

عضو

عضو

Source: State Security Court of the Hashemite Kingdom of Jordan, Decision 545/2003, Case of Laurence Foley. Author's archives.

IV

Death Sentence of Abu Musab Al-Zarqawi Pronounced by the Jordanian Court
(Translation of the Original)

SENTENCE

DECISION OF THE COURT

For the defendant Ahmad Fadil Nazzal Al-Khalayleh, alias Abu Musab, in flight: We condemn him to death by hanging in accordance with Law 147/178/4 of the year 1960.

Decision of the court for the first, second, third, and sixth culprits and for the fourth, fifth, seventh, eighth, ninth, and tenth culprits in absentia.

In the name of His Majesty King Abdallah III

Read at a public hearing on April 6, 2004.

Presiding Military Judge	Military Judge Taw-fik Al-Qassi Lieu-tenant Ahmad	Colonel Fawaz El Bakour Hayach Al-Hamous
[signature]	[signature]	[signature]

V

Diagram of the Zarqawi Network in Europe Made by Shadi Abdalla During His Interrogation by the German Authorities in 2002

(Photocopy of the Original)

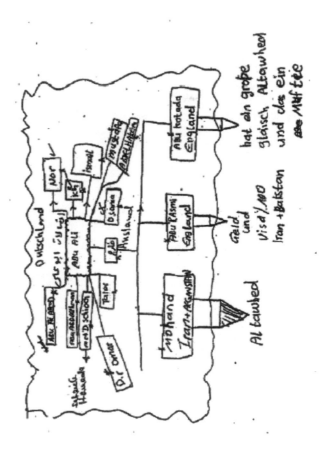

Source: German judiciary proceedings, Al-Tawhid case, testimony of Shadi Abdalla, 2002. Author's archives.

VI

Diagram of the Zarqawi Network in Germany Made by Shadi Abdalla During His Interrogation by the German Authorities in 2002

(Photocopy of the Original)

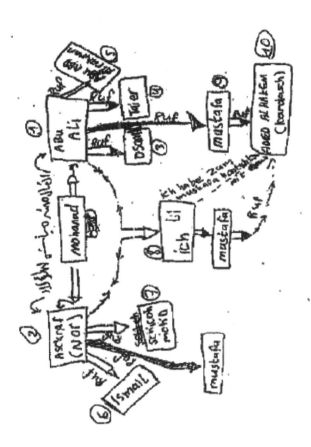

Source: German judiciary proceedings, Al-Tawhid case, testimony of Shadi Abdalla, 2002. Author's archives.

VII

Map of Kabul with Location of Zarqawi's House, Made by Shadi Abdalla During His Interrogation by the German Authorities in 2002

(Photocopy of the Original)

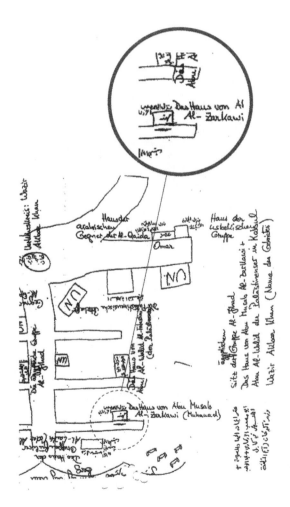

Source: German judiciary proceedings, Al-Tawhid case, testimony of Shadi Abdalla, 2002. Author's archives.

VIII

Letter Signed by Zarqawi, Seized in Iraq in 2004[1]

In the name of God, full of Mercy and Compassion,

From .... to the proudest of individuals and leaders in this time of servitude,

.... To the men on the mountaintops, the falcons of glory, the lions [of the mountains] of Shara, the two honorable brothers ....,

May the peace and mercy and blessing of God be with you.

Even if we are separate in body the distance is small between our hearts.

We find comfort in this word of Imam Malik. I hope we are both well. I ask God the Exalted, the Generous [that] this letter may find you decked in the finery of health and borne with delight by the winds of victory and triumph.... Amen.

I am sending you a report that is appropriate for your situation, revealing and bringing to light all the aspects, positive and negative, contained in the theater of operations in Iraq.

As you know, God has favored the [Islamic] nation with a jihad in His name in the land of Mesopotamia. You are well aware that this is a unique land. There are favorable elements there that do not exist elsewhere, and unfavorable elements that also do not exist elsewhere. One of the most favorable elements is that this is a jihad located in the heart of the Arab region, two steps away from the two Holy Regions and [the mosque of] Al-Aqsa. The religion of God teaches us that the true decisive battle between the infidels and Islam is taking place in this land, that is to say in [Greater] Syria and its environs. This is why we must insistently exert all our efforts to take control of this land, after which God may perhaps let his will be done. In the present situation, O brave sheikhs, it is essential that we carefully consider the issue, relying on our true Law and the reality in which we live. . . .

Here, insofar as my limited vision allows me to see it, is how the current situation appears. I ask God to forgive me my babbling and my faults. I say, after having asked for God's help, that the Americans, as you well know, entered Iraq on the basis of a contract to create the State of Greater Israel from the Nile to the Euphrates, and that this Zionized American Administration thinks that in hastening the creation of the State o[f Greater] Israel it will hasten the arrival of the Messiah. It came to Iraq with all its men and all its pride, full of arrogance toward God and his Prophet. It thought that the operation would proceed quite easily, that even though there would be difficulties it would be a simple matter. But it came up against a completely different reality. The mujahidin brothers launched their operations from the beginning, which complicated the situation a bit. Then the pace of the operations speeded up. This happened in the Sunni Triangle, if that is the exact name of this region. The Americans had to conclude an agreement with the most vile people in the human race, the Shiites. The agreement was concluded on the [following] basis: the Shiites would get two thirds of the booty in recompense for having joined the ranks of the Crusaders against the mujahidin.

First: The Composition [of Iraq]

In a general sense Iraq is a political mosaic, a country where the ethnic groups are mixed together and where there exist side by side various confessions and sects with many and complex differences, which only a strongly centralized power and a mighty leader have ever been able to govern from the time of Ziyad Ibn Abihi[2] to Saddam. Difficult choices are on the horizon for the future. This is a country in which everyone, whether or not he acts serious, is undergoing harsh ordeals and great hardships. . . .

Now for more detail:

1. The Kurds
Cut into two halves, the Barazani and the Talabani, they have given

themselves over heart and soul to the Americans. They have opened their land to the Jews, who have made it their fallback position and a Trojan Horse for accomplishing their aims. They (the Jews) are infiltrating everywhere in their territory, draping themselves in their faded finery and depending on them in order to get financial control and economic hegemony; they also use them as a spy network, for which they have set up a structure proliferating in all parts of the region. The voice of Islam has faded away for most of them (the Kurds) and the light of religion is no longer more than a weak flickering in their homes. The Iraqi Da'wa ["call" or "invitation"] has intoxicated them, and those among them who remain honorable, few as they are, are oppressed and live in fear of being snatched away by the birds [of prey]...

3.[*sic*] The Shiites

[They are] the insurmountable obstacle, the prowling serpent, the crafty, evil scorpion, the enemy lying in wait, and biting poison. Here we are entering a battle waged on two levels. On the first, manifest and declared, we are grappling with an enemy who is the aggressor and with the most blatant of infidels. [The other is] a harsh, difficult battle that sets us against a sneaky enemy who presents a friendly face, showing good will and appealing for comradeship, but who in truth harbors dark designs and is busy hiding his true nature. These are the heirs of the Batini groups who have marked the history of Islam, leaving scars on it that time cannot erase. Whoever takes the time to look carefully at the situation will realize that Shiism is the greatest danger threatening us and the real challenge we must confront. "They are the enemy. Do not trust them. Fight them. God is our witness that they are liars." The message that History delivers is confirmed, as we see in the current situation that clearly shows that the Shiite religion has nothing in common with Islam, except in the sense in which the Jews have something in common with the Christians insofar as both are Peoples of the same Book. These confirmed polytheists, who stand and pray at gravesides, who organize funeral processions, who treat the Companions [of the Prophet] as infidels and insult the mothers of the faithful and the elite of this [Islamic] nation, do all they can to distort the Koran, presenting it as an offshoot of

logical thought in order to disparage those who have a correct knowledge of it; in addition, they speak of the infallibility of the [Islamic] nation, they claim that it is essential to believe in them, they assert that they
have received revelation, and in many other forms they give clear proof
of the atheism that abounds in their authorized works and original
sources (which they continue to print, distribute, and publish). To believe, as do some sweet dreamers, that a Shiite can forget [his] historical
heritage and the dark ancestral hatred of the Nawasib [those who doom
the descendants of the Prophet to hatred], as they whimsically call them,
is tantamount to asking a Christian to give up the idea of the crucifixion
of the Messiah. No one, unless he is not of sound mind, could bring himself to do that. Those are the people who have aggravated their infidelity
and their atheism by engaging in political maneuvers and doing all they
can to take advantage of the crisis of the government and the balance of
power; they are trying to outline a new State, setting up guidelines from
the perspective of their political parties and organizations in cooperation with their secret allies, the Americans.

At all periods of history and since the dawn of time they have been a sect
of deceivers and traitors, The principles they profess are aimed at fighting the Sunnis. When the foul Baathist regime fell the Shiites' slogan was,
"Vengeance, vengeance, from Tikrit to Al-Anbar." This is sufficient proof
of the extent of the hidden resentment they harbor with regard to the
Sunnis. Yet their "ulemas" have been able to keep control of matters in
their sect, lest the battle setting them against the Sunnis turn into openly
partisan war, for they know that this is not how they will be victorious.
They know that if a partisan war were ever to break out, there would be
many in the [Islamic] nation who would support the Sunnis in Iraq. As
worthy adepts of a religion that advocates dissimulation, they have pro-
ceeded in another way, one that is craftier and more elaborate. They
began by seizing institutions of the State, its security, military, and economic structures. As you know, may God bless you, security and the
economy are the two essential components of any country. They have
infiltrated all the way into these institutions and their subdivisions. To
return to the matter at hand, here is an example of what I am proposing:

the Badr Brigade, the armed branch of the Supreme Council of the Islamic Revolution, has gotten rid of the Shiite attributes of its clothing and adopted those of the police and the army. It has placed cadres in these institutions and, in the name of the protection of the land and its citizens, it has begun to settle its score with the Sunnis. The American army has begun to evacuate certain cities, and its presence is becoming scarce. It has gradually been replaced by an Iraqi army, and that is where our main problem lies, since the battle we are waging against the Americans is an easy matter. The enemy is apparent, it is in the open and does not know the terrain or the current situation of the mujahidin, since its sources of information are weak. We consider it a certainty that the armed forces of these Crusaders will disappear in short order. When we look at the current situation we may observe how eager the enemy is to put in place the army and the [local] police, who have begun to complete their assigned missions. It is that enemy, composed of Shiites joined by Sunni agents, who are the real danger with which we are confronted, for it is [composed of] our fellow citizens, who know us better than anyone. They have more resources than their masters in the army of the Crusaders, and, as I said, they are already trying to get control of security matters in Iraq. They have systematically and deliberately liquidated many Sunnis and a good many of their enemies of the Baathist Party, along with other allies of the Sunnis. They began by killing many mujahidin brothers, and they then set about liquidating scientists, thinkers, doctors, engineers, and others. God only knows what will happen, but for my part I believe that the worst will not be behind us as long as the American army is standing firmly in its rear positions and the secret Shiite army and its military brigades continue to fight at its side. They infiltrate like serpents to take control of the army and the police forces, which are the primary weapon and iron hand of our Third World, and to monopolize all the economic structures like their supporters, the Jews. With each passing day they grow ever more hopeful of one day seeing a Shiite State established that would extend from Iran to the Papier-Mâché Kingdom of the Gulf, passing through Iran, Syria, and Lebanon. The Badr Brigade arrived, brandishing its vengeful slogan against Tikrit and Al-Anbar, but it quickly took off its faded finery in order to put on the insignia of the army and police so as to oppress the Sunnis and kill the people of Islam in the name of law and justice, and all this is covered with honeyed words. The harmfulness of falsity takes the path of deception. Their Ghunusi religion (based on private and personal illumination) veils itself in lies and conceals itself behind hypocrisy, exploiting the naiveté and goodness of many Sunnis. We do not know when our [Islamic] nation will begin to learn the lessons of History and build on the evidence of past epochs. The Safavid Shiite State was an insurmountable obstacle on the road to Islam, for it was like a dagger plunged in the heart of Islam and the back of its people. An Orientalist will rightly declare that ["]if the Safavid State had not existed, we who live in Europe would be reading the Koran like the Berbers of Algeria.["] To be sure, the troops of the Ottoman State halted at the gates of Vienna, and those ramparts failed to fall before them, [which would have enabled] Islam to spread glory and jihad throughout Europe under the sign of the sword. But those armies were obliged to turn back and retreat because the army of the Safavid State had occupied Baghdad, demolished its mosques, killed its people, captured its women, and confiscated its riches. The armies returned to defend the sanctuaries and people of Islam. The fierce battles that followed for about two centuries ended only when the power and influence of the Islamic State had evaporated and the [Islamic] nation had fallen asleep—before the fifes and drums of the Western invader awakened it with a start.

The Koran teaches us: the machinations of the hypocrites, the deceptions of the fifth column, and the maneuvers of those of our fellow citizens whose mouths are full of honey but who have a devil's heart in a man's body—that is where the gangrene is hidden, that is the secret reason for our disarray, that is the worm in the apple. "Those are the ones who are the enemy. Do not trust them." Sheikh Al-Islam Ibn Taymiyya spoke the truth when he said (after speaking of what they, the Shiites, thought of the people of Islam): "This is why, deceitful and sneaky, they help the infidels against the masses of the Muslim people and are the primary cause of the sudden appearance of Genghis Khan, king of the infidels, in the lands of Islam; the entry of Hulagu into Iraq; the capture of Aleppo; and the sack of Al-Salihiyya, among other things. This is why they pillaged the troops of Muslims when they encountered each other for the first time on the road to Egypt. And this is why they stop Muslims on the border roads and rob them. And this is why they lend their support to the Tartars and the Franks against the Muslims. They felt great sadness at the victory of Islam, since they were the friends of the Jews, the Franks, and the polytheists against the Muslims. Those are some of the ways of these hypocrites.... Their heart is full of vinegar and a rage like no other against all Muslims, old and young, the most impious and the most fervent.

"Their greatest [act of] devotion is to curse the Muslim friends of God unto the last one. Those are the people most desirous of dividing the Muslims. Some of their most important principles enjoin them to accuse of infidelity, curse, and insult the elite among the leaders, like the ortho-dox caliphs and the 'ulemas' of the Muslims, for they think that whoever does not believe in the infallibility of the Imam (something that does not exist) does not believe in God and his Prophet, may God bless him and grant him health....

"The Shiites love the Tartars and their State, for thanks to them they have won the glory that the Muslim State did not bring them.... They were the most fervent supporters [of the Tartars] when the latter seized the lands of Islam, killing Muslims and capturing their women. The story of the Caliph and the men of Ibn Al-Alqami in the episode of Aleppo is famous. Everyone knows it. If the Muslims triumph over the Christians and the polytheists, this saddens the Shiites. If the polythe-ists and the Christians conquer the Muslims, the Shiites celebrate the event with joy."—Al-Fatawa, 28th Part, pages 478 to 527.

Glory be to God, it is as though the hidden truth had been revealed be-fore his eyes (Ibn Taymiyya), offering itself to his gaze and inspiring in him limpid words based on a careful examination of the facts. Our imams have clearly shown the path to be followed and have revealed the true nature of these men. As Imam Al-Bukhari says: never in my home do I pray behind a Shiite or behind Jews or Christians. They are not welcome, One must not celebrate them on the occasion of religious holidays. One must not marry them. They cannot bear witness. One must not eat the animals they kill.—Khalq Af'al Al-'Ibad, page 125.

Imam Ahmad said (he had been asked who had cursed Abu Bakr, 'Umar and 'A'isha, may they find favor in the eyes of God): "I do not see him in Islam." Imam Malik said: "He who curses the Companions of the Prophet, may God bless him and grant him health, that man is not part of Islam." —Kitab Al-Sunna of Al-Khallal, number 779.

Al-Faryabi said: "I see only atheists among the Shiites." —Al-Lalika'i, 8th part, page 1545.

And when Ibn Hazm brought irrefutable evidence against the Jews and the Christians, who had deflected the Torah and the Gospels, they could say nothing in their defense except that the Shiites among them were speaking of distortions of the Koran. He said: ["]May god have pity! The Shiites of whom they are speaking, who claim that a substitution has been made, are not Muslims. They belong to a sect following the paved path of lies and infidelity traced by the Jews and the Christians." —Al-Fasl, 2nd part, page 78.

Ibn Taymiyya said: "This clearly proves that they are more evil than the members of sects and that they deserve to be fought more fiercely than the Khariji. It is for this reason that, in everyone's opinion, the Shiites are a nation of heretics. The truth is spreading among the masses: the Shiites are the opposite of the Sunnis, for they refuse to recognize the *sunna* [normative way of life] of the Prophet of God, may God bless him and grant him health, and the Laws of Islam." —Extract from Sa'it Ahl Al-Ahwa', 28th part, page 482.

And he said: "If the *sunna* and the *ijma* [consensus of Islamic legal scholars] agree in saying that if one could [only] reveal to the light of day [the mind of] the Muslim aggressor by killing him, then one would have to kill him even if [all] he had stolen was half a dinar, what then shall we say about those who do not respect the Laws of Islam and fight God and His Prophet, may God bless him and grant him health?"—4th part, p. 251.

And therefore let the people of Islam know that we are not the first to set out on that path. We are not the first to brandish the sword. Those people (the Shiites) keep on killing those who hope and pray for Islam and the mujahidin of the community; they stab them in the back under cover of the complicitous silence of the entire world and even, alas, of the figureheads allied with the Sunnis.

Moreover, they are like a bone stuck in the throat of the mujahidin and like a blade planted in [the back of] their leaders. No one is unaware of the fact that it is by the hand of those people that most of the mujahidin who fell in combat died. In these wounds that have not yet healed over, they continue to twist the dagger of hate and deceit. Night and day they tirelessly go about their task.

2. With Regard to the Sunnis
They are more helpless than orphans at the table of the depraved. They have lost [their] leader and wandered in the desert, robbed of everything, ignored by all, divided and dispersed, and deprived of the key figure who unified them, gathered up the scattered [pieces], and kept the eggshell from breaking. They too appear in [various] guises.

1. The Masses of the People
These masses are the silent majority; they are there but do not exist. "The vandals who were following everybody and his neighbor were starving. They did not seek knowledge or take shelter." Those people, even if they generally hate the Americans and want to see them disappear and the dark cloud with which they weigh down their shoulders vanish, turn in spite of everything toward the promise of radiant tomorrows, a prosperous future, a peaceful life, comfort and its benefits. They await this day with hope and are thus the ideal prey for the cunning tricks of the news [media] and the strategies of seduction of political sirens.... But in any case they are part of the people of Iraq.

2. The Sheikhs and the "Ulemas"
Most of these are Sufis headed for damnation. In matters of religious

practice they are content, on some anniversary, to sing and dance under the leadership of a camel driver and end by wallowing in the pomp of banquets. All they really are is a harmful drug and deceitful guides for an [Islamic] nation groping its way in the dark night. As for the spirit of jihad, the law of the martyr, and the rejection of infidels, they know nothing of this, they are as innocent of it as the wolf before the blood of Joseph, may peace be with him. While horrors and misfortunes are raging, none of them ever speaks of jihad or calls for immolation or self-sacrifice. For those people three is already too much, let alone four. They are unworthy of our task.

3. The [Muslim] Brothers
As you have been able to observe, they trade in the blood of martyrs and build their tawdry glory on the spoils of the faithful. They have debased their horses, set down their weapons, declared "no to jihad"... and they have lied.

They devote all their efforts to extending their political influence and grabbing the seats of Sunni representatives, distributing the pieces of cake in the government that has been formed, even as they try underhandedly, thanks to their financial support, to take control of the groups of mujahidin, and this for two reasons. First, to fuel propaganda and the work of media infiltration abroad so as to attract funds and public sympathy just as they had done at the time of the events in Syria; and their second aim is to control the situation so as to be able to dissolve these groups, once the party is over, and share the spoils. They now have the intention of creating a Sunni *shoura* that would be the mouthpiece for the Sunnis. They have the habit of interfering in things and changing sides according to the way the political wind is blowing. Their religion is fickle. They do not follow any stable principle or rely on any consistent legal foundation. It is from God that *we* have sought help.

D. The Mujahidin
They are the quintessence of Sunnism and the courageous vitality of this country. For the most part they adhere to Sunni doctrine and, nat-

urally, to the Salafist credo. The Salafists formed a rebel group only when the path veered off in a new direction and the people of [distant] regions set out behind their convoy. Generally speaking these mujahidin have the following distinguishing traits:

1. Most of them are uneducated and inexperienced, especially when it comes to organized collective work. They arose, undoubtedly, in reaction to a repressive regime that militarized the country, plunged the population into disarray, spread fear and terror, and sapped the confidence of the people. This is the reason why most of these groups work in an isolated fashion, with no political horizon or vision of the future, and without concern for the heritage of the land. To be sure, the idea is beginning to take root; the tiny whisper has grown louder, and it is with a lot of noise that they now talk of the need to come together and unite under one and the same banner. But this project is just at the beginning stages. With God's blessing we are trying to bring it to fruition as quickly as possible.

2. Here, alas, jihad takes the form of minefields, rocket fire, and the flash of mortars that sound far and wide. The Iraqi brothers still prefer their security and would rather go back to the arms of their wives, safe from all fears. The members of these groups sometimes boast that none of their people have been killed or taken prisoner. We have told them in our many meetings that safety and victory are incompatible, that the tree of triumph and access to power cannot attain its full majesty without dipping into blood and facing death, that the [Islamic] nation cannot live without tasting martyrdom or smelling the perfume of blood shed in the name of God, and that the people will not emerge from their torpor as long as the concern for sacrifice and the account of the martyrs does not occupy them day and night. The issue calls for more patience and conviction. We have great hope in God.

E. The Immigrant Mujahidin
Given the extent of the conflict awaiting us they are still too few in number. We know that the convoys of merchandise are many, that the march

of jihad is following its course, and that, for many of them, only the uncertainty regarding common objectives and the obscurity maintained
around true facts keep them from [responding] to the call to arms. If we
cannot [issue an appeal for] general mobilization, this is because in this
region there are no mountains in which we could find refuge or forests in
whose thickets we could hide. We are exposed, and our movements are
compromised. We are being observed from everywhere. The enemy is in
front of us and the sea is behind us. Many Iraqis would gladly receive you
and open their doors to you in a spirit of brotherly peace, but if it is a matter of transforming their house into a logistical base and a battleground,
suddenly no one is there. This is why we have often made sacrifices to
shelter and protect the brothers. The training of new recruits is all the
more difficult; we are so to speak moving forward with a millstone around
our necks, even if, God be praised and thanks to our tireless efforts and
the persistence of our quests, we have taken possession of an increasing
number of strategic sites, God be praised, for welcoming our brothers
who stoke [the fire] of war and lead the population of the country into the
furnace of battle so that a real war can break out, God willing.

Second: The Current Situation and the Future

There is no doubt that the Americans are suffering very heavy losses
because they are deployed over a large part of the territory and within
the population, and because it is easy to procure weapons, which makes
them ideal targets and tempting for the faithful. But America did not
come here to turn around and go home, and it will not leave no matter
how important the wounds inflicted on it and the amount of blood it
will have to shed. Its immediate objectives are to be able to withdraw to
its bases in compete safety, to have its hands free, and to entrust the Iraqi
battlefields to the government they installed, to which they have added
an army and police forces that will turn Saddam and his acolytes over to
the populace and let it decide their fate. There is no doubt that our
room to maneuver has decreased and that the yoke strangling the mujahidin has become tighter. This deployment of soldiers and police
forces is an omen of a frightening future.

Third: Where Are We Now?

Despite the scantiness of support, the desertion of friends, and the harshness of the circumstances, God the Exalted has enabled us to inflict serious harm on the enemy. God be praised, in terms of location, preparation, and planning we have been at the center of all the martyr operations, with the exception of those carried out in the north. God be praised, I have accomplished 25 [of these missions] up to now, including against the Shiites and their figureheads, against the Americans and their soldiers, the police and the army, as well as the forces of the coalition. God willing, others will follow. If we have not acted out in the open up to now, this is because we first wanted to gain ground and finish setting up integrated structures that would enable us to act covertly without incurring the consequences, so as to appear in a position of strength and avoid suffering a reverse. We are seeking the protection of God. God be praised, we have made much progress and gotten through many important stages. As the fateful moment draws near, we feel that [our] presence has expanded, taking advantage of the security vacuum; we have acquired new strategic sites on the ground that will be the nerve center from which we will be able to launch our operations and maneuver on a large scale, God willing.

Fourth: The Plan of Action

After careful study of the situation we are able to identify our enemy by dividing it into four groups:

1. The Americans: These, as you know, are the most cowardly of God's creatures. They are easy prey, God be praised. We ask that God allow us to kill and capture them, so that we can sow panic among those who support them and to exchange them for our imprisoned sheikhs and brothers.

2. The Kurds: They are a foreign body that is strangling us and a wound of which we have yet to rid ourselves. They are the last on the list, even if we did everything we could to get at some of their figureheads, with God's help.

3. Soldiers, police forces, and agents: They are the eyes, ears, and hands of the occupier, who uses them to see, hear, and exert his violence. With God's help we are determined to make them special targets in the coming period before the situation is consolidated and they have the means to proceed to arrests.

4. The Shiites: In our view they are the key element of change. I mean that in making them our targets and striking at the heart of [their] religious, political, and military structures we will trigger their rage against the Sunnis... [forcing them] to bare their fangs and reveal the sly rancor that drives them from deep within. If we manage to draw them onto the terrain of partisan war, it will be possible to tear the Sunnis away from their heedlessness, for they will feel the weight of the imminence of danger and the devastating threat of death wielded by these Sabeans. Weak and divided though they may be, the Sunnis are the sharpest adversaries, the most determined warriors, and the most loyal companions against these Batini (Shiites), who are a nation of traitors and cowards. They are brave only before the weak and attack only fallen men. Most of the Sunnis are aware of the danger these people represent, distrust it, and know what would happen if they let them gain power. If only one had not had to deal with the weakness of the Sufi sheikhs and the [Muslim] Brotherhood, things would have taken an entirely different turn.

Soon the sleepers will awaken from their leaden sleep and will arise, but our operation also requires that we neutralize these Shiites and pull their teeth before the fateful battle; soon we shall also have to kindle the anger of the people against the Americans, who have sowed destruction and are the primary cause of this plague. The people must be careful not to gorge themselves on the honey and the pleasures that were inaccessible to them up to now, for then the men might yield to weakness, preferring the safety of their homes, and remaining deaf to the clash of swords and the whinnying of horses.

5. The Mechanics of Action
Our current situation, as I told you before, makes it necessary for us to

maneuver with courage and precision, and to do so quickly, for [otherwise] we will not achieve any result in keeping with religion. Only God the Exalted knows what will happen, but the solution as we, for our part, foresee it is to draw the Shiites into battle, for this is the only way to prolong the fighting that sets us against the infidels. We say that we must draw them into battle for several reasons, as follows:

1. They (that is, the Shiites) have declared a secret war against the people of Islam. They are the dangerous enemy in immediate proximity to the Sunnis, even if the Americans are also a supreme enemy. The danger represented by the Shiites, however, is greater, and the damage they inflict on us worse and more destructive for the nation [of Islam] than that of the Americans, who by common agreement are to be considered aggressors and killed.

2. They have offered friendship and support to the Americans, swelling the latter's ranks against the mujahidin. They have tried hard, and at present are redoubling their efforts, to put an end to the jihad and the mujahidin.

3. Our fight against the Shiites is the way to draw the nation [of Islam] into battle. What concerns us here are the details of our action. We have already said that the Shiites have put on the uniforms of the army, the police, and the Iraqi security [forces], holding high the banner of defense of the land and its citizens. Rallied under this banner, they have begun to liquidate the Sunnis, whom they accuse of being saboteurs, relics of Baath, and terrorists spreading evil in the country. The guidelines issued to them by the Government Council and the Americans have enabled them to mingle with the Sunni masses and the mujahidin. I shall give an example that will bring us very close to the region called the Sunni Triangle—if that is its exact name. The army and police forces have begun to deploy in these areas and are gaining power from one day to the next. They have entrusted positions of responsibility to agents [recruited] from among the Sunnis and the population of this region. In other words, this army and police forces are sometimes linked to the inhabitants by

kinship, blood, and honor. Truly, this region is the focal point of all our activities. When the Americans disappear from these areas—and they have already begun to withdraw—and are replaced by these agents who share a common lot with the people of this land, what will become of our situation?

If we fight them (and we must fight them), we will face a choice between two possibilities. Either:

1. We fight them, and do so with great difficulty because of the rift that will open up between us and the men of this region. How can we fight their cousins and their sons, and under what pretext, once the Americans, who hold the reins of power from their rear bases, have retreated? When the moment comes this will be up to the true sons of this region to decide. Democracy is on the march: once it comes, we will have no excuse.

2. We pack our bags and go in search of an new country, as was, alas, often the case in the history of jihad, because our enemy is gaining power and consolidating its intelligence sources day by day. By the Lord of the Ka'ba, [this] is leading us to suffocation and then to the death throes of wandering. People follow the religion of their kings. Their hearts are with you, and their swords are at the side of Bani Umayya (the Ummayads), that is, with power, victory, and security. May God have mercy.

I repeat again, our only solution is to strike at the Shiites, attacking their religious, military, and other personnel, coming at them relentlessly until they yield to the Sunnis. Some people may find that we are showing zeal and harshness in this matter, that we are drawing the nation [of Islam] into a battle for which it is not ready, [a battle] that will be repugnant and will see much bloodshed. This is exactly what we want, for in the present situation there are no longer grounds for a distinction between what is just and what is not. The Shiites have put an end to all these notions of balance. The religion of God is more precious than lives and souls. When the overwhelming majority is on the side of truth, this religion requires us to make sacrifices. May blood be shed, and we shall sweeten the fate of good men by hastening their entry into paradise. [As for] those who, on the other hand, spread evil, we shall be free of them, since, by God, the religion of God is more precious than anything and must come before life, wealth, and children. The story of the Companions of the Ditch, blessed by God, is the best proof of this. According to [Imam] Al-Nawawi, this story showed that the city and the desert might as well fight to the point of total annihilation as long as each person did not acknowledge his faith and the oneness of God, and that this would be good. Men live, blood is safe, and honor preserved solely as a result of sacrifice made in the name of this religion. By God, brothers, the Shiites are summoning us to repeated battles and dark nights from which we must in no case turn away. They are threatening us with imminent danger, and the object of the fears we share, you and we, is certainly very real. Know that these [Shiites] are the most cowardly of God's creatures and that in killing their leaders we shall only increase their weakness and their cowardice, for when one of their leaders meets his death the entire sect dies with him. Conversely, when a Sunni leader dies or is killed a *sayyid* rises up. They bring all their ardor to battle and restore the courage of the weakest of the Sunnis. If you knew the fear [oppressing] the Sunnis and their followers among the people, you would shed sorrowful tears over them. How many mosques have been converted to Husayniyyas (Shiite mosques), how many houses have they caused to collapse on the heads of their occupants, how many brothers have they killed and mutilated, and how many sisters have seen their honor sullied at the hands of these depraved infidels? If we manage to get at them with our repeated and painful blows so as to force them to enter into battle, we will be able to deal the cards [in a new way]. Then the Government Council will no longer have any legitimacy or influence, as will be true of the Americans, who will engage in a second battle with the Shiites. This is what we want, and, like it or not, many Sunni regions will stand with the mujahidin. In the end, the mujahidin will seize key areas from which they will be able to launch the offensive against the Shiite strongholds; they will also be able to position themselves more precisely vis-à-vis the media and put in place a solid strategic plan for rallying the mujahidin [in Iraq] and the brothers abroad.

1. We are in a real race against time when it comes to creating companies of mujahidin who will take up positions in the security zones and try to take control of the country and hunt down the enemy (the Americans, police forces, and soldiers) on every road down to the smallest paths. We are continuing to train them in increasing numbers. As for the Shiites, we will hit them in their flesh, God willing, thanks to the martyr operations and car bombings.

2. For some time now we have been making an effort to keep close watch on the theater of operations, selecting those who are trying to find sincere and upright men so as to engage their cooperation in doing good and mounting specific actions with their assistance; we test these men and put them through a hard time with the aim of cementing solidarity and unity. We hope we have made great progress along these lines. Perhaps we will soon decide to make our actions public, even if this must be done gradually, so that we can act openly. We have been hidden for a long time. Right now we are preparing a substantial file, intended for the media, that will reveal the facts, announce our resolutions, and spark determination; in this way the pen will join forces with the sword in the pursuit of jihad.

3. Moreover, we are redoubling our efforts to put an end to the uncertainties that are undermining our enterprise and to explain the rules of *sharia* by means of tapes, written documents, study reports, and training programs intended to raise awareness, implant in people's minds the doctrine of the oneness of God, set up facilities, and fulfill [our] obligations.

5. [*sic*] Operational calendar: We hope to step up the pace of our work, forming companies and battalions of confirmed experts and resisters who are preparing for the fateful moment when we shall begin to act openly; we shall then take control of the territory by night and extend its domain in the light of day, with the permission of God the Supreme and Victorious. We hope that this operation (I mean this fateful hour) will take place around four months before the formation of the government promised by our enemy. As you see, we are in a

race against time. If, as we hope, we are able to deal out the cards differently and thwart their plans, that will be good. If the contrary [scenario comes to pass] (and we beg for God's protection) and the government extends its control throughout the country, then we shall have to pack our bags, strike camp, and head for other lands where we will be able to raise our flag once again and where God may choose to call us to martyrdom in his name.

6. And you? You, my honorable brothers, are the leaders, the guides, and the key figures of jihad and the struggle. We do not consider ourselves worthy to challenge your authority, and we have never sought to win fame for our own advantage. We hope only to become the spearhead, the invigorating vanguard, and the bridge that the nation [of Islam] will cross to reach the shores of victory promised to us and the future to which we aspire. That is our vision, as we have just explained. That is the road open before us, as we have just been tracing it in broad outline. If you are in agreement with us on this point, if you adopt it as our program and the path to be followed, and if you fall in with our idea of fighting the sects of apostasy, we shall be your willing soldiers, we shall work under your flag, we shall comply with your orders, and we shall swear fidelity to you without hesitation, publicly and in the news media, which will foil the infidels and gladden those who preach the oneness of God. On that day the faithful will celebrate the triumph of God. If matters seem otherwise to you, we are brothers and the disagreement will not mar [our] friendship. We are cooperating on behalf of this cause with a view toward doing good and in order to support the jihad. Awaiting your reply, I pray that God will protect you, you who are the keystone of good and the living strength of Islam and its people. Amen, amen.

May the peace and mercy and blessing of God be with you.

Notes

Part I. Genesis of a Terrorist

1. Popular Front for the Liberation of Palestine, a movement of revolutionary tendency and Marxist inspiration founded by George Habash in 1967.

2. Marc Lavergne (2004). Jordanie: fracture sociale et fragmentation spatiale dans un processus de métropolisation. Le cas d'Amman. *Insaniyat* 2. Algiers.

3. Foreign General News. *The Canadian Press*, June 3, 2001.

4. Bomb defendants all deeply religious Muslims. Reuters, May 25, 1994.

5. Can Islamists be democrats? The case of Jordan. *Middle East Journal*, July 1, 1997.

6. Zarqa tribes in disarray ahead of elections while candidates scramble for women's votes. *Jordan Times*, July 11, 1999.

7. Can Islamists be democrats, note 5 above.

8. Zarqa tribes in disarray, note 6 above.

9. This is especially true of the interview we held with Muhannad Hijazi, military prosecutor of the Hashemite Kingdom of Jordan, on September 16, 2004.

10. Al-Zarqawi's tribe cables King Abdallah pledging allegiance. *Al-Ra'y*, May 29, 2004.

11. Ghazi Bin Muhammad (1999). *The Tribes of Jordan at the Beginning of the XXIst Century.* Amman: Turab Press.

12. Jordan tribe voices solidarity with Iraq. *IPR Strategic Information Database,* July 16, 2002.

13. Zarqawi's siblings are Aisha, born in 1963, married, living in Zarqa; Alia, born in 1968, married to Khaled Al-Aruri, living in Zarqa; Fatima, born in 1961, married, living in Amman; Intisar, born in 1970, married, living in Amman; Mariam, born in 1968, married to Haytham Mustafa Obeidat; Rabia, born in 1975, married, living in Amman; Amnah, born in 1973, married, living in Amman; Mohammed, born in 1965, married, living in Zarqa; and Sayel, born in 1959, married, living in Saudi Arabia. (Summary of the BKA [German Criminal Police] on Abu Musab Al-Zarqawi, 2004, in the author's archives.)

14. Interview with Abdallah Abu Rumman, Zarqawi's former prison mate, November 8, 2004.

15. Zarqa police, 2004. Author's archives.

16. Under the microscope. *Al-Jazira,* July 1, 2004.

17. Interview with Zarqawi's former classroom teacher, September 15, 2004.

18. Interview with the wife of Abu Musab Al-Zarqawi. *Al-Dustur,* June 24, 2004.

19. Zarqa Department of Education, 2004. Author's archives.

20. Zarqa police, 2004. Author's archives.

21. Showdown with Iraq. *Los Angeles Times,* March 12, 2003.

22. Interview with Ahmed Firaz, former neighbor of the Khalayleh family, September 15, 2004.

23. Zarqawi's journey: from dropout to prisoner to an insurgent leader in Iraq. *New York Times,* July 13, 2004.

24. Zarqa police, 1987. Author's archives.

25. Report interviews Al-Zarqawi's neighbors, prison mates. *Al-Sharq Al-Awsat,* March 8, 2004.

26. Report, note 25 above.

27. Zarqa police, 1987. Author's archives.

28. Interview with Ibrahim Izzat, September 15, 2004.

29. Interview with the director of security at Suwaqah Prison, September 16, 2004.

30. Interview with Abdallah Abu Rumman, Zarqawi's former prison mate, November 8, 2004.

31. Zarqa police, 1987. Author's archives. See Appendix I, pp. 216–217.

32. Under the microscope, note 16 above.

33. Interview with Mohammed Al-Harahshah, Zarqawi's nephew, September 15, 2004.

34. Arab Afghan says Usama Bin Laden's forces' strength overblown. *Al-Sharq Al-Awsat*, September 6, 2001.

35. Arab veterans of Afghan war bolster Mideast Islamic factions. Associated Press, November 25, 1992.

36. Confessions of Abu Musab Al-Zarqawi, State Security Court of the Hashemite Kingdom of Jordan, decision 95/300, August 31, 1994. Author's archives.

37. Message entitled "Advice of Sheikh Maqdisi to Abu Musab Al-Zarqawi," 2004 (www.ribaat.org).

38. Confessions of Abu Mohammed Al-Maqdisi, State Security Court of the Hashemite Kingdom of Jordan, decision 95/300, August 31, 1994. Author's archives.

39. Confessions, note 38 above.

40. The Russian Supreme Court considers banning fifteen Islamic organizations. Agence Interfax, February 12, 2003.

41. U.S. Department of the Treasury, Suspect List of Special Designated Global Terrorists.

42. State Security Court of the Hashemite Kingdom of Jordan, Bayt Al-Imam case 95/300. Author's archives.

43. Paper questions court ruling on extradition of Jordanian to USA. BBC (Al-Urdum), December 2, 1996.

44. Arrests reportedly linked to masterminds of Khubar blast. BBC (Al-Hadath), May 28, 1997.

45. Arab Afghan, note 34 above.

46. Azmiri, whose real name is Wali Khan Amin Shah, is also known by the names Azmarai, Asmari, Asmurai, and Osmurai.

47. Under the microscope, note 16 above.

48. Summary of the BKA (German Criminal Police) on Abu Musab Al-Zarqawi, 2004. Author's archives.

49. Zarqawi segreto. *L'Espresso* 39, September 30, 2004.

50. Under the microscope, note 16 above. The two citations in the following paragraph are from the same source.

51. Zarqawi took familiar route into terrorism. *Los Angeles Times,* July 2, 2004.

52. Speech delivered on December 26, 2001.

53. Confessions, note 36 above.

54. State Security Court of the Hashemite Kingdom of Jordan, the case of the murder of Laurence Foley, decision 95/300, August 31, 1994. Author's archives.

55. Confessions of Mohammed Wasfi Omar Abu Khalil, State Security Court of the Hashemite Kingdom of Jordan, decision 95/300, August 31, 1994. Author's archives.

56. Report of the National Commission on Terrorist Attacks upon the United States (also known as The 9/11 Commission), July 22, 2004, p. 163.

57. US v. Osama Bin Laden, testimony of Jamal Al-Fadl, February 20, 2001.

58. State Security Court of the Hashemite Kingdom of Jordan, the case of the murder of Laurence Foley, decision 95/300, August 31, 1994. Author's archives.

59. Under the microscope, note 16 above.

60. Arab veterans of Afghan war bolster Mideast Islamic factions. Associated Press, November 25, 1992.

61. Arab veterans, note 60 above.

62. Declaration in support of pretrial detention, US v. Soliman S. Biheiri, case # 03-365-A, declaration of David Kane, August 14, 2002.

63. Also called Omar Mahmoud, Othman, Abu Qatada Al-Filistini, Takfiri, and Abu Ismail.

64. United Nations/2002/127, report of the Hashemite Kingdom of Jordan to the Committee on Counterterrorism, January 21, 2002.

65. Arab veterans, note 60 above.

66. Jordanians jailed for planning grenade attack on Israelis. Agence France Presse, November 26, 1996.

67. Interview with Mohammed Al-Harahshah, Zarqawi's nephew, September 15, 2004.

68. Jordanian daily interviews wife of Abu Mu'sab Al-Zarqawi. *Al-Dustur*, June 24, 2004.

69. Zarqawi took familiar route, note 51 above.

70. Message, note 37 above.

71. *Al-Dimuqratia Din*, http://www.almaqdese.com. This Web site is now inactive.

72. Jordanian militants train in Afghanistan to confront regime. Agence France Presse, May 30, 1993.

73. Confessions, note 36 above.

74. Arrests reportedly linked to masterminds of Khubar blast. BBC (Al-Hadath), May 28, 1997.

75. Confessions of Abu Mohammed Al-Maqdisi, note 38 above.

76. Interview with Muhannad Hijazi, military prosecutor of the Hashemite Kingdom of Jordan, September 16, 2004.

77. Confessions of Abu Musab Al-Zarqawi, note 36 above.

78. Zarqawi's journey, note 23 above.

79. Confessions of Khaled Al-Aruri, State Security Court of the Hashemite Kingdom of Jordan, decision 95/300, August 31, 1994. Author's archives.

80. Confessions of Abu Musab Al-Zarqawi, note 36 above.

81. Confessions of Abu Mohammed Al-Maqdisi, note 38 above.

82. Confessions of Abu Musab Al-Zarqawi, note 36 above.

83. Confessions of Abu Musab Al-Zarqawi, note 36 above.

84. Confessions of Abu Mohammed Al-Maqdisi, note 38 above.

85. Confessions of Abu Mohammed Al-Maqdisi, note 38 above.

86. Interview with Hijazi, note 76 above.

87. Confessions of Abu Musab Al-Zarqawi, note 36 above.

88. Confessions of Abu Mohammed Al-Maqdisi, note 38 above.

89. Papers report revival of Islamic groups. BBC (Al-Hadath), May 12, 1998.

90. Jordan militants jailed for planned Israeli attacks. Reuters, November 27, 1995.

91. *Jordanian Human Rights Practices.* United States Department of State, 1995. (See http://www.usemb.se/human/human95/jordan.htm.)

92. Zarqawi took familiar route, note 51 above.

93. Interview with the director of security, note 29 above.

94. Zarqawi's journey, note 23 above.

95. Message, note 37 above. The quotations from Maqdisi in the two following paragraphs are from the same source.

96. Under the microscope, note 16 above. The following quotation is from the same source.

97. Report interviews, note 25 above.

98. Interview with the director of security, note 29 above.

99. Report interviews, note 25 above.

100. Zarqawi's journey, note 23 above. The following anecdote about Abu Doma is from the same source.

101. Zarqawi took familiar route, note 51 above.

102. Interview with Abdallah Abu Rumman, note 14 above.

103. Zarqawi segreto, note 49 above.

104. Zarqawi segreto, note 49 above.

105. Zarqawi's journey, note 23 above.

Part II. Full-Time Terrorist

1. Abdallah face à la bravade islamiste. *Le Figaro*, September 23, 1999.

2. King endorses general amnesty law. Jordanian TV, March 25, 1999.

3. Jordanian prisoners to be freed under amnesty. Xinhua News Agency, March 25, 1999.

4. Under the microscope. *Al-Jazira*, July 1, 2004.

5. Zarqawi segreto. *L'Espresso* 39, September 30, 2004.

6. Interview with the wife of Abu Mussab Al-Zarqawi. *Al-Dustur*, June 24, 2004.

7. Under the microscope, note 4 above.

8. Showdown with Iraq. *Los Angeles Times*, March 12, 2003.

9. Al-Qa'ida's Abu-Mus'ab al-Zarqawi confirms he is currently in Iraq. *Al-Sharq Al-Awsat*, May 26, 2004.

10. Zarqawi's journey: from dropout to prisoner to an insurgent leader in Iraq. *New York Times*, July 13, 2004.

11. Showdown, note 8 above.

12. Showdown, note 8 above.

13. Testimony of Shadi Abdalla, German judiciary proceedings in the case of Al-Tawhid, 2002. Author's archives.

14. Testimony of Jamal Ahmed Al-Fadl, US v. Osama Bin Laden, New York, February 7, 2001.

15. The Taliban: Exporting extremism. *Foreign Affairs*, November 1999.

16. 30 Arabs escape to Afghanistan to avoid arrest in Pakistan. *The News* (Pakistan), July 17, 2000.

17. Pakistan hands over Bin Laden's aide to Jordan. *The News* (Pakistan), December 18, 1999.

18. Showdown, note 8 above.

19. Testimony of Shadi Abdalla, note 13 above.

20. Interview with Mohammed Al-Harahshah, Zarqawi's nephew, September 15, 2004.

21. Summary of the BKA [German Criminal Police] on Abu Musab Al-Zarqawi, 2004. Author's archives.

22. Report of the September 11 Commission, chapter 4, note 181.

23. Testimony of Shadi Abdalla, note 13 above.

24. Definitive prosecutorial statement of partial dismissal of charges, referral to the magistrate's court, and maintenance in provisional detention. High Court, Paris, case of Beghal et al., 2004. Author's archives.

25. Government evidentiary proffer supporting the admissibility of coconspirator statements. US v. Enaam Arnaout, 02CR892, Northern District of Illinois, Eastern Division, January 29, 2003.

26. Spanish proceedings 35/2001 regarding the activities of Al-Qaeda in Spain. Note from UCIE on the "Afghan Arabs." Author's archives.

27. Testimony of Shadi Abdalla, note 13 above.

28. Internal records of the Al-Qaeda organization seized in Afghanistan in 2001 in a "guest house used by Osama Bin Laden," p. 9. Author's archives.

29. Government evidentiary proffer, note 25 above.

30. Zarqawi took familiar route into terrorism. *Los Angeles Times,* July 2, 2004.

31. Summary, note 21 above.

32. Afghan envoy says Bin Laden masterminded US terrorist attack. *Interfax*, September 13, 2001.

33. Summary, note 21 above.

34. Pakistan hails reopening of Afghan–Iran border. Agence France Presse, November 22, 1999.

35. Iran opening eases chokehold of UN sanctions on Afghans. *Washington Post*, December 22, 1999.

36. FSB says foreign mercenaries fought alongside Chechen rebels. *Interfax*, December 8, 1996.

37. German court proceedings in the Al-Tawhid case, BKA investigation of 2002. Author's archives.

38. Suspects captured in Van, members of "Union of Imams" before Al-Qaida. *Anatolia*, February 19, 2002.

39. Al-Tawhid. *Jane's Intelligence Review*, September 21, 2004.

40. Jordanian security court begins trial of suspected Al-Zarqawi "collaborator." BBC, September 16, 2004.

41. Interview with the head of an Arab intelligence service, July 8, 2004.

42. Al-Zarqawi's aide, terrorist Nidal Arabiyat, killed in North Baghdad operation. *Baghdad*, February 24, 2004.

43. US forces hand criminal over to Jordan. UPI, July 20, 2004.

44. Statement of Azmi Al-Jayusi on Jordanian national television, April 2004.

45. Fourth Jordanian from Al-Salt "martyred" in Afghanistan. *Al-Dustur*, October 24, 2001.

46. Summary report, note 21 above.

47. Under the microscope, note 4 above.

48. Ricin at terror camp. *Daily Star*, April 5, 2003.

49. Jordan unveils group linked to Al-Qaida, Ansar Al-Islam. *Financial Times*, September 13, 2003.

50. Jordan unveils, note 49 above.

51. Definitive prosecutorial statement, note 24 above.

52. State Security Court, Hashemite Kingdom of Jordan, case of the millennium plot, 2000. Author's archives.

53. Military court sentences millennium plot defendants to death. Associated Press, February 11, 2002.

54. State Security Court, Hashemite Kingdom of Jordan, decision 545/2003, case of Laurence Foley. Author's archives.

55. Principaux points de la présentation de Colin Powell. Agence France Presse, February 5, 2003.

56. Security Court, Foley case, note 54 above.

57. Saddam's bankers: "UN is no problem," a manager of Iraq's state-owned bank, Rafidain, says of the international sanctions designed to prohibit transfers of money into the country. *The Gazette* (Montreal), February 21, 2003.

58. Security Court, Foley case, note 54 above.

59. Security Court, Foley case, note 54 above.

60. Security Court, Foley case, note 54 above.

61. Interview with Sean Penn, December 5, 2003.

62. Sean Penn, Commentary, *San Francisco Chronicle*, January 14, 2004.

63. Summary, note 21 above.

64. Summary, note 21 above.

65. Summary, note 21 above. The information in the following paragraph is from the same source.

66. Summary, note 21 above.

67. German court proceedings, note 37 above.

68. Testimony of Shadi Abdalla, note 13 above.

69. On July 1, 2004, the United States government offered the same reward, $25 million, for the capture of each of these men.

Part III. Zarqawi's Iraq

1. Principaux points de la présentation de Colin Powell. Agence France Presse, February 5, 2003. See http://www.whitehouse.gov/news/releases/2003/02/20030205-1.html.

2. Report on the U.S. intelligence community's prewar intelligence assessment on Iraq, Select Commission on Intelligence, U.S. Senate, July 7, 2004.

3. Testimony of Dezcallar de Mazzatedo, former director of National Intelligence Center of Spain. Commission of Inquiry into the Attacks of March 11, 2004, Chamber of Deputies, July 19, 2004. Author's archives.

4. Testimony of Dr. Khidhir Hamza, hearings to examine threats, responses, and regional considerations surrounding Iraq. Committee on Foreign Relations, United States Senate, July 31 and August 1, 2002.

5. Testimony of Dr. Khidhir Hamza, note 4 above.

6. National Public Radio, February 18, 1999.

7. The Immigration and Naturalization Service's contacts with two September 11 terrorists. Office of the Inspector General, United States Department of Justice, May 20, 2002.

8. United Nations envoy confirms terrorist meeting. *Prague Post*, June 5, 2002.

9. Associated Press, April 26, 2001.

10. Testimony of Eleanor Hill, Staff Director, Joint Inquiry Committee

hearings on the 9/11 failures, Joint House and Senate Select Intelligence Committee, September 18, 2002.

11. Spanish proceedings 35/2001 concerning the activities of Al-Qaeda in Spain. Author's archives.

12. Testimony of L'Houssaine Kherchtou, USA v. Osama Bin Laden, trial transcript, February 26, 2001.

13. *New York Times*, October 4, 1998.

14. Remarks by the Under Secretary of State for Political Affairs at the Middle East Institute, Washington, DC, United States Department of State dispatch, November 1998.

15. Statement of James Foley, State Department spokesman. Associated Press, August 26, 1998.

16. National Security Adviser Sandy Berger, press briefing, February 26, 1999.

17. *The Independent*, December 6, 1996.

18. *Sunday Times*, September 16, 2001.

19. Testimony of Jamal Ahmed Mohammed Al-Fadl, USA v. Osama Bin Laden, trial transcript, February 13, 2001.

20. Testimony before the United States Congress presented by Dr. Amatzia Baram, September 24, 2002.

21. Ansar Al-Islam, Ansar Al-Sunnah Army, Abu-Musab Al-Zarqawi, and Abu-Hafs Brigades. *Al-Basrah*, March 14, 2004.

22. Jordan unveils group linked to Al-Qa'ida, Ansar al-Islam. *Al-Ra'y*, September 13, 2003.

23. Paper says Bin-Laden sets up Jund-al-Islam group in Iraq's Kurdistan. *Al-Sharq Al-Awsat*, September 28, 2001.

24. Paper says Bin-Laden, note 23 above.

25. Testimony of Al-Fadl, note 19 above.

26. Spanish proceedings 35/2001, note 11 above.

27. New Kurdish fundamentalist group declares "jihad" against secular parties. *Al-Sharq Al-Awsat*, September 11, 2001.

28. http://www.geocities.com/kordestaan/jundalislamenglish11.htm.

29. http://www.geocities.com/kordestaan/jundalislamenglish9.htm.

30. http://www.geocities.com/kordestaan/jundalislamenglish1.htm.

31. Iraqi Kurdistan: Kurdish leaders cited on activities of Jund Al-Islam movement. *Al-Majallah*, February 10, 2002.

32. http://www.geocities.com/kordestaan/jundalislamenglish2.htm.

33. http://www.geocities.com/kordestaan/jundalislamenglish10.htm.

34. Iraqi Kurdistan, note 31 above.

35. Iraq: United States regime changes efforts and post-Saddam governance. Congressional Research Service, November 25, 2003.

36. Iraq: Ansar Al-Islam leader views United States war, denies Norwegian charges. *Al-Sharq Al-Awsat*, April 25, 2003.

37. Radio France International, September 20 and 29, 2002.

38. Jason Burke (2004). *Al-Qaeda: Casting a Shadow of Terror*. London: Tauris.

39. The enemy of my enemy: the odd link between Ansar Al-Islam, Iraq and Iran. Canadian Institute for Strategic Studies, April 2003.

40. Interview with Mullah Krekar. *Al-Sharq Al-Awsat*, February 21, 2003.

41. Interview with Mullah Krekar. *Nidal Ul Islam*, September 1997.

42. Iraq: Kurdish Islamist leader explains split. *Hawlati*, June 10, 2001.

43. Talks to unite Al-Jama'ah al-Islamiyah, Jund al-Islam in Northern Iraq fail. *Al-Sharq Al-Awsat*, October 19, 2001.

44. Iraq: Kurdish groups agree on the dissolution of armed fundamentalists. BBC, November 28, 2001.

45. Iraq: Kurdish Islamic group wins over previously neutral groups. *Hawlati*, September 16, 2001.

46. Interview with Mullah Krekar, note 40 above.

47. Guido Salvini, #5236/02 R.G.N.R., order of application of the measure of preventive detention, Ordinary Court of Milan, November 21, 2003. Author's archives.

48   See www.cihad.net, the Turkish website of Ansar Al-Islam.

49. Interview with Mullah Krekar, note 41 above.

50. Al-Tawhid. *Jane's Intelligence Review*, September 21, 2004.

51. Ansar al-Islam: Al-Qa'ida's ally in northeastern Iraq. CIA analytic report, CTC 2003-40011CX, February 1, 2003. Report of the Commission of Inquiry on September 11.

52. See Ansar Al-Islam's Web site, www.ayobi.com.

53. *Hawlati*, October 28, 2001.

54. Threat of war: mountain camps: militant Kurds training al-Qaida fighters: extremists suspected of testing chemical weapons and links to Iraq. *The Guardian*, August 23, 2002.

55. Interview with a European antiterrorist official, 2004.

56. UPI, September 2002.

57. *Der Spiegel*, February 10, 2003.

58. Guido Salvini, note 47 above.

59. EFE (Spanish News Agency), November 1, 2001.

60. Mullah Kraykar: I met Ben Laden at a luxurious villa in Arab Afghans' quarter in 1988. *Al-Sharq Al-Awsat*, March 1, 2003.

61. Iraqi Kurdistan: Ansar al-Islam group denies links to Al-Qa'ida, Iraqi regime. *Al-Sharq Al-Awsat*, September 29, 2002.

62. Guido Salvini, note 47 above.

63. During an interrogation a member of the Italian cell of Ansar Al-Islam later confirmed that the Khurmal camp was intended for mujahidin volunteers. See Guido Salvini, note 47 above.

64. Jordan unveils group linked to Al-Qa'ida, note 22 above.

65. Summary report of the BKA (German criminal police) on Zarqawi, 2004. Author's archives.

66. CIA review finds no evidence Saddam had ties to Islamic terrorists. Knight Ridder, October 5, 2004.

67. Guido Salvini, note 47 above.

68. Department of Public Safety, Jordan, document 10/31/C/8846. Author's archives.

69. Guido Salvini, note 47 above.

70. Guido Salvini, note 47 above.

71. Guido Salvini, note 47 above.

72. Ansar Al-Islam reportedly dismissed Mollah Krekar as group leader. *Al-Sharq Al-Awsat*, August 23, 2003.

73. Statement of the Department of the Treasury regarding the designation of Ansar Al-Islam, February 23, 2003.

74. *Hawlati*, November 12, 2003.

75. Ansar al-Islam bolsters European network. *Jane's Intelligence Review*, September 21, 2004.

76. *Al-Sharq Al-Awsat*, March 18, 2004.

77. Intelligence report, interrogation of Khallad, September 12, 2003; CIA analytic report "Iran and al-Qa'ida: ties forged in Islamic extremism." CTC 2004-40009HCX, March 2004, pp. 6-12. Commission of Inquiry into the attacks of September 11.

78. Intelligence report, analysis of Hezbollah, Iran, and 9/11, December 20, 2001. Intelligence report, interrogation of Binalshibh, July 16, 2004. Commission of Inquiry into the attacks of September 11.

79. IRNA (Iran News Agency), June 22, 2002.

80. Iran reportedly rejects Jordanian demand to hand over Al-Zarqawi. *Al-Sharq Al-Awsat*, September 2, 2003.

81. Summary report, note 65 above.

82. German judicial proceedings in the case of Al-Tawhid, inquest of the BKA, 2002. Author's archives.

83. Jordan unveils, note 22 above.

84. Minister says Iran holding senior members of Al-Qa'ida "terror" network. Agence France Presse, July 23, 2003.

85. Iran denies harboring Al-Qa'ida, challenges foreign intelligence services. Agence France Presse, October 14, 2003.

86. Iran reports to UNSC Committee on efforts to block Al-Qa'ida, Taliban. IRNA, October 28, 2003.

87. Ansar al-Islam group threatens to fight Americans, seculars in Iraq. *Al-Sharq Al-Awsat*, June 13, 2003.

88. LBC Satellite Television transcript, August 10, 2003.

89. *Hawlati* reveals the secret of Arbil explosions. *Hawlati*, April 11, 2004.

90. Ansar Al-Sunna. Al-Maqrisi Center for Historical Studies, March 14, 2004.

91. *Al-Hayat*, September 5, 2003.

92. Islamists cited on US-Iraqi-Syrian "deal," "suicide elements" in Iraq. *Al-Sharq Al-Awsat*, April 13, 2003.

93. Message entitled "Advice of Sheikh Maqdisi to Abu Musab Al-Zarqawi," 2004. Author's archives.

94. New al-Qaida spokesman expects "gloomy fate" for US "crusade" on Iraq. *Al-Sharq Al-Awsat*, March 24, 2003.

95. See www.cihad.net, the Turkish Web site of Ansar Al-Islam.

96. Ansar al-Islam bolsters European network, note 75 above.

97. Videotape, May 11, 2004. Author's archives.

98. Press release from Ansar Al-Sunna, November 10, 2004. Author's archives.

99. Internal records of the Al-Qaeda organization seized in Afghanistan in a guest house used by Bin Laden. Author's archives.

100. The Web address is http://www.almaqdese.com.

101. Summary of intelligence report on Abu Musab Al-Zarqawi, Iraqi Provisional Authority, September 23, 2004. Author's archives.

102. Estimates by US see more rebels with more funds. *New York Times*, October 21, 2004.

103. The state security court begins the trial of a collaborator with Al-Zarkaoui. *Al-Ra'y*, September 16, 2004. Killing of Abou-Anas al-Shami was a strong blow to Al-Zarkawi's group. *Al-Sharq Al-Awsat*, September 24, 2004.

104. Message, note 93 above.

105. Un lieutenant de Zarqawi à la tête des rebelles à Fallouja. Agence France Presse, November 19, 2004.

106. Estimates, note 102 above.

107. Jordanian security court begins trial of suspected Al-Zarqawi collaborator. *Al-Ra'y*, September 16, 2004.

108. Al-Qa'ida's Abou-Mus'ab Al-Zarqawi deplores Muslims' "renunciation"

of jihad. *FBIS Report,* January 6, 2004. (FBIS is the Foreign Broadcast Intelligence Service.)

109. Text of Al-Zarqawi message threatening more attacks. *FBIS Report,* April 6, 2004.

110. Press release from the Zarqawi group, October 14, 2004. Author's archives.

111. Deux Libanais sortent vivants de la tanière de Zarqawi [Two Lebanese leave Zarqawi's lair alive]. Agence France Presse, October 14, 2004.

112. Deux Libanais, note 111 above. See also Les deux Libanais libérés en Iraq avaient été enlevés par Tawhid wal Jihad [The two Lebanese freed in Iraq had been kidnapped by Tawhid wal Jihad]. Agence France Presse, October 13, 2004.

113. Al-Arabiya TV, United Arab Emirates, October 10, 2004.

114. Al-Arabiya TV, note 113 above.

115. Wanted rebel vows loyalty to bin Laden, Web sites say. *New York Times,* October 18, 2004.

116. Excerpt from the letter of Abu Musab Al-Zarqawi, Provisional Authority of Iraq, January 23, 2004.

117. Press release from Tawhid wal Jihad, August 3, 2004. Author's archives.

118. *Al-Hayat,* September 10, 2004. The next quotation in this paragraph is from the same source.

119. Text of Al-Zarqawi message, note 109 above.

120. *Voice of Jihad* 1, October 17, 2003. (Middle East Research Institute; www.memri.org).

121. United Kingdom: "Fugitive" Islamist Abou-Qatada interviewed via Internet. *Al-Sharq Al-Awsat,* October 18, 2002.

122. *Al-Ahram Al-Arabi,* February 3, 2001.

123. Muslim cleric calls suicide bombers martyrs. Associated Press, April 25, 2001.

124. Al-Jazira, December 9, 2001.

125. Islamic scholar says anyone killed trying to expel U.S. forces from Gulf is "martyr." *Gulf News,* January 29, 2003.

126. Al-Qaradawi, Saudi clerics call for djihad against the US, support for Iraq. *Al-Quds Al-Arabi*, March 8, 2003.

127. Qatar's Al-Qaradawi resumes anti-US rhetoric. Irak–FMA, FBIS report, September 29, 2003.

128. Friday sermons urge Islamic unity, denounce "aggression" on Palestinians, Iraq. FBIS report, October 3, 2003.

129. Friday sermons denounce bombings, urge resistance, hail Prophet's birthday. FBIS report, April, 30, 2004.

130. Islamic figures, scholars worldwide condemn "US-Zionist" crimes in Iraq, Palestine. *Al-Quds Al-Arabi*, August 23, 2004.

131. Egypt: Muslim cleric Al-Qaradawi calls on Muslims to fight all Americans in Iraq. Teheran Sahar TV 1, September 3, 2004.

132. *Al-Sharq Al-Awsat*, September 2, 2004.

133. *Voice of Jihad* 23: August–September 2004. MEMRI, October 12, 2004 (www.memri.org).

134. Author's archives.

135. Author's archives.

Part IV. A Global Network

1. *Der Spiegel*, November 25, 2002.

2. http://www.treas.gov/rewards/pdfs/terroristlists/list16.pdf.

3. German court proceedings in the Al-Tawhid case, 2002. Author's archives.

4. German court proceedings, note 3 above.

5. As of December 2004 Ashraf Al-Dagma was in preventive detention in Germany, where he was sentenced to ten years in prison.

6. German court proceedings, note 3 above.

7. As of December 2004 Abu Dhess was in preventive detention in Germany, where he was sentenced to ten years in prison.

8. German court proceedings, note 3 above.

9. German court proceedings, note 3 above.

10. Shadi Abdalla spent two years in prison in Germany before being freed in 2004 after cooperating with the German judiciary.

11. As of December 2004 Jamel Mustafa was in preventive detention in Germany, where he was sentenced to five years in prison.

12. German court proceedings, note 3 above.

13. German court proceedings, note 3 above.

14. German court proceedings, note 3 above.

15. Weekly surveys Al-Qaida presence in Germany. *Der Spiegel*, March 22, 2004.

16. German court proceedings, note 3 above.

17. At the present time Maqdisi is in prison in Jordan.

18. Decision of the special court of appeals in matters of immigration, March 2004. Author's archives.

19. Ordinary Court of Milan, Guido Salvini, # 5230/02 R.G.N.R. Ruling for the application of the measure of preventive detention, November 21, 2003. Author's archives.

20. As of December 2004 all but Ben Mouldi were in preventive detention in Italy.

21. Ordinary Court of Milan, note 19 above.

22. Italian judiciary proceedings in the case of Ansar Ai-Islam, 2003. Author's archives.

23. Italian judiciary proceedings, note 22 above.

24. Ordinary Court of Milan, note 19 above.

25. The General Intelligence Department uncovers new al-Qa'ida and Ansar Al-Islam group that planned terrorist operations against tourists, US interests in Jordan, and intelligence officers. *Al-Ra'y*, September 13, 2003.

26. Mahjoub was extradited from Germany to Italy and placed in preventive detention.

27. Spain says three Algerians linked to Iraq attacks. *Washington Post*, May 20, 2004.

28. Italian judiciary proceedings, note 22 above.

29. Analysis by the FSS on Wahhabism in the Caucasus. Author's archives.

30. Space TV, Baku, September 25, 2003.

31. Ordinary Court of Milan, note 19 above.

32. Press release from the ministries of the interior and internal security, December 30, 2002. Author's archives.

33. As of December 2004 Merouane Benhamed, Menad Benchellali, and the latter's father, Chellali Benchellali, were in preventive detention in France.

34. Press release, note 32 above.

35. Press release, note 32 above.

36. Quand le juge Bruguière fait la bombe devant les patrons. *Le canard enchaîné*, October 6, 2004.

37. As of December 2004 Mouloud and Samir Feddag were in preventive detention in Great Britain after being convicted of using false passports.

38. A series of attacks strikes Madrid and leaves over 100 dead. *Le Monde*, March 12, 2004.

39. Des millions de personnes dans les rues, l'ETA dément toute responsabilité. Agence France Presse, March 12, 2004.

40. Hearing of Baltasar Garzon Real, examining magistrate # 5, in the National Law Court, July 15, 2004. Author's archives.

41. Hearing, note 40 above.

42. As of December 2004 Zougam was in preventive detention in Spain. Shawi was released on December 2, 2004 but remains available to the Spanish courts in connection with the ongoing proceedings concerning the attacks of March 11.

43. Both of these men have been released but remain available to the Spanish courts in connection with the ongoing proceedings.

44. Madrid attacks: five arrests. *AP News*, March 13, 2004.

45. As of December 2004 Abu Dahdah was in preventive detention in Spain.

46. Spanish court proceedings #35/2001 concerning the activities of Al-Qaeda in Spain. Author's archives.

47. According to the German court proceedings concerning the attacks of September 11, 2001, Mohammed Fizazi preached in the mosque in 1999 and 2000 when Atta attended services there. Author's archives.

48. Summary report of the BKA (German criminal police) on Zarqawi, 2004. Author's archives.

49. In this connection David Courtailler, sentenced to four years in prison, admitted having met Jamal Zougam in a mosque in Madrid in 1998.

50. Charge brought in case #35, examining judge #5, September 17, 2003. Author's archives.

51. Azizi is a Moroccan national born on February 2, 1968 in Hedami. As of December 2004 he was still at large.

52. Mourafik, too, is being sought by the Moroccan courts in connection with the Casablanca attacks.

53. Charge, note 50 above. As of December 2004 Kattan was in preventive detention in Spain.

54. Charge, note 50 above.

55. Spanish court proceedings, note 46 above.

56. On December 7, 2004 El-Sayed, imprisoned in Italy since June of that year, was extradited to Spain. As of December 2004 Al-Suri was on the run.

57. Definitive prosecutorial statement of partial dismissal of charges, referral to the magistrate's court, maintenance in provisional detention. High Court, Paris, case of Beghal et al., 2004. Author's archives.

58. Spanish court proceedings, note 46 above.

59. As of December 2004 Zouaydi was in preventive detention in Spain.

60. State Security Court, Hashemite Kingdom of Jordan, decision 545/2003, case of Laurence Foley. Author's archives.

61. Jordanian source cited on concern over security of borders. *Al-Hayat*, August 4, 2004.

62. Interview with a Pakistani television news channel in the U. S. Embassy in Islamabad.

63. Echec d'une rencontre secrète. *Intelligence Online*, April 9, 2004.

64. General cites rising peril of terror in Iraq. *Washington Post*, August 22, 2003.

65. General cites rising peril, note 64 above.

66. Powell gives hope for Iraq power handover, UN staff prepare to leave. Agence France Presse, September 27, 2002.

67. An Arab "martyr" thwarted. *New York Times*, November 2, 2004.

68. Minaccia terroristica di matrice islamica; esito attività investigativa esperita sul conto di Remadna Abdelhalim Haded, Chekkouri Yassine, Es Sayed Abdelkader Mahmoud, Benattia Nabil. Procedimento penale n. 13016/99, CAT A4 DIGOS 01, Milan, November 21, 2001.

69. Italian court proceedings in the case of Ansar Al-Islam, 2003. Author's archives.

70. Do the Europeans know more than they now pretend? *National Review*, February 11, 2003.

71. Syrian defense minister blames WTC attacks on Israel. *Jerusalem Post*, October 19, 2001.

72. Syrian president says he doubts Al-Qaeda exists. *Los Angeles Times*, May 26, 2003.

73. Interrogation of Robert Richard Antoine Pierre, Department of National Security, Morocco, July 7, 2003. As of December 2004 Pierre was in preventive detention in Morocco.

74. As of December 2004 Ghalyoun was in preventive detention in Spain.

75. Spanish proceedings, vol. 79, "Juzgado central de Instruccion # 5: contra Imad Eddin Barakat Yarkas; relaciones con extremistas islamicos: con Ghasoub Al-Abrash Ghalyoun. *Summario* 35/2001, November 12, 2001.

76. A transformation in Syria. *Financial Times*, December 6, 2001. See also: Syria's new cabinet is overshadowed by old realities. *New York Times*, January 21, 2002, and A face of terror or benevolence; Enam Arnaout calls his work honorable, but the US says it's a cover for his support of terrorism. *Chicago Tribune*, October 13, 2002.

77. The Hamburg connection. *Toronto Star*, September 29,, 2002.

78. Verband der Vereine Creditreform, Creditreform German Companies, 2002.

79. The Syrian bet: Did the Bush administration burn a useful source on Al-Qaeda? *New Yorker*, July 28, 2003.

80. Deutsch-Syrischer Kaufmann unter Terrorverdacht. *Die Welt*, September 11, 2001. See also: Germany hunts for terror clues. CNN Berlin, September 10, 2002.

81. German proceedings, Erklärung zur Person: Tatari, Mohammed Hadi. Bundeskriminalamt Hamburg, March 12, 2003. See also: Syrische Geheimdienst—Connection zu Hamburger Terror-Piloten. *Der Spiegel*, March 8, 2002.

82. Matthew Levitt (2003). Criminal enterprise in the political economy of Middle Eastern terrorism. *Policywatch*, Washington Institute, January 3. See also: Syrian intelligence linked to Al-Qaeda cell in Hamburg. *Middle East Intelligence Bulletin* 4.9, September 2002; and Robert Baer (2003), *Sleeping with the Devil*. New York: Crown.

83. Trial transcript, USA v. UBL, testimony of Jamal Ahmed Al-Fadl, February 6, 2001.

84. Spanish court proceedings, note 46 above.

85. Déclaration du ministre français des Affaires étrangères, Amman, Jordan, August 31, 2004.

86. Islamic figures, scholars worldwise condemn "US-Zionist crimes" in Iraq, Palestine. *Al-Quds Al-Arabi*, August 23, 2004.

87. See the interview with the supreme leader of the Muslim Brotherhood, *Al-Sharq Al-Awsat*, November 15, 2002.

88. Founding documents of the Muslim Brotherhood. Author's archives.

89. La France pose la question d'un retrait des forces américaines d'Irak. Agence France Presse, September 27, 2004.

90. Al-Manar TV, October 6, 2004. FBIS.

91. Al-Manar TV, August 27, September 24, and October 15, 2004. FBIS.

92. Une enquête mise à mal par les tensions entre parquet et juges antiterroristes. *Le Monde*, June 25, 2004.

93. Une enquête mise à mal, note 92 above.

94. La guerre des juges sauve les jihadistes. *Libération*, June 25, 2004.

95. CIA report on Islamic charitable organizations in Bosnia-Herzegovina, 1996. Author's archives.

96. IIRO raises SR 15m in funds. *Arab News*, December 22, 1993.

97. La justice enquête sur des volontaires français en Irak. *Le Figaro*, September 22, 2004.

98. CIA: Iraq security to get worse. CNN, November 12, 2003.

99. Interview with the author, June 22, 2004.

100. Iraqi PM: Terrorists pouring in. CNN, September 20, 2004.

101. Identification d'un français mort en combattant la coalition en Irak. Agence France Presse, October 22, 2004.

Conclusion

1. *Al-Jihad* 41, April 1988.

2. Internal document of Al-Qaeda. Author's archives.

3. Internal document of Al-Qaeda. Author's archives.

4. Internal document of Al-Qaeda. Author's archives.

5. Internal document of Al-Qaeda. Author's archives.

6. *Al-Bunyan Al-Marsus,* July 1989.

Appendices

1. A letter attributed to Zarqawi, seized by the American forces in Iraq on January 23, 2004, and made available by the Provincial Authority there.

2. Seventh century AD.

Index